Ignored Voices: Public Opinion Polls
and the Latino Community

**CMAS Publications**
The Center for Mexican American Studies
The University of Texas at Austin


General Editor
Ricardo Romo

Managing Editor
Jose Flores


The Center for Mexican American Studies
SSB 4.112
The University of Texas at Austin
Austin, Texas 78712

# Ignored Voices:

## PUBLIC OPINION POLLS
## AND THE LATINO COMMUNITY

**Edited by**
**Rodolfo O. de la Garza**

UT
CMAS

First Edition, 1987

Requests for permission to reproduce material from
this work should be sent to CMAS Publications,
Student Services Building, 4.112,
The University of Texas, Austin, Texas, 78712.

International Standard Book Number 0-292-73844-7
Library of Congress Catalog Number 86-051514

Distributed for CMAS Publications by:
     University of Texas Press
     P.O. Box 7819
     Austin, Texas 78713

*Cover Design*
David S. Cavazos

To Willie Velasquez and SVREP

# Contents

### III. Issues in Polling Latinos

### IV. Latino Public Opinion Research and Databases

# Introduction

Rodolfo O. de la Garza, *University of Texas*

For whom did Latinos vote in the 1984 election? What were their views on the issues and candidates in that election? Surprisingly, reliable answers to these and related questions are unavailable. No independent source—not the national press, not the nation's leading public opinion pollsters, no one—systematically asked Latinos their views or monitored their participation in the 1984 election. On October 18, 1985, journalists, representatives of national polling firms, academic experts in public opinion and Latino politics, and Latino political leaders met in Austin, Texas, to discuss why this was the case. They participated in "Ignored Voices: Public Opinion Polls and the Latino Community in the United States," a conference organized by the Center for Mexican American Studies of the University of Texas at Austin. Participants explored why Latinos' political views have been ignored, the consequences of this neglect, and what can be done to overcome it. This volume includes the papers presented at the meeting and two additional commissioned papers.

The inattention to Latino political attitudes and behavior in 1984 is not surprising, since it is merely one more example of the longstanding disinterest of the nation's leaders to Latino political participation. On the other hand, the 1980s have been widely touted as the "Decade of the Hispanic," and 1984 was the year that Latinos expected to begin making their presence felt as national political actors. Latinos approached the 1980s optimistically because of significant changes in their status over the past 20 years. Among these was their growth from only two major subgroups—Mexican Americans and Puerto Ricans—to several significant subgroups, all of which were viewed as if they constituted a homogeneous Hispanic population.

This more inclusive focus reflects a dramatic increase in the number of Spanish-surnamed U.S. residents. The U.S. Census reports that as of 1980 the Latino population totaled 17.6 million, including 3 million residents of Puerto Rico. This represents a two-thirds increase between 1970 and 1980 compared to an increase of 11% for the total U.S. population. Between 1970 and 1980, the U.S. Census reported that the Latino population living on the mainland increased from 8 to 14.6 million. This growth is reflected in the increased geographic dispersion of Latinos.

Historically, the Latino population on the U.S. mainland has consisted primarily of Mexican-origin residents concentrated within regions of the Southwest and Puerto Ricans in the New York area. Not only are these groups increasing rapidly, but the Latino population now includes rapidly increasing numbers of Caribbean and Central and South American immigrants. Today, these Latinos are scattered throughout the nation. Cities as distant from the historic homeland as Seattle, Washington, D.C., Minneapolis–St. Paul, and Milwaukee have a large and growing population of Latinos of various nationalities. This increase along with the Latinization of cities such as Los Angeles, Miami, and New York has brought Latinos to the nation's attention.

Latino population growth has combined with the increased democratization of the nation's political processes, especially in the Southwest, which has enabled Latinos to convert their expanding population into a political resource. As a result of the Voting Rights Acts of 1975 and 1982 and numerous court decisions requiring single-member districts, there has been an impressive increase in the number of Latino elected officials. In 1984, the National Association of Latino Elected Officials reported that elected Latinos totaled 3,128. Today, Latinos are being elected in jurisdictions such as Phoenix, Los Angeles, and San Antonio where in the past they were systematically denied their political rights. They are also being elected in cities such as Bridgeport, Massachusetts, Dodge City, Kansas, and Wilder, Idaho, which have never been identified as Latino areas. Another indication of this increased national political presence is the change in Latino participation at national political conventions. Between 1976 and 1984, the number of Latinos attending the Democratic and Republican national conventions increased from 271 to 763.

As Latinos have become a larger part of the population and have begun to play a greater role in political decision making at all levels, their presence has begun to alter the nation's political agenda. More than any other minority group, Latinos have stimulated the national debate over bilingual education. To a great degree, the nation's concern regarding immigration reform is a concern about the increased Latinization of the United States—that is, about the continued incorporation of Spanish speakers who are seen as having no absolute commitment to becoming full-fledged Americans culturally, socially, and politically. It is this perception of Latinos that has also given rise to concern regarding the role that Latinos will play in U.S.-Latin American relations.

Their increased numbers have also altered the nation's political agenda in another way. For a variety of reasons, both political parties are actively seeking the Latino vote. Democrats know that they must retain the Latino vote if they are to remain a viable national force. Republicans, perhaps because they are convinced that they have permanently lost the black vote, are working hard not to lose the Latino vote also. Moreover, they seem convinced that as family-oriented Catholics Latinos will find the Republican agenda to their liking. Latinos thus now find themselves courted by the same parties that for decades either exploited or ignored them.

As Latinos have become more visible, the role of Latino spokesperson has become increasingly coveted. Whoever speaks in the name of Latinos is clearly an individual with whom the nation's political elites must reckon. It is not surprising, then, that when Latino leaders speak out on issues they invariably claim to represent all Latinos rather than any specific subgroup such as Mexican Americans or Puerto Ricans. To do so enhances their potential political clout: it is, after all, more significant to speak in the name of the entire Latino community than to claim to represent any subgroup. But while the individuals who claim to be spokespeople for the "Latino community" are taken seriously by the nation's media and political elites, it is virtually impossible to evaluate the legitimacy of such claims since we do not know how Latinos view the political world.

There is no systematic reliable source that tells us what Latinos think about issues or how they view the nation's political leaders. This is especially ironic since there has been such increased effort to court the Latino vote. This lack of attention is even more puzzling in view of how much information we have about the non-Latino American electorate. Public opinion pollsters have for years dissected the American people into many component parts. We know how the gender gap, regional alignments, age cohorts, and income and educational differences affect political behavior. We know about black-white differences, and about the concerns and behavior of Jewish Americans, and of European ethnics generally. But the same sources, including major commercial polling firms as well as academic organizations such as the Institute for Survey

Research at the University of Michigan, have told us virtually nothing about Latino attitudes, opinions, and behavior.

Although scholars disagree regarding how directly public opinion affects any specific political decision, there can be no doubt that public opinion polls have become a major factor in our nation's political life. Polls can and do influence candidate selection and issue resolution. By not having their views regularly reported in polls, Latinos are effectively excluded from influencing both of these outcomes. In a fundamental sense, because of the role that polls play in our political life, being excluded from them is tantamount to partial disenfranchisement.

Why is the Latino population not systematically included in national public opinion polls? What are the consequences of Latinos being excluded? How can this situation be corrected? It was to discuss these and related questions that the conference "Ignored Voices: Public Opinion Polls and the Latino Community in the United States" was held.

As the conference papers illustrate, the meeting did not yield definitive answers to all these questions. It did, however, clarify numerous issues and provide important insights into others. For example, most participants felt that it would be premature if not incorrect to assume that Latinos constitute a coherent political community. The various Latino groups are becoming more culturally alike, as Barbara Caplan states in her paper, and they share general political objectives, a point emphasized by Harry Pachon and Congressman Robert Garcia. But the evidence, especially that presented by Robert Brischetto, indicates that intragroup differences are so significant that if a united Latino political community exists at all it is only at the most abstract level.

This lack of political community is reflected in the profound disagreement on what term to use to identify this population. Frank del Olmo argues for using the term "Latino" and expresses contempt for the term "Hispanic." Those who with equal vigor argue for "Hispanic" are led by Congressman Garcia. The only data available on the issue are presented by I. A. Lewis of the Los Angeles Times Poll who found that in his survey most California Latinos preferred to be identified as "Mexicanos." He noted that this is probably because that is, in fact, what they are.

James Prothro reminds us that deciding which label to use to identify a population is not a trivial issue. With regard to blacks, for example, the transition in self-identification from "Negro" to "Afro-American" to "black" paralleled fundamental political changes among black Americans. It is reasonable to assume a similar process may be underway among Latinos. The existence of this debate and the intensity with which it is sometimes pursued is further evidence that no unified political community exists among Americans of Latin American heritage.

The lack of knowledge regarding how Latinos think and vote is addressed by numerous participants. This ignorance is largely the result of the scant attention paid to Latinos by the commercial political polling community. James Shriver's paper, which presents the Gallup Poll data on Latinos in the 1984 election, illustrates this. When reviewing his paper, it is important to remember that no other major polling group analyzed Latinos more systematically than did the Gallup Organization.

Not only is there a scarcity of data, but questions of interpretation and bias arise regarding existing data. This problem becomes evident when one compares the paper presented by Lance Tarrance with Robert Brischetto's. Tarrance works closely with the Republican party, while Brischetto has worked most closely with Democratic partisans. Each is sometimes seen as partisan, although both insist on the accuracy of their findings. For whatever reasons, their work regularly offers almost contradictory views of the same events and issues. Tarrance's paper, for example, indicates that Latinos are relatively conservative and potentially pro-Republican. Among the examples he offers to support his argument are the results of a survey regarding immigration reform which he conducted for the Federation for American Immigration Reform (FAIR). Yet, during a question and answer period Congressman Garcia cited surveys commissioned by FAIR as illustrative of the kind of research that he disregards because it is so biased. Brischetto, on the other hand, finds that Latinos other than Cuban Americans are much more supportive of Democrats. He disagrees that Latinos are increasingly voting Republican and argues instead that Latinos and Anglos are polarized. F. Chris Garcia's comments suggest, however, that Brischetto may be overstating his case. Garcia notes that, rather than polarization, Brischetto's data may reveal nothing more than a "lead-lag" pattern—that is, that Latinos are following the same pattern toward Republican support that Anglos have followed but are a few years behind in the process. Caplan's paper arrives at a similar conclusion based on her analysis of Latino cultural patterns. Supporting Garcia's critique is the direct correlation between income levels and Republican party preference shown in table 13 of Brischetto's paper. By combining all those who report any Republican party preference one obtains the following:

|                | Percent of Respondents within |
|----------------|-------------------------------|
| Income         | Each Income Category          |
| $  0–5,000     | 6                             |
| $  5–10,000    | 10                            |
| $10–20,000     | 13                            |
| $20–30,000     | 15                            |
| $30–40,000     | 16                            |
| $40–50,000     | 17                            |
| $50,000 plus   | 39                            |

Despite such problems of interpretation raised in the papers by del Olmo and Representative Albert Luna, the data generated by the Southwest Voter Registration Education Project under Brischetto's direction are generally recognized as the best available.

The paper by Bruce Cain and Rodney Kiewiet adds another dimension to our understanding of Latino political reality. Their comparison of Latino, black, and Asian American attitudes identifies significant differences in how each group views issues such as bilingualism and immigration reform. Their findings suggest that it will not be easy for Latinos to develop coalitions with these groups around these issues. (It also is important to note that their findings on Latino attitudes toward immigration issues differ substantially from Tarrance's findings, as do the results of the Los Angeles Times Poll survey cited by del Olmo.)

The conference also underscored several technical issues associated with polling Latinos. The problems encountered by Lewis raise questions about whether it is financially possible to carry out well-designed surveys of Latinos. Joe Belden's paper shows that, while most polling agencies are sensitive to the problems inherent in bilingual polling, few design their work in such a way as to overcome them. Belden further suggests that perhaps too much is being made of the language issue, especially with regard to differences in the Spanish spoken by the various Latino subgroups. Based on the results of exit polls conducted in 1984, Warren Mitofsky even questions whether there is any need for Spanish language interviews when the population is limited to voters.

Among the most interesting points brought out at the conference was how Latino leaders view public opinion polls. Both Congressman Garcia and Representative Luna acknowledge that it is important to have polls of the Latino community. Both, however, express a surprising amount of skepticism about their overall utility. Their attitude appears to reflect the way that polls have been used or abused in the past. Perhaps it is because there is so little reliable information on Latino attitudes that both of these elected officials seem to place so much trust in old-fashioned personal communication. Ben Page advises that it may be wise to rethink that position. He contends that, while polls may be unreliable, other methods of gauging public opinion may be even more fraught with bias and pitfalls. His answer is not to avoid polls but to have good ones.

Finally, what may be the most important point of the conference is provided by Congressman Garcia and Curtis Gans, each from his own perspective. They clearly remind us of the limits of polls. Polls identify the boundaries within which politicians may move most freely. They do not tell us what is right or necessary. Furthermore, as Garcia well notes, the best polls will not produce great leadership, and great leaders may have no need for polls.

By traditional standards, the conference was a success. There were substantive debates, new information was shared, and some old ideas were challenged. What the conference did not do, however, was answer the key question regarding how to have Latinos included in future surveys. How do private pollsters justify excluding Latinos as an identifiable population when they so willingly include smaller groups? Are there really technical reasons for this? If so, why is it that commercial polling firms are so successful in measuring Latino consumer preferences? Why are public pollsters who are funded with tax dollars allowed to continue to define the American electorate in ways that exclude Latinos? Perhaps the answer is that the Latino community is politically so marginalized that its attitudes and beliefs are essentially irrelevant to the nation's leaders and the public at large.

The purpose of this introduction is to somewhat prepare the reader for what follows. The conference addressed many more issues than those I have discussed here, and I am certain that many readers will disagree with my conclusions regarding what the key themes of the conference were and how well each point was made. I would hope, however, that all readers will agree that these papers raise important questions and leave us better informed than we had been.

The volume is divided into four sections. The first examines the importance of Latino public opinion from the perspective of journalists and Latino public officials. The second section reviews the results of surveys examining Latino involvement in the 1984 election. The methods used by pollsters, the problems associated with different types of polls, the relationship between consumer and political polling, and the limits of polls are among the issues discussed in the third section. A final section includes two additional papers that complement the papers presented at the conference. The first is a bibliography of published, politically related research based on surveys that include Latinos among the respondents or that focus exclusively on Latinos. The second describes the publicly available machine-readable files from major studies that include information on Latinos. It also identifies the major studies that have not included Latinos as an identifiable population. Together, these papers constitute an important resource for anyone interested in survey research on the Latino community.

Congressman Bill Richardson's presentation is not included in this work at his request. When he accepted the invitation to participate in the conference, he indicated that he thought he could add more to the event if he spoke off the record.

I would like to express my appreciation to those who made the conference and this volume possible. As stated previously, this conference was hosted by the Center for Mexican American Studies at U.T. Austin. It was funded by the Ford Foundation with the assistance of the College of Liberal Arts, U.T. Austin. I especially want to thank Elizabeth Forsyth and the staff of the Center for Mexican American Studies for all that they did. Forsyth's organizational efforts made the conference a success. The support provided by William Diaz of the Ford Foundation made the conference possible, and his advice made it better than it would otherwise have been. Thanks also go to Dean Robert King of the College of Liberal Arts, U.T. Austin, for his support. Finally, I would like to express my appreciation to those who attended the conference as paper presenters, discussants, moderators, and audience. I hope they benefited as much as I did.

Rodolfo O. de la Garza
The University of Texas at Austin

# Public Opinion Polls and the Latino Community

Robert Garcia, *U.S. House of Representatives*

One of the questions I was asked to address in my presentation is the importance of Latino public opinion to politicians. As a Hispanic politician, I considered it to be very important. Why? Because the Hispanic community is very important to me, and public opinion polls are one of the best ways to keep in touch with the sentiment of the community on any given issue.

I particularly use polls to gauge public opinion within my constituency. They help me get a better reading of how my constituents feel about an issue. Because I am a Hispanic politician, I am often asked to reflect on issues that affect Hispanics not only in my district but also across the nation. Since I can't keep up with every individual community, polls enable me to get a better understanding of what people are feeling.

I have, however, been frustrated by the lack of polls taken of the Hispanic community. This is not to say that these polls do not exist or that the situation hasn't improved over the past few years. It has. Ten years ago there were very few if any polls that dealt with Hispanics. Today there are several.

One of the primary questions, then, when judging the importance of Latino public opinion is why haven't more polls been taken of the Hispanic community? What are some of the problems confronting pollsters in trying to take polls in our communities? While I am not a pollster, and it is not my intention to apologize for them, I can, nonetheless, appreciate some of the difficulties they have traditionally come up against when trying to poll Hispanics and other minorities.

First of all, identifying Hispanics for the purpose of taking a poll can be a problem. You need a specifically designed sample because there are, generally speaking, too few Hispanics interviewed in most general surveys, and some of the specialized surveys have not been well done. It is possible to accurately target

Hispanics, but it can be expensive, primarily because, as I said, setting up a sample is not easy—for instance, how does one determine in an unbiased manner if an individual is a Hispanic?

In addition, when targeting Hispanics, who do you compare them to in order to judge the accuracy of poll results—other Hispanics, blacks, the majority community? How do you devise questions—should they be bilingual? Can a poll taken in Spanish and English accurately reflect the subtleties of the questions being used in the poll?

Then there are the same general problems confronting all pollsters: minimizing the subjectivity, controlling the cost, identifying a representative sample. In a 1981 study issued by the National Academy of Sciences entitled *Surveys of Subjective Phenomena: A Summary Report*, the authors state, "Because poll and survey results can be manipulated . . . one must question the claim that these methods necessarily lead to the democratization of political and social decision making." While this is a problem inherent in all polls, it is a particularly sensitive issue with Hispanics and other minorities when polls are released that allegedly represent the opinion of the community. Perhaps because we have been left out of the decision-making process for so long in this country, we are more defensive about outside organizations speaking for us through the use of selective polls.

Considering all these difficulties, what can we expect from public opinion polls taken of the Hispanic community? We can, at the very least, expect them to be as accurate as possible. We can also expect them to survey issues of critical importance to our community, from immigration reform to bilingual education to Central America. We can further ask that groups and organizations conducting polls not have a particular bias or point of view that they are trying to promote through the use of a poll. Finally, politicians' expectations of opinion polls should be no different from those of business executives or reporters. Polls should be looked upon as a way to measure public opinion, not to create it.

That is why it is so necessary to make polls as unbiased as possible. This is crucial for politicians. We use polls to get a better understanding of what our constituents are saying. It is important to keep in mind that politics is not really a science. A seasoned politician relies a great deal on instinct, and public opinion polls help to clarify our instinct. They bring a little science to the politician's craft. A biased poll can therefore throw a politician off, eroding his or her ability to judge a situation.

The greatest damage done by an inaccurate or poorly designed poll is that it misrepresents the community. This degrades both the poll and the community. Fortunately, there have been polls and polling organizations that have dealt with the Hispanic community in a fair and accurate manner. For instance, the Spanish International Network (SIN) commissioned Yankelovich, Skelly and White to do a study of the Hispanic market in this country. While the study dealt with economic and social characteristics and not political opinions, it did represent an in-depth survey of certain characteristics of the Hispanic community, and it can be used as an excellent example of how to conduct a survey or poll of the Hispanic community.

There have been other polls taken of Hispanics on a variety of subjects. A 1983 poll taken by the Midwest Hispanic Political Leadership Conference in Chicago covered a number of political issues. A 1982 survey of Hispanics conducted by the New York Archdiocese discussed the community's views on the Catholic Church. The point is, there have been accurate and relatively unbiased surveys taken of our community despite the obstacles, and these polls have proven useful to politicians, business executives, and even religious leaders.

In summary, I have a few comments and recommendations on public opinion polls and the Hispanic community that I hope will prove useful.

First of all, since these polls seem to have become a permanent fixture of modern life, there is little to be gained by ignoring them and much to be gained by putting them to good use and making certain that they accurately reflect the opinion of our community.

Second, any poll conducted by an organization with an obvious bias on a subject of particular interest to that organization ought to be stamped with the warning "Reader, beware!" In other words, if my wife conducts a poll on the best-looking Hispanic politician in the country and the poll names me, then there may be reason to question the accuracy of the poll. We have to carefully scrutinize not only the results of a poll but the methodology as well. If polls are judged to be fair, then more attention will be paid to them.

Third, since polls can be useful it would be worthwhile for members of the Hispanic community to become more involved with the poll taking by designing questionnaires, conducting the polls themselves, and in analyzing the results of the polls.

Fourth, we must learn to make better use of polls in order to fashion solutions to our problems. This gets back to the original question of how important polls taken of our community are. If we properly utilize them, they can be of great advantage to us, and the size and economic power of our community will increase the more interested those outside the community become in these polls.

Finally, and this ties in with the previous points, it is essential that we encourage the taking of even more polls of our community. The more polls that are taken, the better our ability to perfect the process and the more accurately we can make comparisons.

One final comment. As chair of the House Subcommittee on Census and Population, I have been involved with statistics and statistical analyses of a number of issues from immigration to census undercounts. I believe I have an appreciation of the usefulness of statistics. They can help us get a more complete picture of an issue. I put public opinion polls in the same category as statistics. They can help us get a more complete picture of our community. There is still a great deal to be learned about Hispanics in this country, and public opinion polls are an important way to broaden our general knowledge about the Hispanic community.

# Public Opinion and the Minority Legislative Agenda

Albert Luna III, *Texas House of Representatives*

Assisted by Brian A. Quintero, *Mexican American Legislative Caucus*

There is an erroneous assumption in politics about how to provide for the needs and opinions of the less fortunate: throw them more welfare, give them a few more seats in the Legislature, and then turn your backs on them. Unfortunately, many policymakers in our country fail to see the potential ramifications of ignoring the nonaffluent.

It wasn't too many years ago—in 1936, to be precise—when the *Literary Digest*, the most respected polling authority of that time, predicted that a fellow named Alf Landon would be the next president of the United States. From their preelection boasting, you would have thought that America didn't even know that Franklin Delano Roosevelt had just turned the country around. Well, one year later Landon wasn't in the White House, and three years later the *Literary Digest* was out of business.

How did a respected authority make this grave error in prediction? The *Digest* had mailed out 10 million polls and tabulated their results from the 2 million that were mailed back at respondent's cost. The *Digest* chose the original 10 million from a list of registered telephone and auto owners at that time. Unfortunately for the *Digest*, it was very unlikely that the heartbeat of post-Depression America could be judged from a group of citizens that all had phones, automobiles, change for postage, and time to fill out a questionnaire.

Now, almost half a century later, America has learned better polling procedures, but it still struggles to obtain the opinions and insights of those who aren't in the socioeconomic mainstream.

This paper will provide my reflections on public opinion and polls. However, you should be advised of three things. First, what I will say to you about the normative operation and abuses of politics and public opinion polls may be a rude awakening for our many colleagues and friends who assemble and publicly disseminate polls for every occasion. I specifically address these remarks to students of the statistical sciences; they should never believe that a poll is valuable just because it meets some objectivity criteria. Second, my reference base is as an aficionado of government, an elected official for five years, and chair of the Texas House of Representatives' 30-member Mexican American Legislative Caucus (MALC). The Caucus is composed of 19 Mexican Americans, 10 Anglos, and 1 black. Membership is generally open to those who demonstrate an interest in issues that specifically affect Hispanics. The members come from districts with a significant number of Mexican Americans. The group is nonpartisan, although I would suggest that it tends to be progressive in keeping with the many problems that face our communities. Third, on the basis of my observations over the years, I believe that race makes a significant difference in outlook on policy. According to the Gallup Poll, in 1973 85% of blacks preferred the Democratic party while only 38% of whites preferred this party over all others. Although Latinos were not singled out as a class in that poll, I believe our percentages would have closely resembled those of blacks. These gaps have decreased somewhat with the changing political times and the social advancement of minorities, but as I will explain later racial struggles and differences are still manifested in the polls.

My insights should be interpreted in the context of my work. I hope students of public opinion will understand and appreciate that a poll to the legislator is more a two-edged instrument of war than a peaceful olive branch.

### Elected Officials and Local Public Opinion in Their Districts

It's important to know where the state representatives, particularly Latinos, gather their opinions from. Unlike others who can write about opinion from arm's length with no worries, elected officials must have a precise knowledge of district concerns. In Texas, most state representatives with Latino-majority districts have very population-dense districts—we differ from many of our colleagues who have to drive substantially more hours to cover their districts. Legislators spend a considerable amount of time in neighborhood meetings and extracurricular events, and it is natural for people to approach us with their problems. Generally, these problems are not of global concern, but they are the most important thing to that person—specifically, that voter—at that time.

If it cannot be handled with a quick phone call, visit, or government form, then it necessarily becomes a deficiency in the system, that is, a problem which the legislator must make mental note of it to see if further action is needed.

In the 19 months between regular sessions (January through May every two years, special sessions excepted), a legislator has made a lot of mental notes. Usually, patterns start to emerge, particularly if her or his district is concentrated with civic and trade associations. You can sort out the issues between "district-specific" and "larger appeal." My Legislative District No. 143 consists of Houston's East End (our large Latino barrio), the Houston Ship Channel, and two blue-collar cities with populations of nearly 10,000 each. According to the 1980 Census, my district is 59% brown, 27% white, and 13% black, with 92% of the owner-occupied housing valued at less than $50,000. My experiences during the year tell me that my constituents want me to address problems concerned with transportation, inhalant abuse, union rights, and educational opportunities. They have also expressed concern on occasion about immigration reform, health and welfare services, and interest rates for housing and private loans. In general, it is from personal contact with the community that I form my local opinions.

While some officials do their polling through community contacts, a few others choose to send out questionnaires using certain budget allotments. Although this works for some areas, I have found that this does not work in most Hispanic districts. Consider the problem that arose with the Franklin Delano Roosevelt/Alf Landon poll. The poll was contingent upon a precise mailing identification of the subjects, and upon the return of a representative number of surveys. It helps to guarantee return postage on these surveys, but this can be costly and the return is generally imprecise. At best, a legislator may be able to discern what voting positions could be fatal to reelection, as those most likely to respond will be the ones who go to the polls for revenge.

Minority elected officials, more than their counterparts, meet with community leaders, particularly church and service organizations members, to ask for additional opinions and reports on the needs of the community. The rise in interfaith groups like Communities Organized for Public Service (COPS), Valley Interfaith, and The Metropolitan Organization (TMO) have been instrumental in raising the social conscience of the state. However, it should not be assumed that elected officials have issues first called to their attention by these groups—elected officials oftentimes are researching and negotiating ways to solve these problems long before community organizations unite on them.

Also, Latino elected officials are human, so they will have many innate biases that will affect their voting and service records. Like many other groups, Mexican Americans discuss issues and philosophically lean toward the opinions of their families, friends, community officials, co-workers, and church groups. To the extent that these ideologies and opinions are passed on from generation to generation, deep biases are formed. These may affect the political orientation and agenda setting of Latino elected officials.

### Elected Officials and Nonlocal Public Opinion

Above I suggested how a large number of Latino elected officials obtain the sense of public opinion for district concerns. The problem of greater academic concern is how Latino elected officials in the Texas House, ostensibly in a minority, choose to balance their knowledge of their districts with the needs of colleagues and the state as a whole.

The primary way that we determine what public opinion is and what the minority agenda will be is through candid, informal discussions with each other about our findings and experiences during the interim. Despite the undocumented nature of our revelations, we consistently find that we share the same problems and desires. Parents in McAllen and San Antonio are no different from parents in Houston trying to find ways to curb inhalant abuse among teenagers.

Oftentimes you will see similar goals in several legislative packages on the same issue, unless there is a representative who has a history of working on that particular issue. In such a case other members will usually defer to that representative through professional courtesy and only that representative will introduce a bill. Thus, if 30 different members do not introduce separate bills on one issue, it does not mean that they are not all interested in the matter. In reality, there is a better chance of getting good legislation passed if just one person sponsors a bill on an issue and others cosign or cosponsor it. This prevents duplication, eradicates hurt feelings, and minimizes the possibility of a bad version inadvertently becoming law.

People jokingly state that they breathe easier once the Legislature leaves town, and in fact losses can be substantial if bad representation or information influences decisions. Because of the gravity of this situation, we pool our personal polls, and then evaluate other polls for possible use. If necessary, we expose the shortcomings of polls. In chronological order, here are the criteria that Latino legislators usually apply in evaluating polls:

1. Whether they come from reputable, nonhostile sources
2. Whether they include Hispanic and other minorities, and if so whether we are analyzed as a separate group, a percentage of the population at large, or both
3. Whether the topics are of interest to the Latino elected official
4. Whether they can be effectively used in the course of the legislative game
5. Whether their results suggest other areas that need to be worked on in future legislative sessions.

The remainder of the paper discusses these criteria. Few polls meet these criteria, and thus the accomplishments of the Mexican American Legislative Caucus this past session (and others in the past) were not due to the use of commercial polls. However, if given the chance to participate in creating good polls from the start, I believe that in the future the Caucus would be ready to use them, and that they could further the interests of Mexican Americans and the state as a whole. This would mean the opportunity to participate in identifying the issues and framing the questions.

### Analyzing the Poll's Source

In general, a polling source needs to build a reputation for excellence before it is relied on, but it will be forever discounted if it is grossly incorrect or tends to stray into areas despised or intentionally ignored by the legislator.

During a legislative session, and even during the interim, legislators have no shortage of information provided to them; many agencies and special interests employ people just to provide legislators with opinions and data. As a general proposition, polls that we see are provided through special funds or interests. During the regular session of the Sixty-ninth Legislature, advocates of pari-mutuel betting supplied legislators with Wall Street economic impact studies and a poll conducted by Lance Tarrance & Associates (February 19, 1985) showing that pari-mutuel betting was favored by a majority of Texans. The bill, however, was defeated by almost two-thirds of the House of Representatives. It is doubtful that the advocates would have presented a poll indicating anything less than majority support for their issue. One battle that the Caucus and I fought was against the repeal of pesticide safety regulations for farmworkers. One of the key reasons behind the repeal's defeat was the use of erroneous polls from various industrial and farm interests showing that a majority of the House and the state were in favor of gutting the regulations. After House members realized that they had been misled on polls and vote counts, they responded by killing the legislation.

Polls sponsored by government agencies and reputable non-profit research groups receive most-favored treatment and often control sizable votes. During the Education Special Session, surveys from such groups as the Texas Research League and the Equity Coalition aided minorities and the Legislation as a whole.

### Determining if Hispanics Are Included in a Poll

As a general proposition, most polls lump Mexican Americans, Cubans, Puerto Ricans, and other peoples of Spanish descent together as "Hispanics." With the recent influx of many immigrants from Central America, it has become harder to distill what "Latino" public opinion is because of complications in identification, tracking, and subculture.

The problem that state legislators have with state data and surveys is that in the past Latinos were (and in many cases still are) put in the category of "White" or "Other." Thus such data cannot be used to examine areas of specifically Hispanic concern. For example, recent studies indicate that Hispanics may be more susceptible than the general population to various cardiovascular diseases, yet a broad-based research effort on Hispanic cardiovascular diseases using state databanks cannot be carried out. The reason is that Hispanic birth certificates would be needed for this research, but they cannot be retrieved as a group; many were coded as "White" or "Other." And it would be difficult if not impossible to retrieve them by surname. A majority of Hispanic birth certificates would have to be amended for this information to become accessible. Although there can be other justifications for amending Hispanic birth certificates, such as pure ethnic pride, there are potential fraud problems, and we would have to convince others that the amendments were justified despite the cost.

Still another problem relates to obtaining adequate polls based on person-to-person interviews. Legislators must seriously question the poll that claims to have "gone into the heart of the barrio." A poll that goes into the barrio must be done on foot, and few polls are willing to go to such expense. (Polling experts indicate that a good poll consists of at least 500 samplings, and the cost per person can range from $7 for a methodologically weak poll to $45 for a sound, top-rate survey.) In addition, there are other problems associated with person-to-person surveys such as length of time to compile, the risk of shortcuts taken because of the costs involved, and the general reluctance of Hispanics to open up and give their opinions to strangers. Phone polling of Hispanics, however, is not the solution; it has been repeatedly viewed as inaccurate not only because of Hispanic mistrust of strangers but also because of the complexities of designing a poll that can be answered by a cross section of a group with such a high disparity in educational levels.

Finally, Latino elected officials must rely on federal estimates of the size of the Hispanic population. Although the U.S. Census has been fairly predictable for the last decade and criteria have remained consistent, many feel our numbers are being underestimated.

The point that I want to stress here is that Latino elected officials are less likely to use outside polls than their Anglo colleagues because they must reject polls in which their people have not been adequately questioned and included; they are trustees for a population that affords substantial deference to elected officials, and unskilled acceptance of such a poll would be inexcusable. For example, a colleague who wants my vote brings me a poll showing that a "majority of Texans" feel a certain way on an issue. It would be a crime for me to forget who makes up the majority. According to the 1980 Census, Hispanics make up some 21% of the state's population. More likely than not, my colleague's poll has already discounted the Hispanic vote, if it bothered to put it in at all. My colleague's majority could be 51% all-white agreement, while all 21% Hispanics, all 23% Blacks, and 5% Others disagree. Thus, Latino officials must dissect polls and research before they decide whether they can support an issue.

### Deciding Whether the Topics Are on the Hispanic Agenda

People have always tried to pin us down on what specifically the "Hispanic agenda" is—that is, what they can expect to see us work on in terms of research, committee debates, press conferences, and vote gathering. Here I make three observations: one, the agenda is extremely fluid on specific issues; two, the agenda has actually been consistent on broad issues; and three, there is a tremendous internal debate about revealing the agenda to persons not immediately involved in the Latino policy process, since they might reveal it to those who may not agree with us on that series of issues.

Specific issues are raised constantly and generally don't disappear until they are statutorily corrected. These issues can be broken down into (1) issues awaiting further evaluation ("fresh issues"), and (2) issues that the legislator has already deemed meritorious but must postpone to a future date for various reasons. An example of a fresh issue is the "No Pass, No Play Rule" recently mandated for Texas secondary schools (in the Education Reform Act of 1984, also known as H.B. 72, which was passed in the second called special session of the Sixty-eighth Legislative Session). The legislators have all received substantial commentary on the rule, both pro and con. Although members may already have their personal opinion on the matter, they must still await results before deciding on any action. Examples of the latter type of specific issues include job training, minority business enterprises (MBE), low-income housing, and bilingual services. Here minority legislators have committed themselves, yet shortfalls in state revenue or a hostile political climate may bar them from any effective action.

Drawing upon many years of experience, I would say the broad issues are:

1. Education
2. Vibrant economic activity where we live
3. Preservation/creation of services, such as child support and food programs, so that those at the bottom of the social ladder can move up.

In government, it is especially interesting to see all types of Latinos uniting for these causes—rich, poor, educated, illiterate, and so on. Why is it that those who are well-to-do still advocate these positions to us, even if it may cost them a little more? Alan Monroe sets forth a good paradigm in his analysis of the black experience:

1. Middle-class blacks have experienced economic poverty in the recent past and have a continued identification with

the community they left behind. This makes them more sympathetic than whites, hence economic liberals.
2. Minorities are more enthusiastic about the efficacy of government, since it was the public arena that yielded many of their recent social gains.
3. Being liberal implies a rejection of some traditional values. Such traditional values are often strongly perceived by blacks as norms of the white society which they reject.

One difficult—and often overlooked—decision minority legislators must sometimes make is to downplay their legislative intentions even when it disappoints the public. During the recent session, for example, the press and citizens alike asked the Caucus to stir up support for indigent health care and farmworker bills. Rather than draw attention and risk complications, the Caucus quietly steered bills on these issues through both houses, defeating all sabotage attempts. We also had realized that minority business enterprise would not pass this session, so we diverted our resources away from this issue. We received much private criticism from minority chambers of commerce, yet we knew that running with MBE proposals would have hurt other bills. The horse-racing bill that died this session presents the clearest example of anti-MBE sentiment: conservatives were torn on the issue so they tacked on an MBE amendment in order to kill the bill on final reading. We have looked at their postsession newsletters and seen that they used the MBE/Minority Welfare issue to silence those voters who wanted to race and breed horses. We have found, and the public has discovered, that there are House members who will consistently work against issues that benefit minorities and the poor in general.

**Why Good Polls Can't Always Be Used**

Some polls and data—like U.S. Census reports, housing surveys, and reports on financial conditions—can be used for many years and still be valuable sources of information. However, most polls are not as broad in scope, so they must be tested for timeliness. Unfortunately, many good polls and surveys of public opinion must be rejected for untimeliness. Polling the Latino community accurately is very time-consuming, and it's virtually impossible to get quick responses back. On emotional issues, the date the poll is taken can be critical. For example, one colleague ran a minipoll of some constituents to see how effectively human resource services were being distributed. In that particular week DHR employees were experiencing contractual problems with the state, so public support for employee efforts was unusually low.

Even if we receive good polls, it may be too early or too late to introduce them into the policymaking process. A poll commissioned in 1985 by minority chambers of commerce saying Anglos favored government support for minority business enterprises would be irrelevant if decided by a slim margin like 55%, and would have very little value in 1987. Conversely, a poll that reported Texans favored preservation of general social services was useful because it reflected a broad proposition. Moreover, the respondents spoke for the future.

## Polling in the Future

There are five points concerning future polling which, if followed, would make it incumbent on elected officials to take a greater interest in polls.

First, the challenge for the future will be the assembly of impact statements for services increase or curtailment. Since the legislative process is often reduced to a game of numbers, it is important that we in government have our own numbers to check outside reports. In addition, state agencies such as the Department of Community Affairs compile user profiles, and it is important that these be continued. We cannot keep track of all agency activity, and reports from and about the individuals served are useful in committee testimony. For us to obtain the information critical in providing our constituents' social services, the government needs to do more polling. For many logistic reasons, government polls are very economical. There are, however, caveats. Where there is a shortage of funds (as Texas is experiencing right now), there will be little appropriative support. Also, it is very likely that most government entities would have to bring in professional help to ensure objectivity and accuracy.

A second point is that polling by government agencies and officials with particular concerns can be very effective. The recent survey by MALC on surplus scholarship monies in state universities has influenced policymaking in that area, hopefully to the benefit of Hispanics. Private surveys we have been doing on agency performance, particularly in minority employment practices, are compelling these agencies to listen when minorities knock on their doors. It is an exciting thing we are doing as the people's representatives to the state, and we should increase our polling and research efforts. Also, I expect many Latino legislators to become public informants—that is, move into the business of governmental relations—so that our experience with polls can be used.

Third, there is a great absence of polls on the Latino middle class and middle-income businesspeople. (We have an abundance of data on the poor, and *Forbes* and *Nuestro* are more than happy to tell us about the rich.) I don't have an answer to how we can get these polls and who will pay for them, but I can say that they should be immediately useful for two things: they would show how such individuals and their families moved into the middle class, and what elements (ignorance, discrimination, and so on) are preventing them from moving into the upper class.

Fourth, the polls have told us that the Latino is generally unaware of available benefits, laws pending, and rights in general. Polls to tell us how we can achieve greater social awareness would be helpful. (We have surveys on what media and community services the Latino gets information from, but there is a disparity between information dissemination and actual awareness of its significance.) I can think of no better example than the Latino's current struggles with the tax system.

Finally, as Latino officials move into greater political prominence, they will need polls to improve their political mobility. Polls that assess their saliency, their opponents, their chances in other races, and their overall performance and framing of issues will be in great demand as we start to run for higher offices.

## Summary

At this point in time, Latino elected officials do not rely on many polls. However, their inability to rely on polls is not of their choosing, and they must compensate for it by searching out opinion at many different levels.

Latino elected officials do evaluate polls, but their concerns and experience prevent them from accepting the common will of the majority, which they often determine from conversations with their closest colleagues. They are in a trusteeship position.

It is the intent of Latino elected officials to use polls when they can get more actively involved in them. It would be ideal to generate polls from within the government, but there are fiscal concerns. The polls of outside pollsters could be made a lot more attractive to Latino legislators if they were able, from the start, to participate in the production of the polls.

This Latino official has identified many areas where polls could be useful. Some of the most pressing needs include polls on the Latino middle class, polls on how to raise Latino awareness of rights and benefits at reasonable costs, polls and data on how services are reaching the people, and opinions on Latino elected officials in general.

# A Journalist's View of Latino Public Opinion Polls

Frank del Olmo, *Los Angeles Times*

I have been a reporter and columnist on the staff of the *Los Angeles Times* for 15 years. During that time I have often been asked to write reports that attempt to assess the views of Los Angeles' large Chicano community on social and political issues—from busing for the purpose of school integration to immigration reform. Additionally, in almost every major election campaign during that period I have also written reports on how Latino voters might cast their ballots in specific political races, from mayor to president of the United States. As a working journalist who has had to rely on poll results for help in writing news stories and opinion columns, I have reached two conclusions about public opinion polling as it affects the Latino community.

First, while polling among Latinos is done better today than 15 years ago, it can still be improved and refined. Specifically, it should be focused on subgroups or specific communities within the overall Latino population of the United States. I have found that polls attempting to gauge Latino sentiment on issues or candidates seem to be more reliable when they focus on a specific national group like Cuban Americans or Puerto Ricans, or on a particular community like San Antonio or East Los Angeles, than when they deal with Latinos as a national bloc.

Second, the most significant result of the past shortcomings of public opinion polling among Latinos has been an unfortunate tendency by political activists of all persuasions to use dubious or slanted polling results for their own ends. Usually this has involved trying to prove that their party or candidate or issue has significant support in the Latino community as a whole.

Because I am no expert on polls or how they are conducted, I am more comfortable dealing with this second point. I can, in fact, get myself pretty worked up about the misuse of sketchy or misleading poll results because I have seen it happen so often. It has been a consistent source of frustration to me while working at the *Times*.

My first experience with the lack of reliable polling among Mexican Americans was during the 1972 presidential campaign. Beginning with the California Democratic primary fight between South Dakota Senator George McGovern and Vice President Hubert Humphrey, I had a hard time coming up with a trustworthy and independent assessment of how the candidates and their campaigns were being received by the state's Mexican American voters, who represent a significant number of the state's registered Democrats. The only preelection poll I could find, Mervin Field's California Poll, had McGovern dramatically ahead, 55% to 22%. The only other way I had to assess Latino community reaction to the campaign was random interviews with Mexican Americans and with leaders of community organizations, trying to focus on those who were reputable and neutral in the Democratic race. Most of these sources saw the McGovern versus Humphrey race as a much tighter contest than the Field Poll indicated, as it eventually turned out to be.

My frustration grew later that year because of the vocal and highly visible effort by the La Raza Unida party to become a national Chicano political organization. I often wondered how much of their activity would translate into real votes, but again I had no polls to rely on. Obviously the lack of any real evidence that they commanded popular support, except in a few small Texas cities where their candidates had won local elections, did not stop La Raza Unida leaders from claiming that they spoke for the nation's Chicano voters. La Raza Unida leaders even went so far as to hold a national convention in El Paso where the delegates decided to support neither McGovern nor Richard M. Nixon in the presidential election.

But my greatest frustration stemmed from the fact that Nixon's now-notorious Committee to Reelect the President (CREEP) made an unprecedented effort to woo Latino voters in 1972, and I was unable to adequately determine how sincere or effective that campaign was prior to election day. My suspicions about CREEP's Latino effort were fed by occasional press leaks from the campaign committee. One of the more noteworthy was a campaign memo I obtained which indicated that a negative campaign was being waged among Latino voters by the Nixon people. Their intent was not so much to get Latinos to vote for Nixon as it was to "keep the electorate home." That memo quoted a poll taken by "a top reputable political survey company" in Los Angeles, San Antonio,

New York, and Chicago which found, among other things, a 74% disapproval rate among Puerto Ricans for Nixon. Clearly it was preferable to keep people who felt that way about Nixon away from the polls. I was never able to obtain a copy of the survey mentioned in the memo, or even find anyone who admitted having read it. But that memo and others raised legitimate suspicions about CREEP's Latino effort. What was needed were independent surveys to weigh against the Nixon campaign's claims.

After Nixon swamped McGovern, I tried to assess how well his highly visible and expensive campaign had done among Latino voters. Unfortunately, little effort was made by any of the major polling organizations to do exit surveys in Latino communities. In the only independent poll that I am aware of, Richard Scammon, polling for the NBC network, showed Nixon winning 18% of the Latino vote nationwide, an improvement of only 3% over his 1968 total of 15%.

Sources in the Nixon campaign, of course, were eager to offer their own specially compiled results that showed otherwise. After saying that they had hoped for modest support, perhaps 20% among Latinos in California, they proudly made available precinct results from Latino areas in middle-class cities like Whittier, Pico Rivera, and Monterey Park, where Nixon got voter support ranging from 50% to 66%. In precincts in heavily Latino Northeast Los Angeles, Nixon's support ranged from 26% to 35%, still impressive according to GOP campaigners. As a result of their survey of selected precincts and counties, Nixon's Latino supporters claimed that he had increased his 1968 vote among Mexican Americans from 10% to 35% and among Puerto Ricans from 17% to 27%, while losing ground with Cuban American voters, 70% to 60%. Because these results came from specially selected precincts I was initially reluctant to use them. When I finally did so, I tried to put them in perspective and to counterbalance them with rebuttals from Democratic party leaders, who often referred to Scammon's findings. My 1972 experience has made me cautious with poll results ever since.

(I must add at least one self-serving note on the 1972 election at this point. While it was dissatisfying to use CREEP figures that had clearly been slanted in favor of Nixon, it did help me establish a good relationship with the sources who gave them to me, both in the Nixon campaign and among the Nixon administration's Latino appointees. Most of those sources proved valuable to me later, when the Watergate scandal broke. Several of them provided me with papers and information on the activities of a small clique known as the Brown Mafia, a handful of Latinos who worked for the administration who were caught using political appointments and government grants to sway Latino leaders and community groups to support Nixon. It was a minor, but nonetheless telling, Latino angle to the larger Watergate scandal.)

There has been more polling of Latinos since 1972, although I am not so sure the polls have been any more accurate. And I know they have not made much difference to the politicians, both Latino and otherwise. The politicos still have a fondness for tossing around figures that support what they want to believe, while ignoring anything that contradicts them.

Looking over my notes and reports for the 1976 campaign between former Presidents Jimmy Carter and Gerald Ford, for example, the only figure that leapt out at me was a quote from Kansas' Republican Senator Robert Dole, who was Ford's running mate that year. Dole told a meeting of Latino political activists in Los Angeles that Ford would win more Latino votes than the "35%" Nixon got in 1972. Apparently the GOP liked that number enough to repeat it as a matter of faith.

In the 1980 election between President Carter and Ronald Reagan the problems posed by the lack of detailed and rapid exit-poll results from Latino precincts again became obvious. Within days of the Reagan victory, Latinos active in the Republican campaign were claiming that Reagan had outdone Nixon's '72 effort, again using results from specially selected areas. This time, however, the Southwest Voter Registration Education Project (SVREP) in San Antonio had made an independent effort to conduct its own assessment of the Latino vote. Unfortunately, the project's tally was compiled very slowly and was not available to the press for several weeks. SVREP determined that Reagan apparently did no better than Nixon had done, and perhaps worse, with 20% to 30% of the Latino vote. Unfortunately, SVREP's exit poll did not receive the wide publicity that some of the claims made by Reagan supporters got.

In 1984, by way of contrast, I had for the first time several estimates of the Latino vote to work with in the immediate aftermath of the race between Reagan and former Vice President Walter Mondale. I attribute this to the fact that the Reagan campaign had made no secret of the fact that it intended to focus on Latino voters to offset the president's unpopularity among blacks and his gender gap with women voters. The lowest figure was NBC's, which put Reagan's Latino support at 33%. ABC had the highest figure, 50%. The Spanish International Network, CBS

News, and I.A. Lewis, who conducts the Los Angeles Times Poll, had Reagan getting 43% of the Latino vote.

Again, however, when the SVREP compiled the results of its own surveys later on, all these initial estimates were determined to be on the high side. Reagan's support nationally among Latinos was in the range of 25% to 40%, according to the project's survey. More significantly, the project for the first time in my memory broke down the results by national origin and local communities, finding that Reagan's support ranged from a low of 18% among Mexican Americans in the Midwest to 93% among Cuban Americans in Miami.

Sadly, these not-so-subtle differences have apparently meant little to Latino Republicans who have been loudly proclaiming the emergence of a "real two-party system" among Latinos nationally. While they are entitled to boast about their achievements, they would be better off if they focused on their real gains rather than illusory triumphs. The difference between 18% and 93% is more than trifling, and should call into question the viability of a Latino coalition in support of a specific candidate whether a Democrat or a Republican, a liberal or a conservative. The longer Latino activists continue to posture about bloc voting power, the more they will appear to be little more than amateurish shams to the news media, their own party leaders, and other political professionals, all of whom can read those numbers more carefully than some ardent activists care to.

The tendency to overlook national and cultural differences in gauging Latino opinion is not just evident in the variable support a politician like Reagan gets from Chicanos and Cubanos, or in East Los Angeles and the South Bronx. It is also evident when Latinos are polled on key public issues like illegal immigration.

Immigration, of course, is a complex and emotional issue. Not surprisingly, different polls of Latino views on the subject have arrived at variable results. Once again, people on particular sides of the issue have tended to focus on the findings they think back up their point of view.

The most notorious in this regard, from my experience, has been the Federation for American Immigration Reform (FAIR). They are no longer satisfied with citing all the opinion polls (Gallup, Roper, etc.) that indicate most Americans want the kind of immigration reforms FAIR is pushing for, such as sanctions against employers who hire illegal immigrants. Part of their campaign has been to portray Latino activists—who have been their most visible, if not most effective, opponents in the congressional debate on illegal immigration—as isolated from the mainstream of Latino community opinion. Time and again FAIR spokespersons have tried to prove that Latinos favor employer sanctions and other restrictionist positions on immigration. The latest instance was in FAIR's most recent newsletter (September 1985) which cited a poll taken for the *Corpus Christi Caller-Times* by Texas A&M University in July 1985. The survey found that 63% of Latino respondents favored employer sanctions. The item concluded that "every major poll of Hispanic Americans has shown overwhelming support for employer sanctions legislation."

This is not true, of course. To the chagrin of FAIR officials, the major poll taken by I.A. Lewis of the Los Angeles Times Poll as part of our Pulitzer Prize-winning series on Los Angeles' Latino community came out quite differently. Our poll of 1,498 California residents included 568 Latino respondents. The survey found that 57% of the Latinos opposed employer sanctions, compared to 34% who supported the idea. And on the issue of amnesty for illegal immigrants, our Latino respondents favored it by 75% to 18%.

I cite these results not to engage in a pointless debate with FAIR over immigration reform, but to suggest that when reputable pollsters come out with such dramatically different results perhaps they are missing something. In this case I suspect it is the subtle nuances of the divided feelings Latinos have about immigration.

The immigration issue is, after all, not just a political abstraction to Latinos, but often a deeply personal concern. That is why a pollster like Gallup can ask a question, in English, about "illegal aliens," and get many Latinos (who like most Americans want "solutions" to "problems" like illegal immigration) to say they favor a solution like employer sanctions. But when a Spanish-speaking pollster, like those employed by Lewis for our survey, asks a similar question, in Spanish, the nuances can be quite different. Often, so is the answer. When a Latino is asked about "workers without proper papers" instead of "illegal aliens," for example, different feelings arise. Almost every Chicano in this country has relatives somewhere in Mexico, and she or he may well answer one way when asked if illegal aliens should be stopped from crossing the border and another way when asked if Uncle Carlos should be kept from entering the United States the next time he wants to come here.

Until public opinion polls can take these kinds of distinctions into account, the results will remain subject to dispute, whether they focus on public issues or on individual candidates in political campaigns.

# Polling the Latino Community: Does Anybody Have the Numbers?

Daniel J. Balz, *Washington Post*

Who won the Latino vote in the 1984 election? The answer to that seemingly simple question is more puzzling than revealing. On a grand scale, the answer is obvious. Democrat Walter F. Mondale captured a majority of the national vote among Hispanics or Latinos, despite President Reagan's 49-state landslide victory. Just how sizable Mondale's victory was among these traditionally Democratic voters is another question. According to exit polls conducted for NBC, Mondale won 68% of the Latino vote nationwide to Reagan's 32%. CBS exit polls showed it as Mondale over Reagan by 61 to 37. ABC's margin was even narrower: Mondale 56, Reagan 44. Other exit polls showed Mondale with an even narrower margin. The variety of the findings is all the more perplexing when contrasted to exit poll findings on the white vote and the black vote, which varied only a few percentage points among the network polls.

How did Reagan do among Hispanics in Texas? According to NBC, the president lost to Mondale by a margin of 65 to 35. ABC, on the other hand, said it was Reagan losing by 76 to 24. And what about Reagan's home state of California? There ABC found the tighter outcome, with Mondale defeating Reagan 57 to 42. NBC said it was Mondale over Reagan 76 to 24. CBS found common cause with each of the other networks. In Texas, CBS saw it about like NBC: Mondale 66, Reagan 34. In California, CBS called it almost precisely the way ABC did: Mondale over Reagan by 56 to 43.

What about New York, which has the third largest concentration of Latinos in the nation? The ABC exit poll said Mondale captured 60% of the Hispanic vote in New York compared to Reagan's 40%. CBS said Reagan won it by 50 to 46, but the sample size makes the figures unreliable. And NBC? Based on the postelection booklet issued by the network, which was said to contain "the major findings of 15 separate Election Day Voter Polls," the information doesn't exist. The Hispanic vote presumably would be found in one of two categories, race or ethnic background. The racial breakdown covers whites and blacks. The ethnic breakdown covers the New York of an earlier era: Italians, Germans, Eastern Europeans, and Irish. What happened to the Puerto Ricans?

Such are the frustrations of a journalist seeking to understand what happened in 1984—and this in a year in which more attention was paid to Latino and other minority voters than ever before. Until it was clear the president was destined to bury Mondale and the Democrats in a victory of historic proportions, one of the principal themes of the coverage of major newspapers, newsmagazines, and television networks was the potential for a significant increase in voter registration and turnout among women, minorities, and the poor. That also was one of the fundamental elements of the Democratic party's strategy. The Democrats' analysis of the American electorate, based on the results of the 1982 midterm elections, said that if the vast numbers of unregistered voters among groups that traditionally supported the Democrats could be mobilized, it would tip the balance against Reagan. Among minority voters, blacks were the main focus of attention, in part because of the historic presidential candidacy of the Reverend Jesse L. Jackson. But Latinos were a close second. As Haynes Johnson and Thomas B. Edsall of the *Washington Post* wrote in March 1984, "In Texas, a vital state for the Democrats if they are to regain the White House, the path to victory lies in the ability of (voter registration organizers) to produce a record turnout of Mexican American voters in November." That was a common assessment at the time, not just in Texas but in many other states.

Ultimately, Hispanic voters turned out in record numbers. (Registration alone was up 27% over 1976.) But everyone's analysis came up short. Overall, the increase in minority registration and turnout was less than the Democrats had predicted—and it does not appear to have changed the outcome anywhere in the country.

Today, nearly a year after election day, there is considerable disagreement over how Latinos voted and why. The examples cited earlier are hardly insignificant and make interpretation of the 1984 election something of a guessing game. The results uniformly show that Reagan won more Hispanic votes in 1984 than in 1980, but the variations among the network exit polls affect a journalist's ability to decide whether Reagan simply captured slightly more Hispanic votes than the historical norm for a Republican or whether he made dramatic inroads into a once strongly Democratic constituency. Which is it? Who should be believed? Given the intense interest in the issue of party realignment nationally and the role Hispanic voters may play in such a shift, the absence of better information about 1984 leaves analysts rather empty-handed.

Even more confusing are the findings for Texas and California. NBC found that Mondale's margin over Reagan was 30 points in Texas but a whopping 52 points in his home state. ABC, on the other hand, found Mondale a 52-point winner in Texas but a much narrower 15-point victor in California. How do you analyze that? Adding to the puzzle are findings from exit polls conducted by the Southwest Voter Registration Education Project. SVREP's findings mirror NBC's in Texas and ABC's in California. The group sampled "Texas Mexicans" and "Los Angeles Mexicans," admittedly samples somewhat different from those in statewide exit polls by the networks. But what SVREP found was Mondale over Reagan 76 to 24 in Texas and 72 to 28 in Los Angeles.

The more journalists—and presumably political campaign managers—analyze the available data on the Latino vote from 1984 and previous elections, the more exasperating it becomes, giving rise to the oft-quoted statement that Hispanics are not only the fastest-growing minority group in America but also the least understood.

In recent years, an enormous information base about the nation's Hispanic minority has been amassed. We owe much of the credit to the Census Bureau, which in 1980—at the urging of Latino officials around the country—undertook the most systematic count ever of Hispanics. As a result, more now is known about this group than ever before. And yet, despite this growing database, the Latino community remains a political enigma.

## Latino Power versus Potential

The Hispanic community continues to have more political potential than impact. One overriding reason is that the percentage of Latinos who register and vote remains smaller than that of other groups in the country, including blacks. The higher percentage of noncitizens among Latinos means that, even in a year when there was a dramatic increase in voter registration and turnout, the percentage of the voting age population that actually went to the polls remained well below 50%. That fact alone severely limits the power of the Hispanic community and makes it less urgent for politicians of all stripes to respond to the needs of the Hispanic community, or even to work hard to understand how those citizens feel about certain issues. To have political impact, a group needs both size and the ability to demonstrate its clout. Significant advances have been made in the past decade, both in voter turnout and in the election of Latinos to office. But despite large and generally successful voter registration and mobilization drives, the Latino community has yet to fully demonstrate its clout in national politics.

The other reason the Hispanic community has had less impact than some people had predicted is the nature of the "community." It is divided geographically and culturally. As Robert R. Brischetto of the Southwest Voter Registration Education Project wrote in a paper delivered to a League of Women Voters conference in July 1985, "There is not one but a number of Latino electorates in the United States, each with its unique historical experience rooted in its country of origin." About 9 million or almost 60% of the 14.6 million Latinos in the United States as of 1980 were of Mexican origin; about 2 million or 13% were of Puerto Rican origin; while 1 million or 7% were of Cuban origin. The remaining 3 million or roughly 22% were of Other Spanish origin, according to the Census Bureau. California and Texas accounted for roughly 50% of the Hispanic population in the United States, but Latinos were also concentrated in several other states: New York with 11%, Florida with 6%, Illinois with 4%. Another 9% of Hispanics lived in Arizona, Colorado, and New Mexico. New Jersey accounted for slightly more than 3%.

Brischetto's paper contained a breakdown of the voting age population in those states that revealed interesting differences within the Latino community in states that have been stereotyped by politicians and the press. Texas and California both share their southern borders with Mexico, but while 91% of Hispanics in Texas are of Mexican origin, only 78% are in California. In New York, 56% of Latinos are of Puerto Rican origin, with Other Spanish accounting for 35%. In New Jersey, 44% are of Puerto Rican origin, 33% of Other Spanish origin, and 20% of Cuban origin. In Illinois, 63% of Hispanics are of Mexican origin while 19% are of Puerto Rican origin. In Florida, 59% of Hispanics are of Cuban origin, but another 24% are of Other Spanish origin. Arizona and New Mexico offer another striking contrast. In Arizona, 89% of Hispanics are of Mexican origin, but next door in Mew Mexico the percentage is just 47.5, with the bulk of the rest being of Other Spanish origin.

"One must never lose sight of the diversity within the Hispanic population," Thomas Cavanagh wrote in a paper also delivered at the League of Women Voters conference, "The Puerto Ricans of the Northeast are as strongly Democratic as the Cubans of Florida are Republican, while the Mexican Americans of the Southwest are somewhat similar in political leanings to blue-collar urban ethnics of the Frost Belt: New Deal liberals on economic issues, generally conservative on social issues and highly patriotic. The socioeconomic and cultural differences even within these groups make generalization across the entire spectrum of the Hispanic population somewhat suspect."

Consider some other variations. There is no question that the Latino community is growing much faster than the population at large, but even this statistic shows the danger of sweeping generalizations. Between 1970 and 1980, the total national population grew by 9%, while the increase among "Hispanics" was 61%, according to the Census Bureau. But while the increase among those of Other Spanish origin was just 19%, the increase among those of Mexican origin was 93%. (Both Cubans and Puerto Ricans grew by more than 40%.)

There are other demographic differences. That the Hispanic population is younger than the population at large is well known. But among Hispanics, Cubans have a median age of 38 years, which is higher than the overall population. Mexicans and Puerto Ricans, however, have a median age of just 22 years. That Hispanics generally earn less money than the general population is also well known ($16,200 versus $22,000 per family). But while Cuban families had a median income of $18,800 in 1980, Puerto Rican families had a median income of just $11,150. Recent studies of New York Hispanics found a similar breakdown within the state. According to the 1980 Census data, Puerto Rican households in New York City had a median income of $8,181. The average for all Hispanic households was $9,676 (and for black households it was $10,716). Most Hispanics live in metropolitan areas, but Cubans and Puerto Ricans are more likely to live in areas of more than one million persons. For Cubans, the percentage is 83; for Puerto Ricans 73, and for Mexicans 55.

The immigrant status of the Latino community, an important element in any political analysis, illustrates another area of misunderstanding. About one-third of all Hispanics living in the United States in 1980 were born outside the country. But here again the breakdown among states reveals significant differences. In Florida, for example, 61% of Hispanics were foreign-born, largely the result of Cuban immigration over the past three decades. In California, 37% were foreign-born. But an identical percentage of Illinois Hispanics also were foreign-born, underscoring that many of the most recent arrivals in the United States are spreading far beyond the states closest to the Mexican border. In contrast, in Texas, which is usually the location for newspaper or magazine articles that describe the influx of undocumented workers from Mexico, the percentage was just 19. And in New Mexico, the state with the highest percentage of Hispanics in its population, only 6% of the Latinos were foreign-born.

It is easy to dwell on all this diversity, but the sad fact is that the significance of those differences isn't well understood. Whether such differences in age, income, place of birth, immigrant status, and the like mean much in terms of either voting behavior or attitude is not terribly clear. Whether the figures that suggest those differences are even accurate also is not clear. As a result, the coverage of Latinos by the national media continues to focus on several large, seemingly immutable facts.

### The Discovery of the Latino Community

The national media discovered the emerging power of the Latino community in the late 1970s, and they have been trying to understand the phenomenon ever since—with mixed results. It was not until the spring of 1978 that my own newspaper, the *Washington Post*, splashed a multipart series across its front pages that began: "A nation within a nation is emerging in the Southwest. Its language is a hybrid of English and Spanish. Its culture is a blend of modern, technological United States and developing but still rural Mexico. Its existence is most evident along the 1,933-mile border that the United States shares with Mexico, but it is highly visible as well in such diverse nonborder cities as Los Angeles, Phoenix, Albuquerque, Houston, and Denver. Its existence poses a threat to the American melting pot ideal greater than ever faced from the Irish, the Czechs, the Italians and the Poles." Later, the article quoted the late author and historian Carey McWilliams this way: "A binational, bicultural, bilingual regional complex or entity is emerging in the borderlands. Nothing quite like this zone of interlocking economic, social, and cultural interests can be found along any other border of comparable length in the world."

The *Post* was one of the first among major newspapers, magazines, and television networks to bring this to the attention of a general national audience, but others quickly followed, often with distinction. In 1981, John Crewdson, then of the *New York Times* and today a *Chicago Tribune* reporter based in Los Angeles, won a Pulitzer Prize for his coverage of the immigration issue. That same year, Joel Garreau (who edited the 1978 *Washington Post* series) published his book *The Nine Nations of North America*, which described the region from Texas to California (on both sides of the border) as the emerging nation of MexAmerica. In 1984, the *Los Angeles Times* won a Pulitzer Prize for its reporting on the Latino community.

And yet the national media continue to rediscover the obvious: the growing power of the Hispanic population and its potential for changing the nation. The most recent example came barely two months ago when *U.S. News & World Report* carried a cover story, entitled "The Disappearing Border," that posed the question: "Will the Mexican Migration Create a New Nation?" Its opening had a familiar ring. "Now sounds the march of new conquistadors in the American Southwest. The heirs of Cortés and Coronado are rising again in the land their forebears took from the Indians and lost to the Americans. By might of numbers and strength of culture, Hispanics are changing the politics, economy and language in the U.S. states that border Mexico."

In the half-dozen or so years in which the national media have paid attention to the Latino community, the coverage has gone through a number of stages that appear to have brought us almost full circle, if the *U.S. News & World Report* cover story is any indication. First came awareness of the fact that there were increasing numbers of Latinos in this country. Out of that awareness came the recognition on the part of public officials, political organizers, and the media that this new minority was likely to have a powerful impact on American politics in the not-too-distant future. But the more reporters looked, the more they realized they did not know much about Latinos—and there were few places they could turn for reliable information. As the conflict in Central America heated up and the problems of Mexico's economy worsened, attention shifted back to the issue of immigration and whether there really is a nation growing within a nation.

The allure of this "new group," however, has triggered a biennial stampede among political journalists, who with each election cycle discover the potential of the Latino community and point out the fact that Hispanic voters hold the key to victory in one state or another. (Those pilgrimages usually include a visit to the Southwest Voter Registration Education Project, which has been a leader in trying to assemble information about political habits of Mexican Americans and other Hispanics in the Southwest.) These kinds of stories surfaced prominently in 1980, when Jimmy Carter was struggling to hold on to his presidency. Texas emerged as a pivotal battleground state—no Democrat in this century has won the White House without winning Texas—and the changing demographics of the state, especially the potential power of Mexican American voters, formed the basis of much of the analysis of the election there.

The same thing happened in 1982, especially in the coverage of the Texas gubernatorial race. The 1980 election suggested Mexican Americans in Texas might be ready to vote Republican in greater numbers, and Republican Governor William P. Clements courted them furiously during his term in office. Throughout the campaign, his strategists closely monitored the Mexican American vote and confidently predicted that Clements would make a dramatic breakthrough on election day. Instead he was buried by an outpouring of Democratic voters, including Mexican Americans who had been specially targeted by Democratic strategists. Again in 1984, the coverage focused more on the potential of the Latino community than on the reality.

### The Media's Knowledge Gap

Because there is so little reliable information about Hispanics nationally, the media's coverage of Latino political behavior often has been one-dimensional, based largely on population projections that suggest a growing importance of Mexican American, Cuban American, or Puerto Rican voters that may continue to be out of proportion to reality. Lacking more concrete information about attitudes and voting behavior, much of the political reporting about Hispanics has taken on a kind of gee-whiz quality. "Gee, there certainly are a lot of Mexicans coming across that border!" It is the journalistic equivalent of spreadsheet analysis on computers, with journalists plugging in variables on population increases, registration, and turnout and then analyzing these possible new worlds. It's fun, but so far it has not always proven to be well grounded.

The fault lies not just with the media, but also with those who help supply the information that reporters use to describe this phenomenon. Some journalists have become so frustrated in their search for accurate information about the Hispanic population that they have come to distrust almost all survey research data that is publicly available. Pollsters are similarly frustrated by their inability to gauge accurately the sentiments within the Latino community.

Ironically, this comes at a time when many Latino elected officials are seeking to break the stereotype that they and their constituents have few interests beyond the issues of immigration reform and social welfare. Democratic Representative Bill Richardson of New Mexico writes in the fall 1985 issue of *Foreign Policy* magazine that Hispanics are "slowly but steadily and conscientiously becoming involved in foreign-policy issues." Willie Velasquez, who heads the Southwest Voter Registration Education Project, said in the spring of 1984: "The 1984 election is an excellent time to inaugurate a new era. We used to be concerned about paving streets. Now, for the balance of this decade, we're going to be concerned about U.S. public policy questions. After this election, people are going to learn about us." Are these statements correct or are they simply wishful thinking on the part of leaders of the Latino community who resent being narrowly categorized?

Many of the questions reporters began asking almost a decade ago remain unanswered, but they are no less urgent today. Who are the Latinos and where do they live? Why aren't more registered to vote? Why are so many slow to seek U.S. citizenship? How have they voted and why? Can the Republican party make significant inroads into the Hispanic vote, or are Hispanics likely to remain solidly Democratic for years to come? Is the Latino community essentially an immigrant community in attitude, or is it divided between those concerned primarily with issues of jobs and social welfare and those who have entered the economic mainstream? What do Hispanics think about illegal immigration? Is it a threat to their own well-being, or are efforts to reform the nation's immigration laws likely to increase discrimination against Hispanics? How are Latino attitudes affected by country of origin, by age, by place of residence, and by education? Are Hispanic attitudes on arms control, tax reform, and the trade and budget deficits significantly different from the Anglo community's? And what if they are? Will that or should that affect public policy?

Finding the answers to such questions in most national polls is impossible, if only because the sample is so small—and as we've seen so diverse—as to be statistically insignificant. State-by-state polls, which next to national polls are the most common in the context of political campaigns, often undercount Hispanics, and thus underrepresent them in the findings. Even poll takers who want to include a representative sample of Hispanics often find the obstacles too great to overcome. Polls that survey only Hispanics have certain built-in limitations. One is that the organizations that usually conduct them have a vested interest in enhancing the power of the Latino community in state, local, or national affairs. Another is that they tend to be more static than other polls. Sample sizes often are smaller and geographic sweep limited. Also, there aren't many of these polls, meaning they lack the kind of timeliness most useful to journalists reporting on breaking events or evolving public policy issues.

Until that kind of information is routinely available to the public, until it is easier to compare Hispanics to the rest of the population on a variety of issues, until the differences within the Hispanic community are better understood, the task of interpreting the importance of the Latino vote will remain severely limited. So far, it's not clear that either the major polling organizations or the networks and newspapers that conduct their own survey research are prepared to do that, leaving unanswered the question of who won the Latino vote in 1984. Will the same confusion exist after 1988?

# Comment: Why Polls Matter and Why Latinos are Ignored

Benjamin I. Page, *The University of Texas at Austin*

My comments must be rather deferential. I am by no means an expert on Latinos, and I expect to gain more from this conference than the conference gains from me. I will simply offer a few general observations from the perspective of a student of public opinion and survey research.

The papers for this first panel have done an excellent job of raising the issues of the conference as a whole. Not only has the special concern of our panel (the importance of public opinion and of poll data) been brought up, but also the problems of incompleteness and inaccuracy in polling Latinos. I will deal with each of these topics in turn.

First, I think Representative Garcia and others are entirely correct in arguing that poll data are quite important in helping public officials represent the needs and desires and preferences of Latinos. It is very difficult to represent opinions that are unknown. If Latinos' voices are to be heeded politically, someone must hear those voices.

To be sure, as State Representative Luna points out, there are often reasons to be distrustful of polls; and polls are quite costly, especially for small constituencies, where the expense of a good survey can be nearly as great as it would be for a sample of the whole country. Moreover, as he notes, alternative means of ascertaining people's opinions are available. Many political leaders (no doubt including Representative Luna himself) have an uncanny ability of figuring out what their constituents want by talking with people and reading their mail. This is especially feasible in small homogeneous constituencies, and for experienced politicians with close ties to the community, though even they can go astray.

I want to emphasize, however, that most of the alternative methods of learning about public opinion have grave deficiencies. Many of them are not feasible at all for learning about opinions on a statewide or national basis. The timeworn technique of talking with taxicab drivers and barbers and bartenders obviously produces a biased sample of opinions that can differ—in extreme and sometimes bizarre ways—from what the average person thinks. Representative Luna's much more systematic (and extremely burdensome) method of going door to door is superior and, taken to the limit, it will produce a perfect picture of opinions in his district if he talks with everyone. But of course it is not generally feasible to talk with everyone, even in a local district, and it is utterly impossible statewide or nationally. Anything short of completeness creates problems. The people contacted may be atypical because they are willing to talk (political supporters tend to talk more readily than opponents) or happen to be at home (the unemployed or homemakers, rather than those employed outside the home) or happen to live in a convenient neighborhood. Their opinions may not represent constituents' opinions generally. Even if they do, the door-to-door contractor will have a hard time remembering exactly how often people favored or opposed a particular policy. The contractor cannot possibly keep track of which sorts of people (young, old, male, female) thought what, or how various opinions interrelated with each other, as survey tabulations can do.

Mail questionnaires are often worse. Frequently the questions are written in misleading or self-serving ways. Even if not, the responses will almost always be biased. Much research has shown that those of higher income and formal education (and supporters of the questioner) more often fill out questionnaires, so the results give a false picture of public opinion. Opponents and the poor and alienated get left out.

Still worse is unsolicited mail. Not everyone has a secretary to fire off a letter; not everyone has a typewriter or the time and articulateness and self-confidence to write to officials. Those who do so generally have relatively high incomes or a special interest in the topic, and their letters will not tell much about what ordinary people think. To pay attention to them as being the "intense" or the only relevant people distorts the idea of democracy.

Worst of all, as a source of information about public opinion, is the input of group leaders and lobbyists. They have their own agendas, which may be quite different from what the public wants. And, as Rudy de la Garza reminds us, unless we have solid data on what the people think we cannot be sure which leaders to believe.

Survey research is not perfect. But for many purposes it is, as the saying goes, the only wheel in town. There is no other reliable way to get an accurate picture of what thousands or millions of Latinos are thinking. That information (concerning the opinions of noncitizens as well as citizens, I might add) is important for legislators in deciding what bills to introduce or how to vote, for candidates deciding what stands to take, for parties picking candidates and platforms, for executives writing regulations and enforcing the law. Polls are an essential device for helping Latinos get their needs and wants attended to.

I would add that surveys can be useful for at least two other purposes. First, studies of Latinos' political behavior can show politicians to what extent they had better pay attention if they want to win elections. Of course, reality counts; if people don't actually vote, they become easier to ignore. But survey research can show politicians what will happen if they do ignore Latinos. Furthermore, polls and surveys of Latinos can be useful in a different way—to study aspects of their characteristics and behavior that are directly relevant to policy making. Only survey evidence, for example, can demonstrate whether or not recent immigrants (including undocumented workers) pose the kinds of threats and problems that some non-Latinos seem to fear, or whether this is mostly mythology. The existing survey evidence points toward the conclusion of mythology, but more evidence is needed.

If surveys of Latinos are such a wonderful idea, why aren't there more of them, and more accurate ones? Frank del Olmo and Daniel Balz and paper givers on the other panels cite a good many examples of neglect and of noncredible or discrepant findings, especially in election polls. Why is this? I do not want to minimize the importance of deliberate self-serving biases in surveys. It is all too easy to pick your favorite precincts (in Whittier and Monterey Park and so forth) and find a lot of Republican Chicano voters, or to ask questions with loaded phrases like "illegal aliens" and find a lot of antiimmigration sentiment. But in a sense this problem is easy to solve. All it takes is increasingly sophisticated consumers of polls and vigorous exposure of those who engage in trickery. It is much harder to deal with the fundamental problems of polling Latinos, problems that must be faced by those with the best will in the world.

First is the small size of the Latino population: millions of people, yes, but only perhaps 6 to 7% of the U.S. population and 5 to 6% of the U.S. electorate. This means that in a standard national sample of 1,500 respondents, which gives a very accurate picture of the "average" American, only some 90 or 100 Latinos may be included. That is not enough to give an accurate picture of Latinos. It is possible to oversample: to interview, say, twice or three times the number of Latinos who would appear in the sample by chance. But this is very expensive, and it complicates the use of the data. It will generally be done only when there are compelling political or financial reasons to do it—as in some surveys that oversampled blacks in the 1960s. If you want oversampling, organize!

The second problem, the really serious one, is that Latinos live in several quite different, geographically clustered and homogeneous communities. As Daniel Balz points out, Miami Cubanos are very different from East Los Angeles Chicanos and South Bronx Puerto Ricans. This problem interacts with the way surveys are conducted to produce some appalling results. Most surveys, whether national samples or exit polls or whatever, don't rely on truly random samples; they cluster their sampling units geographically to make life easier (and cheaper) for interviewers. Thus a survey may heavily include one Latino community but ignore another, while a different survey does just the opposite.

I believe that this is a major reason for the conflicting poll results. A survey with lots of Cuban American respondents will give different results from one with many Chicanos. A survey with many high-income Chicanos will differ from one with many poor Chicanos. One solution is to stratify, to deliberately include interviews in many diverse Latino areas. Another is to conduct random-digit-dialing telephone interviews, which are more scattered geographically, although telephone interviews may be especially problematic with Spanish-speaking respondents unless interviewers are bilingual. Still another solution is to focus sharply on studying individual Latino communities, using common questionnaires, and then reaggregate the results up to a national sample of Latinos. All these solutions are expensive and require political pressure and financial resources. (Again, organize!) All require the cooperation of pollsters, which this conference ought to be very helpful in enlisting.

There are plenty of other technical problems in polling Latinos. One, a very central one, is defining just who is and isn't Latino, and identifying her or him. Having a Spanish surname is neither a necessary nor a sufficient condition for being a Latino. Screener questions about ethnic identification would seem to be the answer, but they are not easy to devise or use. Actually finding and interviewing Latinos can be difficult, especially in the case of non-citizens and—all the more so—undocumented workers, who may shrink from contact with official-looking and official-sounding strangers. The language of interview is tricky; English may be uncomfortable or unavailable for some respondents, but how can a Spanish-speaking interviewer always be available (for example, when a Latino turns up in an unexpected place)? And how can Spanish and English questions be made comparable? Finally, as Frank del Olmo so tellingly pointed out, subtleties of question wording can distort the responses of Latinos just as thoroughly as the responses of anybody else.

Such technical issues will be addressed by experts later in the conference. I do not want to overstay my welcome. I would close by noting that polls and surveys can do a great deal for the Latino community if they are properly conducted; and the means of properly conducting them are known or at least knowable. I hope this conference will help promote a flowering of survey research on the political opinions and behavior of Latinos.

# Latinos and the 1984 Election:
# A Comparative Perspective

Bruce E. Cain, *California Institute of Technology*
D. Roderwick Kiewiet, *California Institute of Technology*

With the burgeoning of the Latino population and the widening recognition of its political power, there has been a marked increase in the number of Latino-focused polls. These surveys have emanated from such diverse sources as newspapers, candidates, scholars, political parties, campaign consultants, and nonpartisan organizations, and ranged from extensive statewide studies to small community analyses. Their focus, with only a few exceptions, has been exclusively Latino and not comparative across racial and ethnic groups. To be sure, a good deal has been learned about Latino political attitudes and behavior from this effort. Polling areas of high Latino concentration and using statewide samples of Spanish-surnamed individuals are effective means of ensuring large enough samples of Latinos to permit detailed analyses of them.

But while much has been gained from an exclusively Latino focus, something has been lost also. In particular, it has been hard to tell from exclusively Latino surveys how unique or similar Latino attitudes and political behaviors are to those of other racial and ethnic groups in the electorate. If the questions asked the Latino polls are similar in design to those in national polls administered at approximately the same time, the Latino sample can be compared, of course, with the national population. And since the Anglo majority constitutes the bulk of the interviewees in national election studies, it is also possible to compare Latino interests with those of the Anglos. But for the same reasons that Latinos are represented in small numbers in national studies, other minorities (with the exception of blacks) will be sparsely represented in them as well. As a consequence, if the other minority groups are not polled simultaneously, it is hard to make any cross-ethnic/racial comparisons.

How much of a loss is this—what is the importance of a cross-minority perspective? In light of the 1984 elections, there are several good political and academic reasons for taking a comparative approach. For instance, one issue that came up during the 1984 primaries was whether Latinos and Asians would join blacks in a rainbow coalition to support the Jesse Jackson candidacy. A cross-ethnic design would have helped illuminate whether there was a basis for such a coalition. Or, to take another example, Republicans questioned whether all minority groups would automatically join the Democratic camp or whether the Republicans could win some minority support. In the nineteenth century, European Catholics were pushed towards the Democratic party by nativist hostility to them. Is there a similar movement on the part of Asians and Latinos toward the traditional party of the minorities, or are their backgrounds and political agendas so diverse that the newest immigrants will move in different directions from the previous ones? Apart from the issue of broad partisanship, there is the question of whether Asians and blacks share the same perspective with Latinos on policy matters. This question arose most frequently in 1984 over Simpson-Mazzoli, but could also be asked of other issues that are salient to Latinos such as bilingualism, aid to Central America, the funding of government services, and the like.

From a political perspective, Latino leaders will be more effective in forging coalitions if they learn more about the preferences of their potential coalition partners. This is particularly important with respect to Asians, who are a fast-growing immigrant group. Whereas black interests are fairly well understood, Asian political interests are still relatively unknown. Black-Latino relations are far from ideal (especially in Florida), but at least there is a history of interaction between them to base expectations upon. By comparison, Asian-Latino relations are less well understood because interactions between them are more recent. Much can be learned about this potential coalition from a cross-ethnic perspective.

From an academic point of view, it is possible to discover more about the uniqueness and similarity of Latino opinions and interests by studying them in comparative perspective. How much do Latino attitudes and behavior owe to the experience of being a minority group in America per se, and how much to the unique cultural and historical experience of being Latino? In addition, a comparative approach will tell us more about how ethnic and racial groups acquire partisanship and come to participate in American politics.

The purpose of this paper is to point out the complexities, advantages, and disadvantages of a comparative approach to minority politics, using the Caltech 1984 poll as an example. We will begin with a detailed description of our poll and the difficulties of its design. The fruits of a comparative approach come with a price: the design problems of any poll designed to pick up several minority groups are compounded. We will then illustrate what can be learned from a cross-minority perspective by discussing some of the findings in that poll. Finally, we will make some suggestions about future cross-minority research.

**Survey Design Discussed**

The major problem we faced in designing the survey was that of efficiently reaching large numbers of adult individuals from the three major racial and ethnic minorities in California—Latinos (primarily Mexican Americans), blacks, Asians who, according to the 1980 Census, constituted 19%, 8%, and 5% of the state population respectively. Because of the younger age structure of the groups, the percentages of black and Latino adults are somewhat smaller than the percentage of adults for the total population. Given a large enough budget—say, several hundred thousand dollars—we would probably have preferred a Michigan-style areal sampling framework with a field staff going door to door to interview respondents in their own homes. Most comparisons between in-person interviews and telephone interviews indicate that the former technique entails a lower refusal rate and less bias in the resultant sample of completed interviews. To be sure, one worries about how well in-person interviews would work in neighborhoods with large proportions of recent Asian or Latino arrivals, in that undocumented residents might be extremely suspicious of interviewers coming to their doors. Telephone interviews would seem far less obtrusive, and possibly preferable for that reason.

The main reason we chose to do telephone interviews, however, was that of cost, as our budget constraints simply ruled out the extremely expensive alternative of in-person interviews. With telephone interviewing, the most common sample selection technique is of course random digit dialing. This method is not without problems. In many areas there still exists some bias resulting from the not quite complete saturation of telephone ownership. And although we have seen no reference to this problem in the literature on polling, we suspect that an increasingly important source of bias here is the growing use of telephone answering machines to screen incoming calls. More serious of course, is the unavoidable selection bias resulting from the fact that participation in this or any other opinion survey is voluntary. The potential for biases resulting from the differential incidence of telephone ownership and differential refusal rates is likely to be more serious in surveys in which minority group members constitute a large portion of the target population.

Whatever the case, the virtues of sampling via random digit dialing have made it the standard choice in telephone surveys. In large part because of its sampling virtues, however, random digit dialing is an extremely inefficient method for contacting members of minority groups, at least in California. Ideally one could draw a sample of telephone exchanges via probability weights which would yield the desired minority group proportions. In fact, if one were interested only in oversampling blacks, this technique would suffice. For Latinos and for Asians, however, the high level of residential segregation and resultant strong correlation between telephone exchange areas and census units (the necessary demographic data are not available for telephone exchanges) which are needed for this technique to be effective simply do not exist. This problem is bad enough for contacting Latinos. Asians, however, are an extreme case in this regard. Of the 5,050 census tracts in California in the 1980 Census, only 33 (0.6%) were 40% or more Asian. Even if telephone exchanges could be weighted in a skewed enough fashion to increase significantly the probability of contacting Asian respondents (something we are not altogether sure of), the resultant sample of Asians interviewed would be problematic. Most blacks live in neighborhoods which are predominantly black. The vast majority of Asians, however, do not live in predominantly Asian neighborhoods, and so a sample based primarily on those who do would likely be quite unrepresentative.

Given these problems, we decided that the least problematic way of generating the Latino and Asian subsamples would be on the basis of surnames. Oversampling of blacks, on the other hand, could be done on the basis of residence. We therefore began by randomly selecting a list of 300 census tracts in California. DialAmerica Corporation of Cleveland, Ohio, provided us with the names, current phone numbers, and addresses of 80 to 100 individuals per tract for approximately 90% of the tracts, which yielded a list of 24,523 names. We ran these through Hispanic and Asian surname dictionaries, yielding subsamples of 3,306 and

1,170, respectively. We then drew a 20% sample of the remaining 20,047 names, weighting the census tracts corresponding to each name so as to generate another subsample which would contain roughly equal proportions of whites and blacks.

As indicated earlier, one of our chief interests was to compare the experiences and attitudes of Asians who had recently immigrated to this country with those of recently arrived Latinos. In order to increase our sample of recent Asian immigrants, we drew a supplemental sample of Korean surnames from the 1984 *Korean Telephone Directory of Southern California*. The creators of this directory believe that it contains the telephone numbers and addresses of over 75% of all Koreans in Southern California. We ultimately conducted interviews with 80 Korean Americans via this supplemental sample.

According to Leuthold and Scheele, samples which are derived from telephone directories will, relative to random digit dialing, undersample blacks, individuals who are separated or divorced, and city dwellers. Although the percentage of individuals in our base sample of 25,523 who were Asian—4.8%—was almost identical to the 1980 Census figures, the number of Latino names drawn was definitely less than that in the background population—13.5%, compared to 19% in the 1980 sample. The fact that we ultimately interviewed about 25% more whites than blacks also suggests that there were fewer blacks in the base sample than there should have been.

In and of itself, of course, the only problem this might entail is that our subsamples were not as large as we might have desired. What is a real potential problem is that the individuals we interviewed, regardless of whether they were white, black, Asian, or Latino, all had listed telephone numbers and addresses. This could obviously make them somewhat unrepresentative sets of people.

As we have intimated, however, we were more worried about refusal rates than many other potential sources of bias. Given the large number of minority group members in our target population, we expected relatively high refusal rates. This in fact turned out to be the case—only 44% of the individuals we contacted who were eligible to be interviewed agreed to be. Although we cannot be sure about the characteristics of the people who refused to be interviewed, it appears that refusal rates were particularly high among Asians and those who were likely to be black. As far as we could tell, however, refusal rates were no higher among Latinos than among whites. All said and done, we completed interviews with 409 whites, 335 blacks, 593 Latinos, and 305 Asians.

Given the potential problems we faced, we were understandably interested in how well the characteristics of the people we interviewed matched up with data from the 1980 Census. The figures reported in table 1 indicate that in some respects the individuals in our four subsamples were quite representative, while in other respects they were somewhat unrepresentative. In all four subsamples the reported figures for family income and country of birth were quite consistent with figures derived from the 1980 Census. There are, however, some discrepancies. The percentages of blacks and Latinos in our sample who reported being homeowners were higher than the Census figures. And for reasons that are not altogether clear to us, we also tended to oversample Asian men and black women. Reported education, though, was the source of the largest discrepancies. Individuals in all four subsamples were considerably more likely to report having attended college than the 1980 Census figures indicate should be the case. However, we are inclined to blame very little of the education bias we observed on

**Table 1**
Comparison of Sample and Census Characteristics

|  | White | Black | Latino | Asian |
| --- | --- | --- | --- | --- |
| Male |  |  |  |  |
| Sample 1984 | 49% | 38% | 49% | 60% |
| Census 1980 | 49 | 49 | 51 | 48 |
| Owner occupiers |  |  |  |  |
| Sample 1984 | 66 | 64 | 52 | 64 |
| Census 1980 | 62 | 45 | 44 | 62 |
| Family income less than $10,000 |  |  |  |  |
| Sample 1984 | 12 | 25 | 21 | 9 |
| Census 1980 | 16 | 34 | 27 | 14 |
| Family income $10,000–$25,000 |  |  |  |  |
| Sample 1984 | 44 | 41 | 47 | 35 |
| Census 1980 | 40 | 40 | 48 | 37 |
| Family income more than $25,000 |  |  |  |  |
| Sample 1984 | 44 | 33 | 32 | 56 |
| Census 1980 | 44 | 26 | 25 | 49 |
| Native-born |  |  |  |  |
| Sample 1984 | 94 | 98 | 60 | 38 |
| Census 1980 | 90 | 98 | 63 | 42 |
| Some college or higher |  |  |  |  |
| Sample 1984 | 60 | 53 | 34 | 77 |
| Census 1980 | 44 | 36 | 20 | 54 |

our use of a telephone directory sample versus random digit dialing. Warren Miller indicates that the sample of individuals interviewed in the 1984 Michigan Rolling Cross-section (which was a telephone survey) had a considerably higher average education than those interviewed in person in the traditional postelection survey.

Because participation in opinion surveys is voluntary (at least in liberal democratic societies), we believe that regardless of the sampling framework employed there is an irreducible element of self-selection bias generated by the differential propensity of different types of people to submit to an interview. In political polls this self-selection bias is quite naturally related to the extent to which the potential respondent is intellectually involved with things political—people are more likely to talk to strangers about subjects they care about and know something about than about subjects they don't know or care about. This bias will yield us samples which are, compared to the population at large, more educated, more literate, more interested, and more knowledgeable about ongoing political issues. Any incidental bias deriving from telephone directory versus random-digit-dialing sampling was, at least for us, apparently minimal.

It is important, therefore, to think carefully about whether or not the self-selection bias present in any survey is really a serious problem or not. The most important rule of thumb, or course, is that so long as the bias is not related to the dependent variable of interest we can probably live with it. If, for example, we wanted to estimate the effects of religion, income, and age, on levels of political interest and information, we would likely be in serious trouble. If, on the other hand, we were interested in the effects of these same variables on attitudes toward abortion or bilingualism, our parameter estimates would be far less likely to be compromised.

It occurs to us, however, that there is another way of thinking about the inferences we can make from sample surveys which we know contain disproportionately high numbers of people who are politically attentive and informed. Consider two people who are alike in every way except one is politically attentive and informed, the other is not—we are considerably more likely to complete an interview with the first. If for some reason the second person did become interested in politics, concerned about public affairs, and so on, would her or his beliefs, preferences, perceptions, and opinions be likely to differ systematically from those of the first person? In most cases we think not.

**The Values of Cross-Ethnic/Racial Polling: Some Illustrations**

We suggested earlier that there were political and academic interests that could be served by employing a cross-ethnic/racial
polling framework. To illustrate this point better, we will use
evidence from our poll to explore the question of how Latino attitudes differ from those of blacks and Asians. In thinking about
this question, it is important to realize that the circumstances of
minorities in California vary considerably, and hence there are
reasons a priori to expect differences in policy positions across
groups.

At the risk of oversimplification, we can think of minority groups
as varying along two dimensions of characteristics:
socioeconomic status and recency of migration. Needless to say,
there will be much variation among individuals within any one
ethnic or racial group, and thus we are necessarily referring to the
mean, median, or modal circumstances of members in that group.
The first dimension, socioeconomic status, will of course influence the preferences that individuals have concerning the provision of social services, economic policy, the role of the government, and other issues that roughly fall on a traditional left-right
continuum. The second dimension, the recency of migration, matters for both different and related reasons. It matters for different
reasons in the sense that, irrespective of socioeconomic status,
individuals who come from foreign cultures and speak foreign
languages must adjust to a new language and culture and overcome inevitable barriers of discrimination and prejudice against
them. Generally speaking (but not always), the longer individuals
have been in a country, the more linguistic and cultural differences
lessen and associated problems recede.

It is also possible for the two dimensions to be correlated—for
instance, because cultural and linguistic barriers obstruct social
mobility, groups may find it harder to move out of the lower
socioeconomic levels. However, for the sake of simplicity, let us
for the moment disregard the issue of interactions to make the
point that the political attitudes of a group will depend on its position in these two dimensions. In the most extreme cases, a group
that has long resided in the country and is at the upper end of the
socioeconomic scale will have a different perspective from a recent immigrant group at the lower end of the scale.

Using this simple framework, we can loosely place the different
racial and ethnic groups in this matrix. Latino immigrants fall into
the   lower   left   quadrant   (recent   immigrants   and   lower

socioeconomic status), blacks in the upper left quadrant (long established and lower socioeconomic status), most California Asian groups with the exception of the Japanese in the lower right quadrant (recent immigrants and upper socioeconomic status), and most of the older white ethnic groups in the upper middle to right region. In other words, many Latinos differ from blacks in the recency of immigration dimension and from most Asian groups in the socioeconomic status dimension. If these dimensions correlate in significant ways with policy positions, then we should expect policy attitudes to vary as well.

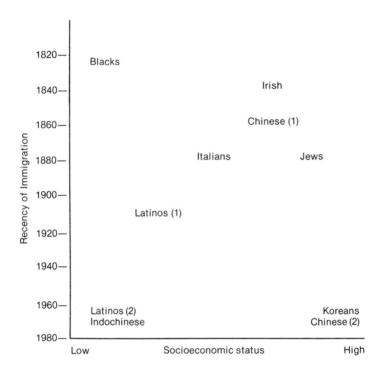

Fig. 1. Distribution of Ethnic and Racial Groups

We anticipate that there might be differences in the attitudes of these ethnic and racial groups, but do we find evidence of this? The Caltech poll contains a number of items that bear on this question, but given the illustrative nature of this exercise we will consider only a few of them—namely, similarity in attachment to the

United States, language usage and policy, partisanship, attitudes toward immigration, and perceptions of discrimination.

We will begin our analysis with table 2, which lists a series of five items dealing with the general theme of attachment to the United States broken down by racial and ethnic grouping. The central issue here is how foreign-born Latinos compare with other foreign-born individuals in terms of their attachment to the United States. Is it the case that Latinos are slower, faster or about the same in cutting ties to the homeland and committing themselves to reside in the United States?

The first row of table 2 displays the percentage of noncitizens as a fraction of the total population of each racial and ethnic group, demonstrating clearly that both the Latino and Asian groups have a large noncitizen component in our sample populations (almost one-third). The second row suggests, however, that Asian foreign-born may be making the transition into citizenship more rapidly than their Latino counterparts, since a higher fraction of the Asian than Latino foreign-born have become citizens. However, in most other respects, Latinos are no more attached to their homeland than the Asians. Considering only those who were foreign-born, roughly equal percentages of Asians and Latinos maintain social links with their country of origin, send money back to relatives in the homeland, and intend to stay in the United States. The percentages of Latinos maintaining social links and intending to stay in the United States are also quite comparable to the white foreign-born in our sample. Latino and white foreign-born differ in the slowness with which Latino foreign-born become citizens and the lower percentage of white foreign-born who send money back

**Table 2**
Attachment to United States

|  | White | Black | Latino | Asian |
|---|---|---|---|---|
| Noncitizen/group population | 4% | 1% | 28% | 28% |
| Noncitizen/non-United States-born | 48 | 44 | 69 | 48 |
| Social links versus country of origin (non-United States-born) | 72 | 78 | 79 | 78 |
| Money sent to country of origin (non-United States-born) | 25 | 33 | 42 | 35 |
| Intention to stay in United States (Non-United States-born) | 91 | 100 | 89 | 86 |

home. The latter is probably attributable to the fact that Latinos and Asians (with the obvious exceptions of the Indo-Chinese and the Central Americans) are mostly economic refugees who came to the United States for the greater economic opportunities whereas this is less true of the Europeans. In general, then, Latinos resemble the Asians a good deal in these matters and the white foreign-born somewhat less so.

Consider now a second area of concern, language usage and policy. We said earlier that language issues are particularly important because language can be a formidable barrier to social mobility. In the United States, the debate over bilingual education programs and ballots has commanded considerable public attention in the past decade. How similar are the different ethnic groups with respect to language use and attitudes on bilingualism?

Table 3 contains two pieces of information. First, it displays the percentage of each racial/ethnic group indicating that English was not their primary language, and next it shows which language was spoken most frequently at home by those who did not regard English as their primary language. Not surprisingly, Asians and Latinos are most similar in both respects. About half of the Latinos and Asians in our sample said that English was not their primary language, and of those less than 20% spoke English most frequently at home. By contrast, only 8% of the whites in our sample and 2% of the blacks did not regard English as their primary language. Also, if the figures are to be believed (and one must be cautious because of the small numbers involved), it appears that the foreign language whites more quickly adopt English at home than do either the Asians or Latinos.

**Table 3**
Language Usage

|  | White | Black | Latino | Asian |
|---|---|---|---|---|
| English is not primary language | 8% | 2% | 57% | 52% |
| Language used at home when English is not primary |  |  |  |  |
| Non-English more | 22 | 14 | 43 | 47 |
| English/Non-English equal | 13 | 29 | 38 | 37 |
| English more | 65 | 57 | 19 | 16 |

Given the similarities in the language usage patterns of Latinos and Asians, one might expect them to have similar positions on bilingual programs. However, as table 4 reveals, this is not the case.

Respondents in the poll were asked to say how they would have voted on election day if they had been presented with certain propositions. Among these were: "Bilingual education programs. In other words, teaching non-English-speaking students in their own language as well as English," and "Providing non-English voters in an election with ballots printed in their own language." Respondents were given the choice of saying they favored the measure, opposed it, or did not have an opinion one way or the other. In addition, an item on our survey asked those who spoke a foreign language and who voted in 1984 whether they voted with an English or non-English ballot.

As can be seen, Latinos were the most enthusiastic supporters of both bilingual education programs and bilingual ballots. However, only a slight majority of Asians favored bilingual education programs and less than a majority favored bilingual ballots. Latinos were also the most likely to have used a bilingual ballot in the 1984 election. Surprisingly, blacks were the closest allies on bilingual education and ballots, although their support for the latter was much weaker than for the former. Why would Asians be less supportive of bilingual programs and blacks more supportive? Why would blacks be less supportive of bilingual ballots than bilingual education programs when bilingual ballots would seem on the face of it to have direct political advantages for them (that is, raising the turnout of a coalition partner)? These questions clearly demand further study.

Another policy area of particular salience to immigrant groups is immigration reform. While the 1965 immigration reform lifted

**Table 4**
Bilingualism and Education

|  | White | Black | Latino | Asian |
|---|---|---|---|---|
| **Bilingual Education Programs** | | | | |
| Favor | 42% | 63% | 69% | 51% |
| Oppose | 51 | 25 | 22 | 40 |
| No Opinion | 7 | 12 | 9 | 9 |
| **Bilingual Ballots** | | | | |
| Favor | 29 | 49 | 60 | 43 |
| Oppose | 67 | 38 | 31 | 50 |
| No Opinion | 4 | 13 | 9 | 7 |
| **Non-English Ballot Usage** | | | | |
| Used non-English ballot in 1984 | 7 | 0 | 8 | 4 |

quota restrictions on Asians and Latinos, a sizable number of Asian immigrants have entered the country by unauthorized means in recent years. In the debate over immigration reform, however, the Asians have been relatively silent, leaving the task of minority leadership on this issue almost exclusively to the Latino congressional caucus, the Mexican American Legal Defense and Educational Fund (MALDEF), and the League of United Latin American Citizens (LULAC). Table 5 may give some insight into why this has been the case. Respondents were asked to say whether they favored amnesty for illegal immigrants and the use of employer sanctions. Latinos most heavily favored amnesty and were the most opposed to sanctions of all the groups, although it is significant that Latinos themselves were almost evenly divided on the latter. Asians more closely resembled the blacks on these issues—that is to say, a small plurality favored amnesty and a somewhat larger one favored the use of employer sanctions. The whites were closest to the positions of the other groups on amnesty and most sharply diverged from them on employer sanctions. Once again we are left with the question of why Latino and Asian opinion diverges on an issue on which it would seem plausible for communities with large numbers of foreign-born individuals to have a common perspective.

**Table 5**
Immigration Issues and Ethnicity/Race

|  | White | Black | Latino | Asian |
| --- | --- | --- | --- | --- |
| Amnesty for Illegal Immigrants |  |  |  |  |
| Favor | 44% | 41% | 61% | 43% |
| Oppose | 40 | 35 | 20 | 33 |
| No Opinion | 16 | 24 | 19 | 24 |
| Use of Employer Sanctions |  |  |  |  |
| Favor | 62 | 52 | 40 | 51 |
| Oppose | 25 | 33 | 42 | 34 |
| No Opinion | 13 | 15 | 18 | 15 |

A third area of concern to immigrant and minority groups is discrimination. Immigrants are often discriminated against for reasons of language, culture, and race. The political bonds created between groups have historically reflected the degree of discrimination the groups have experienced. Thus, it is relevant to ask whether perceptions of discrimination are widely held among Latinos and Asians, and if so, how close are their perceptions to those of the black population?

Our evidence on this point is displayed in table 6. There were a number of items in our poll that dealt with the issues of prejudice and discrimination. For the purposes of discussion, we will focus on two of these. The first asked those of non-Western European race or ethnicity the following question: "Have you yourself personally experienced discrimination because you are _____ ." The follow-up question was then: "Thinking of the most serious discrimination you have experienced, was it in getting a job, or getting into a school, in getting a house or apartment, in a social situation, or in some other respect." On the basis of our data at least, discrimination is much less a problem for Latinos and Asians than it is for blacks: whereas 62% of the blacks claimed to have personal experience of discrimination, only 36% of Latinos and 47% of Asians reported experiencing discrimination. Moreover, the nature of the discrimination experienced by the groups varied significantly. A majority of the black respondents said that they experienced job-related discrimination (overwhelmingly in getting the job as opposed to discrimination on the job) while the largest category for the Latinos and Asians was discrimination in a social setting. The difference in this regard is most clear between blacks and Asians.

**Table 6**
Perception of Discrimination

|  | Black | Latino | Asian |
|---|---|---|---|
| Personal experience of discrimination | 62% | 36% | 47% |
| Type of discrimination |  |  |  |
| Job-related | 52 | 32 | 23 |
| School-related | 8 | 13 | 8 |
| Getting house/apartment | 7 | 12 | 6 |
| Social situation | 28 | 42 | 59 |
| Other | 5 | 1 | 4 |

In sum, we have looked so far at three areas—language policy, immigration, and discrimination—in which the similarity of Asian and Latino circumstances with respect to immigration might have created common interests. What we have found so far is that on several of these issues Latinos are more closely aligned with blacks than with Asians. However, the contrast between Asians and Latinos is even more stark when we move away from issues in which foreign-born individuals might have a common interest to purely partisan questions. In the latter, we find that Asians were far more inclined than Latinos to have voted for Reagan in 1984 and to have identified with the Republican party. Indeed, they were more heavily registered and identified with the Republican party and more supportive of Reagan than even the white population in California (see table 7).

**Table 7**
Partisanship and Ethnicity/Race

|  | White | Black | Latino | Asian |
|---|---|---|---|---|
| Reagan vote 1984 | 50% | 6% | 36% | 67% |
| Partisan identification |  |  |  |  |
| Democrat | 51 | 89 | 74 | 42 |
| Republican | 38 | 6 | 17 | 41 |
| Independent | 11 | 4 | 8 | 16 |
| Other | 0 | 1 | 1 | 1 |

We do not propose to explain these differences in this paper, since doing so would require careful and complex analysis (which we expect to undertake in future work). Certainly, for instance, one plausible explanation for the variations in attitudes we have reported is that there are important differences in the aggregate socioeconomic circumstances of these groups—that is, the horizontal axis of figure 1. Another explanation could be that the political norms of the societies that these ethnic groups have come from have residual effects on their political attitudes in this country. Our more limited point in this paper has been to show that there are variations in political attitudes across groups and that a cross-ethnic/racial perspective can be used to study and explain these differences.

## Conclusion

There is a need to study Latinos from a more comparative perspective. Latino interests and preferences diverge from those of other minority groups in complex and important ways. Class differences between the various minority groups are complicated by religious, linguistic, and cultural differences. Thus, a middle-class minority group like Koreans might have common interests with Latinos on educational issues and lessening discrimination, but not have overlapping concerns on welfare and abortion; or a lower-income group with common social service needs such as blacks might coalesce with Latinos on the role of government, but favor the use of employer sanctions to control undocumenteds more effectively. These kinds of coalitional issues are best studied in a comparative framework. As we have suggested, however, comparative surveys are uniquely difficult to design and administer, particularly for minorities that are not residentially concentrated. However, we maintain that the potential rewards make the effort of designing comparative studies well worthwhile.

# Hispanic Vote Behavior: Selected Findings from Past Research Conducted by Tarrance & Associates

Lance Tarrance, Jr., *Tarrance & Associates*

Since its founding in 1977, Tarrance & Associates has been significantly involved in researching the opinions of Hispanics, especially those of Mexican Americans. Although Tarrance & Associates has a national client base, the firm is perhaps the political polling community's most experienced organization in three key states with large Hispanic populations: Texas, California, and New Mexico. As table 1 demonstrates, Hispanics are a major political force in all three states. In fact, in no other states do Hispanics constitute a larger share of eligible voters or elected officeholders.

**Table 1**
Hispanic Political Power, 1984

| State | Eligible Hispanic Voters | % of Voting Age Population | Hispanic Elected Officials |
|-------|--------------------------|---------------------------|----------------------------|
| Texas | 1,414,000 | 18 | 1,427 |
| California | 1,501,000 | 16 | 460 |
| New Mexico | 286,000 | 33 | 556 |

Although exact records of the number of Hispanics interviewed by the firm are not maintained, a conservative estimate for these three states would be in the range of 22,000. This includes 13,104 in Texas, 5,793 in California, and 3,200 in New Mexico.

The firm's interest in Hispanics has not been limited to voters only. For example, in June 1980, Tarrance & Associates conducted a comprehensive study of the opinions of Hispanic leaders in three South Texas counties. Neither has the company's focus been solely regional. Two major national studies—one of Hispanics and blacks (conducted with Peter D. Hart Research for the Federation for American Immigration Reform) and one of American ethnic groups (one of which was Hispanics)—were undertaken in 1983 and 1982, respectively.

The pages that follow include descriptions and key findings from studies of Hispanics conducted by Tarrance & Associates.

**Overview of Partisan Vote Behavior and Ideology
among Texas Hispanics
(Texas Time Series, 1978–85)**

**Table 2**
How Texas Hispanics Voted, 1978–84
(%)

| | |
|---|---|
| 1978 Texas Governor's Race | |
| Clements | 34 |
| Hill | 53 |
| 1980 Presidential Race | |
| Reagan | 40 |
| Carter | 45 |
| Anderson | 3 |
| 1982 Texas Governor's Race | |
| Clements | 28 |
| White | 72 |
| 1984 Presidential Race | |
| Reagan | 43 |
| Mondale | 53 |
| 1984 U.S. Senate Race | |
| Gramm | 31 |
| Doggett | 66 |

Note: Data were gathered by Tarrance & Associates in statewide postelection telephone surveys of Texas voters. Dates of the surveys and sample sizes follow: November 1978, total N = 1,000 (Hispanic N = 79); November 1980, total *N = 1,000 (Hispanic N* = 80); November 1982, *N* = 500 (Hispanic *N* = 25); November 1984, *N* = 1,000 (Hispanic *N* = 120).

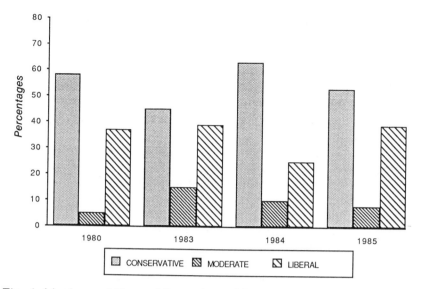

Fig. 1. Ideology of Texas Hispanics, 1980-85

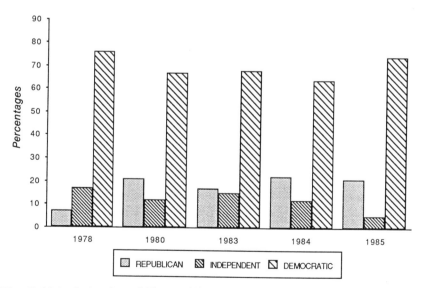

Fig. 2. Vote behavior of Texas Hispanics, 1978-85

## South Texas Hispanic Survey (May 1982)

### Scope and Method

The South Texas Hispanic Study consists of 600 interviews conducted by telephone with 600 Mexican American voters living in a "quadrant" of Texas bordered by Bexar, Nueces, Cameron, and Webb counties.

Data were obtained from the Census Bureau which provided the percentage of the population in each county that was Hispanic, and from the Texas Secretary of State who listed the number of registered voters by county. The number of respondents to be contacted in each county was then determined by (1) taking the percentage of Hispanics in the general population and taking the same percentage of registered voters, (2) summing up the result for all counties in the quadrant, (3) determining each county's percentage contribution to the total, and (4) multiplying the resulting percentage by 600. The resulting number of interviews was then conducted using Spanish surnames taken at random from registered voter lists for each county. The fieldwork began on May 10, 1982.

Table 3
A Comparative Demographic-Political Profile of South Texas
and Statewide Hispanic Registered Voters

|  | South Texas Hispanics[a] (N = 600) | Statewide Hispanics[b] (N = 92) |
|---|---|---|
| Length of Residence |  |  |
| 1975–82 | 3% | 1% |
| 1970–74 | 3 | 3 |
| 1960–69 | 2 | 1 |
| Before 1960 | 19 | 10 |
| Native | 73 | 85 |
| Political Party Primary Preference |  |  |
| Republican | 5 | 13 |
| Democrat | 77 | 74 |
| Age |  |  |
| Young adult | 33 | 37 |
| Family adult | 37 | 43 |
| Older adult | 30 | 20 |

[a] Data are from May 1982 Tarrance & Associates telephone poll.

[b] Data are from February 1982 Tarrance & Associates telephone poll (see table 4).

This particular geopolitical region in Texas has strong cultural ties with Mexico (that is, San Antonio functions within the Texas culture somewhat like Santa Fe functions within the New Mexico culture). More than 50% of the Hispanic population in Texas resides in it.

A demographic-political profile of South Texas Hispanic registered voters based on data from this survey is presented in table 3. Table 4 then presents the statewide distribution of Texas Hispanic voters from a survey carried out in February 1982. Data from the statewide survey are compared to data from the South Texas survey in table 3.

**Table 4**
Statewide Distribution of Hispanic Registered Voters
(February 1982 Survey; *N* = 92)

|  | %<br>(Approxi-<br>mate) | *N* |
|---|---|---|
| South Texas |  |  |
|   McAllen, Laredo, Corpus Christi, and San Antonio | 50 | 47 |
| El Paso/Trans Pecos |  |  |
|   El Paso to San Angelo | 20 | 18 |
| Dallas/Fort Worth and Houston metroplexes |  |  |
|   Dallas, Fort Worth, and Houston SMSAs | 20 | 16 |
| Balance of Texas |  |  |
|   Panhandle, Northwest, etc. | 10 | 11 |
|     Total | 100 | 92 |

Note: Data were gathered by Tarrance & Associates in telephone interviews. Only demographic data can be released from this study which was privately commissioned.

## Special Leadership Survey of
## Hispanic Community Leaders (June 1980)

### Background and Objectives

Given the growth of the two-party system in Texas, traditional Democratic strongholds are becoming vulnerable to recruitment by the Republican party. One such Texas group is the Hispanic community—strongly consrvative, family-oriented, traditional, and economically upwardly mobil.

The following study, which was conducted in June 1980, surveyed the leadership segment of the Hispanic community in three South Texas counties (Nueces, Cameron, and Hidalgo) to obtain information about Hispanic leadership in the following areas:

Involvement/interest in politics and elections

Political party identification

Goals and outlook for Texas and evaluation of Texas political party to accomplish state goals in the 1980s

## Sample Overview

*Size.* The sample of respondents for the Hispanic Leadership Study consisted of 300 Hispanics.

*Sources.* The sample was constructed using the following four sources in each county:

1. Business owners/leaders. Local chamber of commerce Hispanic membership lists were sampled to obtain business and industry leaders (27% of sample).
2. Professionals. Community professional Hispanic membership lists were sampled to obtain professional respondents in the following areas: medical, legal, insurance, dental, real estate, and accounting (40% of sample).
3. Positional. Calls to local business firms identified Hispanic managers and department heads. These respondents constituted the "key employees" group (33% of sample).
4. Reputational. Respondents were asked to indicate individuals they felt were thought and opinion leaders in the Hispanic community. These respondents were classified in categories 1–3.

*Population Demographics.* The sample drawn in the Hispanic Leadership Study can be used to describe this leadership group in Texas. Table 5 presents the demographic data for the Hispanic leadership community gathered in the survey.

As might be expected, the Hispanic leadership group is concentrated in the family adult state between ages 35 and 54 (61%), and is predominantly male (89%). In addition, the Hispanic leadership group is predominantly native Texan (79%). The Hispanic leadership group also shows a Democratic voting record, with only 12% of the Hispanic leaders calling themselves Republican.

**Table 5**
1980 Texas Hispanic Leadership Population Demographics
(*N* = 300)

|  | % |
|---|---|
| *Age* | |
| Young adult (18–34) | 26 |
| Family adult (35–54) | 61 |
| Older adult (55 + ) | 13 |
| *Education* | |
| Less than high school | 13 |
| High school graduate | 24 |
| Some college | 25 |
| College graduate | 38 |
| *Ideology* | |
| Very conservative | 11 |
| Conservative | 44 |
| Moderate | 12 |
| Liberal | 24 |
| Very liberal | 7 |
| *Voting* | |
| Mostly Republican | 6 |
| Slightly Republican | 7 |
| The Candidate | 20 |
| Slightly Democrat | 26 |
| Mostly Democrat | 40 |
| *Political Target Group* | |
| Republican | 12 |
| Ticket-splitter | 22 |
| Conservative Democrat | 34 |
| Liberal Democrat | 32 |
| *Turnout Probability* | |
| High | 35 |
| Medium | 54 |
| Low | 11 |
| *Residency in Texas* | |
| 1970–80 | 9 |
| 1960–70 | 5 |
| Before 1960 | 7 |
| Native Texas | 79 |
| *Sex* | |
| Male | 89 |
| Female | 11 |
| *Occupation* | |
| Business owner | 27 |
| Professional | 40 |
| Key employee | 33 |

**Key Findings and Implications**

The key findings of the Hispanic Leadership Survey are as follows:

1. The Hispanic leadership segment is significantly interested in elections and the political process.

    Interest in politics: Very 59%; Somewhat 30%; None 11%.

    Importance of politics: Strong 38%; Moderate 47%; Low 15%.

    Importance of Hispanic vote: Extreme 54%; Very 39%; Not 6%.

2. The Hispanic leadership is predominantly interested in the local, not state, level of government. (See table 6.)

**Table 6**
Level of Government Most Important to Hispanic Leadership
(%)

|  | Local | State | National | Combina-tion |
|---|---|---|---|---|
| Statewide Results | 52 | 7 | 12 | 28 |
| *Geographic Area* | | | | |
| Nueces | 54 | 6 | 14 | 25 |
| Cameron | 50 | 6 | 13 | 30 |
| Hidalgo | 52 | 10 | 8 | 30 |
| *Voter Group (N = 37)* | | | | |
| Republican | 62 | 3 | 14 | 22 |
| Ticket-splitter | 42 | 3 | 12 | 40 |
| Conservative Democrat | 60 | 9 | 9 | 23 |
| Moderate or liberal Democrat | 47 | 10 | 14 | 29 |
| *Age/Education* | | | | |
| Under 35/no college (N = 18) | 72 | 6 | 17 | 6 |
| Under 35/some college | 52 | 14 | 7 | 26 |
| 35–54/no college | 50 | 13 | 14 | 22 |
| 35–54/some college | 54 | 2 | 12 | 33 |
| 55 & over/no college (N = 22) | 41 | 0 | 18 | 41 |
| 55 & over/some college (N = 19) | 47 | 11 | 5 | 37 |
| *Sex* | | | | |
| Male | 52 | 6 | 11 | 30 |
| Female (N = 34) | 53 | 15 | 15 | 18 |
| *Occupation* | | | | |
| Independent professional | 51 | 10 | 13 | 26 |
| Business leader/owner | 54 | 8 | 12 | 27 |

Table 6—*Continued*

| | | | | |
|---|---|---|---|---|
| Key employee | 51 | 5 | 10 | 32 |
| *Inflation effect* | | | | |
| Hard | 49 | 5 | 12 | 32 |
| Not so hard | 55 | 10 | 11 | 24 |

3. As a whole, the Hispanic community is split concerning Hispanic influence in Austin.
   Hispanics have influence in Austin: 54%
   Hispanics have no influence in Austin: 43%
4. Most Hispanic leaders see themselves as Democrats.
   Past voting record: Democrat 66%; Republican 12%; Ticket-splitter 34%.
   Party ideological stand: Democrat 45%; Republican 20%.
5. However, Hispanic leadership concerns for the future and for Texas share a Republican view. (See table 7.)

**Table 7**
Reasons Why Hispanics Identify with Republicans
among Hispanic Republican Party Identifiers
($N = 60$)

| | % Response |
|---|---|
| Disagree with Democratic social policy | 55 |
| Giveaway programs/welfare (36%) | |
| Too liberal (14%) | |
| Communistic (5%) | |
| Democratic leadership poor | 22 |
| Carter weak/inept (15%) | |
| Crooks in party (7%) | |
| Republican philisophy | 8 |
| Disagree with Democratic economic policy | 3 |
| Other | 12 |
| Other reasons mentioned (7%) | |
| No answer (5%) | |

6. Most Hispanic leaders think there is positive opportunity for Hispanic economic advancement in Texas: Excellent 24%; Good 39%; Only Fair 26%; Poor 8%.

7. When asked which party would be most likely to accomplish their goals for Texas, the Republicans are mentioned out of proportion to either respondents' voting records or party identification.
   Democrats: 31%
   Republicans: 22%
   Neither party: 18%
   Both parties: 15%
8. Finally, the Hispanic leadership indicated their present (June 26, 1980) voting preference in the federal election as follows:
   Reagan: 40%
   Carter: 36%
   Anderson: 7%
   Undecided: 1%

**Conclusion**

The results of this leadership analysis indicate that while a plurality of the Hispanic community leaders are predisposed toward Democratic candidates and the Democratic party, many hold values and attitudes which are compatible with Republican party position. This is not to say that it will be easy to enlist their support on behalf of the Republican party.

In large part, Hispanic leaders feel a larger sense of political efficacy at the local level rather than at the state level. Consequently, it is likely that Hispanic support for Republican candidates will increase at the local level (for example, mayor and city council) before expanding into state politics at the legislative level.

**National Hispanic Study (July 1983)**

This report presents the findings of a survey conducted jointly by Tarrance & Associates and Peter D. Hart Research Associates, Inc., on behalf of the Federation for American Immigration Reform. The study was designed to examine attitudes toward U.S. immigration policy among representative national samples of Hispanic and black respondents.

The interviews for this study were conducted by telephone between June 24 and July 12, 1983, using the phone bank facilities and professional field staff of Tarrance & Associates. The data are based on completed interviews with scientifically selected random samples of 800 Hispanic respondents and 800 black respondents. The sample of Hispanics includes 266 respondents who were interviewed wholly or partly in Spanish. Among the Hispanic respondents, 76% reported that they were U.S. citizens and 24% reported that they were not U.S. citizens.

**Survey Highlights**

Majorities of both Hispanics and blacks rate the issue of immigration as having above average importance as a matter of the government's attention.

Both with regard to legal and illegal immigration, substantial portions of the Hispanic and black communities perceive a need for change in American immigration policies—with pluralities and majorities of respondents emphasizing the need to put greater controls on immigration.

Substantial majorities of both Hispanics and blacks favor proposals to curb illegal immigration by having penalties and fines for employers who hire illegal immigrants, and by making major increases in the amount of money the federal government spends on patrolling the borders to stop illegal immigrants from entering the country.

Hispanics tend to be strongly sympathetic to the idea of an amnesty program for illegal immigrants who have been in the country for a certain period of time; a majority of blacks also support this idea but with less intensity. When asked to volunteer how long an illegal immigrant should have been in the country to qualify for amnesty, 28% of Hispanics mention a period of four years or less, 32% suggest five years, 29% volunteer a period of more than five years, and 5% stress their opposition to any sort of amnesty. Among blacks, 21% mention a residency requirement of four years or less, 27% specify five years, 34% mention a period of more than five years, and 10% say no illegal immigrant should be granted amnesty.

Pluralities of Hispanics and majorities of blacks believe that the United States should admit fewer immigrants into the country legally than has been the case in recent years.

Substantial majorities of Hispanics and blacks believe that illegal immigration hurts the job situation for American workers by taking away jobs that Americans might fill. Sixty-nine percent of all blacks say this is a major problem, as do 51% of Hispanics who are U.S. citizens.

There is no clear consensus among Hispanics or blacks with regard to the argument that restricting illegal immigration would be harmful to the economy because illegal immigrants work at low-paying jobs that would not otherwise get done.

Throughout the survey results, there are substantial differences in attitudes toward immigration policy between Hispanics who are U.S. citizens and who are noncitizens—with Hispanic citizens significantly more likely to favor restrictions on immigration.

Low-income blacks are particularly likely to feel an economic threat from illegal immigration.

**Major Findings**

1. Among both Hispanics and blacks, there is a broad degree of concern with the issue of immigration. This is particularly true among Hispanics, 72% of whom rank immigration as having above-average importance among the range of issues with which government deals—including 31% who say immigration is one of the most important issues facing government and 41% who rank it as very important. Among blacks, 57% assign above average priority to the issue of immigration.

2. There is a widespread perception that illegal immigrants hurt the job situation for American workers by taking away jobs that Americans might take. Fully 82% of all blacks say that illegal immigrants hurt the job situation for Americans. Sixty-nine percent of all blacks believe that this situation is a major problem. Blacks with incomes under $10,000 are particularly likely to feel that job losses caused by illegal immigration are a major problem (76%). Among Hispanics, a 58% majority believe that illegal immigrants take jobs away from Americans who might want them, and 46% of all Hispanics consider this to be a problem of major proportions. Fifty-one percent of Hispanics who are U.S. citizens consider the impact of illegal immigration on American employment to be a problem of major proportions, compared to 28% among noncitizen Hispanics.

3. The large majority of blacks (71%) believe that illegal immigrants cause general pay rates and wages in America to be lower than they otherwise would be, and 6 out of 10 blacks term

the impact of illegal immigration on wage rates a major problem. Attitudes among Hispanics on this question are somewhat more divided—52% say that illegal immigrants undermine American wage rates, while 40% do not believe this is the case. Among Hispanics who are U.S. citizens, 55% say illegal immigrants undercut wage rates in the country, including 43% who deem this to be a major problem. Among noncitizen Hispanics, 42% say that illegal immigrants undercut wages, and the issue is considered a major problem by 26%.

4. Attitudes among both Hispanics and blacks are divided with regard to the assertion that restricting illegal immigration would be harmful to the economy because low-wage jobs now done by illegal immigrants would not get done or employers would be forced to pay higher wages. Among Hispanics, 51% agree and 40% disagree. Among blacks, 48% agree and 44% disagree.

# Latinos in the 1984 Election Exit Polls: Some Findings and Some Methodological Lessons

Robert R. Brischetto, *Southwest Voter Research Institute*

This paper examines the results of exit polling among Latino voters in the 1984 presidential election with two purposes in mind: to report what has been found with respect to Latino voting patterns and party identification from 1980 to 1984; and, by reflecting on these findings, to highlight some of the problems associated with most polling among Latinos.

## Data Sources

For the most part, the tables which follow are based on secondary analysis of data collected by the various national media pollsters. In addition, the results of an exit poll conducted statewide in Texas and in 11 other localities throughout the nation among more than 6,000 Latino voters are presented. This poll was a combined effort by the Midwest Voter Registration Education Project of Columbus, Ohio; the Hispanic Women's Center of New York; the Cuban American Committee of Washington, D.C.; and the Southwest Voter Registration Education Project of San Antonio, which coordinated it.

## Latino Political Demography

To study the Latino vote, some basic geopolitical facts must be understood. First, there is not one but a number of Latino electorates in the United States, each with its unique historical experience rooted in its country of origin. These various cultural histories are manifested in differences in voting and ideology. Each of the major political parties considers one or more Latino national origin subgroup to be a natural constituency.

Table 1 shows the distribution of voting age persons of Spanish origin in states with major Hispanic populations in 1980. The various Latino national origin groups are fairly geographically discrete. About 6 in 10 Latino adults are of Mexican origin, three-fourths of them concentrated in California and Texas. Puerto Ricans—13% of all Latinos in the nation—are found in the Northeast, fully half of them in New York and two-thirds in New York, New Jersey, and Illinois. Cubans—about 7% of all U.S. Latino adults—live mainly on the East Coast with 6 of 10 in Florida and 8 in 10 in Florida, New York, and New Jersey. Persons of "Other Spanish" origin—22% of all U.S. Latino adults—live for the most part in California, New York, and New Mexico.

**Table 1**
Voting Age Hispanics by Origin in Nine States, 1980

|  | Hispanic Voting Age Population | % Mexican | % Puerto Rican | % Cuban | % Other Spanish |
|---|---|---|---|---|---|
| California | 2,775,170 | 77.5 | 2.2 | 1.7 | 18.4 |
| Texas | 1,756,971 | 91.5 | 0.9 | 0.6 | 7.0 |
| New York | 1,061,852 | 2.3 | 56.7 | 5.8 | 35.1 |
| Florida | 629,292 | 7.6 | 9.9 | 58.9 | 23.6 |
| Illinois | 379,208 | 63.4 | 19.4 | 3.8 | 13.4 |
| New Jersey | 307,321 | 2.7 | 44.0 | 20.4 | 33.0 |
| New Mexico | 292,714 | 47.5 | 0.3 | 0.2 | 52.0 |
| Arizona | 256,688 | 89.1 | 1.0 | 0.3 | 9.6 |
| Colorado | 204,301 | 59.6 | 1.4 | 0.6 | 38.5 |
| Nine-State Total | 7,663,517 | 59.7 | 12.5 | 7.4 | 20.4 |
| U.S. Total | 8,980,717 | 57.5 | 13.4 | 6.8 | 22.2 |

Source: U.S. Bureau of the Census, *United States Census of Population, 1980, Characteristics of the Population*, ser. PC80-1B.

A second politically important demographic fact is that Latinos are concentrated in a few states, states which are often viewed as key ones in a close national election. Some 85% of all Latinos are in nine states listed in table 1; these states control 193 electoral votes, 72% of the 270 votes needed to win the presidency.

A third important demographic fact that seemed to indicate Latinos might have made a difference on election day is their tremendous growth relative to the rest of the population. Just as the national campaigns were being launched, data released by the Census Bureau indicated that voting age Latinos experienced a 77% increase from 1970 to 1980, seven times the 11% increase for the rest of the nation. Over the decade, Latinos had increased from 4.5% to 6.4% of the U.S. population, and by election day in 1984, they were about 7% of the total population.

Those are some of the demographic factors that contribute to the growing importance of Latinos in national politics. There are also some factors which tend to diminish Hispanic political clout: their younger age and the large proportion of Hispanics who are not citizens. In 1980 the median age for Latinos was 22.1 years, compared to 31.0 years among non-Latinos. While 7 in 10 in the total population were of voting age in 1980, the proportion for Hispanics was 6 in 10.

According to the 1980 census reports, 74% of Hispanic adults were citizens, compared to 97% of the total population. Census demographers Warren and Passel note that the 74% estimate is a high one, since there is overreporting of naturalized status. The true proportion of Hispanic citizens is probably closer to 68%, which is the same proportion reported by the Current Population Survey for voting and registration in 1984.

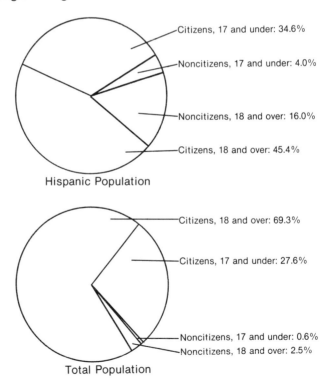

Citizens, 17 and under: 34.6%

Noncitizens, 17 and under: 4.0%

Noncitizens, 18 and over: 16.0%

Citizens, 18 and over: 45.4%

Hispanic Population

Citizens, 18 and over: 69.3%

Citizens, 17 and under: 27.6%

Noncitizens, 17 and under: 0.6%

Noncitizens, 18 and over: 2.5%

Total Population

Fig. 1. Population Eligible to Vote

The political bottom line of all these demographics is that, while they are an increasing proportion of the total electorate, there is some reason to expect that Latinos will never attain the full representation warranted by their numbers. Although 7 in 10 persons in the United States are eligible to register and vote, only 45% of Latinos are eligible (See fig. 1).

## Latino Participation in 1984

The combined impact of attention to the Latino electorates by the media, the political parties, and the nonpartisan voter registration groups shows in the statistics on voter participation in 1984. As table 2 shows, Latino voter registration rose 27% from 1980 to 1984, three times the increase for whites over the same period and very similar to the 24% increase among blacks.

**Table 2**
Registration by Race in the United States, 1972–84
(In thousands)

| Year | Latinos | % Increase | Blacks | % Increase | Whites | % Increase | Total | % Increase |
|------|---------|------------|--------|------------|--------|------------|-------|------------|
| 1972 | 2,495 |    | 8,837 |    | 88,987 |    | 98,480 |    |
| 1976 | 2,494 | 0  | 8,725 | -1 | 88,329 | -1 | 97,761 | -1 |
| 1980 | 2,984 | 20 | 9,849 | 13 | 94,112 | 7  | 105,035 | 7  |
| 1984 | 3,794 | 27 | 12,223 | 24 | 102,211 | 9  | 116,106 | 11 |

Source: U.S. Bureau of the Census, "Voting and Registration, 1972-84," *Current Population Reports*, ser. P-20.
Note: Percent increases are increases in number registered since previous election.

Of course, part of the large increase in Latino registration is due to the increase in the Latino population of voting age generally. However, the 1984 election was particularly noteworthy in that it marked the reversal of a decline in Latino voter participation during at least the past three presidential elections (national Latino participation data were not available until 1972). Latino (and black) voter participation was up in 1984, both in gross numbers and as a proportion of eligible voters; and it was up more among minority voters than among whites (see fig. 2).

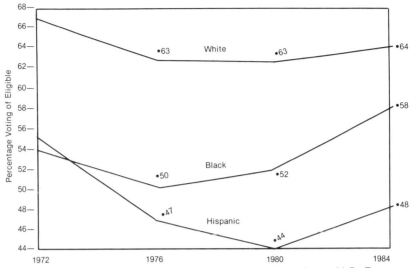

Fig. 2. Voter participation by ethnic group. (Data from U.S. Bureau of the Census, "Voting and Registration, 1972-84," *Current Population Reports*, ser. P-20.)

### How They Voted: Latino Voting Patterns, 1980–84

Unfortunately, the results of national network exit polls tended to cast more shadows than light on the "Hispanic vote" in 1984. The reasons are not complicated, but they are methodological.

First, national origin groups among Latinos are not all the same; they have varied political histories. Yet all the various Latino electorates were lumped together into a single national group for analysis. When this is done, the differences in voting patterns between Cuban Americans, Mexican Americans, and Puerto Ricans are masked and blurred into an average. A more sensible approach to studying Hispanic voting patterns would be to analyze each national origin group separately. This is most easily accomplished by conducting statewide exit polls.

Second, the national pollsters made no attempt to oversample Hispanics and thus their samples were too small to be reliable, ranging from 219 in CBS/New York Times polling to approximately 350 at NBC. Assuming a national random sample, the margin of error associated with the NBC sample, for instance, would be plus or minus six percentage points with 95% confidence, whereas the margin of error for whites would be plus or minus 1%.

The results of the five national exit polls show the extent of their unreliability in estimating the Hispanic vote. Hispanic voting for Ronald Reagan varies from 32% by NBC to 46% by the Los Angeles Times poll, a 14-point spread. Among blacks, the results of the various exit polls vary by only two percentage points. (See table 3.)

**Table 3**
Exit Poll Estimates of Vote for President by Race, 1980 and 1984

| | NBC NEWS | | CBS/NYT | | ABC/WP | | LAT | SIN |
|---|---|---|---|---|---|---|---|---|
| | 1980 | 1984 | 1980 | 1984 | 1980 | 1984 | 1984 | 1984 |
| Whites | | | | | | | | |
| Democrat | 35% | 34% | 36% | 35% | 34% | 36% | 33% | |
| Reagan | 56 | 66 | 55 | 64 | 55 | 63 | 66 | |
| Others/not voting | 9 | — | 9 | 1 | 11 | 0 | 1 | |
| Number | 10,350 | 9,920 | 13,562 | 8,010 | 7,788 | 8,677 | 5,331 | |
| % of electorate | 89 | 85 | 89 | 87 | 88 | 87 | 78 | |
| Blacks | | | | | | | | |
| Democrat | 90% | 91% | 85% | 89% | 82% | 89% | 90% | |
| Reagan | 7 | 9 | 11 | 9 | 14 | 11 | 10 | |
| Others/not voting | 3 | — | 3 | 2 | 4 | 0 | 0 | |
| Number | 930 | 1,167 | 1,458 | 801 | 766 | 845 | 772 | |
| % of electorate | 8 | 10 | 10 | 9 | 9 | 8 | 13 | |
| Latinos | | | | | | | | |
| Democrat | 64% | 68% | 56% | 61% | 52% | 56% | 51% | 55% |
| Reagan | 30 | 32 | 35 | 37 | 39 | 43 | 46 | 45 |
| Others/not voting | 6 | — | 9 | 1 | 10 | 0 | 3 | — |
| Number | 233 | 350 | 323 | 219 | 174 | 286 | 254 | 2,145 |
| % of electorate | 2 | 3 | 2 | 2 | 2 | 3 | 5 | |

Note: CBS/NYT-CBS/New York Times; ABC/WP-ABC/Washington Post; LAT-Los Angeles Times; SIN-Spanish International Network.

## Comparison of Voting Patterns: 1980 and 1984

The three major networks provide some comparative data on voting in 1980 and 1984. The percentage voting for President Reagan increased among both Anglos and Hispanics in 1984, although because of their small sample sizes the differences are statistically significant in only one case. Among blacks, the percentage voting for Reagan seems to have declined slightly according to results from two of the three networks.

While the increase in support for President Reagan was generally acknowledged in the news, what was not well reported was the degree of polarization between white and minority voters. This "ethnic gap" can be measured by subtracting the amount of support Reagan received from minority group voters from the support he received from Anglo voters for each election year and comparing the gap across elections. For example, the smallest white-black Reagan vote gap in 1980 is calculated at 41% by using ABC/Washington Post poll figures. The largest gap is 49%, provided by NBC figures. The gap between whites and blacks in support for President Reagan had increased to 55% by 1984, according to NBC and CBS/New York Times polls; to 56% in the Los Angeles Times poll; and to 52% in the ABC/Washington Post exit survey.

The white-Hispanic Reagan vote gap shows a similar pattern. Although less severe, the difference in 1980 ranges from 16% provided by ABC/Washington Post figures to 26% using NBC's estimates. Polarized voting between Anglos and Latinos in 1984 increased. The gap ranges from 20% in the ABC/Washington Post and Los Angeles Times polls to 28% as reported by NBC News.

### Latino National Origin Group Voting, 1984

An approximation of how the various Latino national origin groups voted can be obtained from the statewide exit polls conducted by some of the networks in some of the states.

*Texas Mexicans.* Nine in 10 Hispanics in Texas are of Mexican ancestry. The Mexican American vote for President Reagan in Texas was found by the network exit polls to range from 24% to 35%. Data are available for 1980 only from NBC; they indicate an increase in support for President Reagan among Mexican Americans in Texas. (See table 4.)

Results of the Southwest Voter Registration Education Project (SVREP) exit polling among 2,040 Latinos in Texas are identical to the findings of the ABC poll: 3 out of 4 Texas Mexicans voted for Mondale. The SVREP sample in Texas was selected to be representative of 75% of all Latinos in the state in precincts where 20% or more of the registered voters have Spanish surnames. One might speculate that Mexican Americans who lived in less densely Hispanic precincts not covered by the sample may have voted differently from those sampled; they may have voted more like their Anglo neighbors. But even if we assume that those excluded from the sample were evenly divided in their vote for president, the estimate of Mexican Americans in Texas voting for President Reagan would increase to no more than 30%.

**Table 4**
Latino Vote for President in Texas Exit Polls, 1984

|  | ABC/WP | SVREP | SIN | CBS/NYT | NBC News | NBC News (1980) |
|---|---|---|---|---|---|---|
| Democrat | 76% | 75% | 68% | 66% | 65% | 78% |
| Reagan | 24 | 24 | 32 | 34 | 35 | 20 |
| Number | 75 | 2,040 | | 142 | 288 | 264 |
| % of electorate | 7 | 9 | | 7 | 10 | 9 |

Note: ABC/WP-ABC/Washington Post; SVREP-Southwest Voter Registration Education Project; SIN-Spanish International Network; CBS/NYT-CBS/New York Times.

A more detailed analysis of how the various subgroups of Texas Mexicans voted may provide some insights into the character of their vote. There was no gender gap in presidential preference among Mexican American voters in Texas in 1984. Men and women were virtually identical in their vote for president. The largest differences were found among age groups. Fewer than 1 in 10 persons over age 65 reported voting for President Reagan, whereas he received support from 3 in 10 in the under-35 age group. Different Mexican American education and income groups voted as predicted, but the differences were not very dramatic. Those with less than a high school diploma gave the greatest support to the Mondale-Ferraro ticket. The two extreme groups were in sharpest contrast: 85% of those with less than $5,000 income voted for Mondale, whereas a majority of those with $50,000 or more supported Reagan. (See table 5.)

*California Mexicans.* Almost 8 in 10 (78%) Hispanics of voting age in California are of Mexican origin. Network estimates of the Latino vote in California vary widely, ranging from 24% to 51% for President Reagan. This large variation is probably for the most part due to their small sample sizes. The two pollsters which have results for both 1980 and 1984 show conflicting trends among Latino voters. CBS/New York Times polling shows that both parties gained about equally from 1980 to 1984. NBC shows that

**Table 5**

Texas Mexican Vote for President in 1984
by Education, Sex, Age, and Income

|  | Mondale | Reagan | Other | % of Group |
|---|---|---|---|---|
| **Education** |  |  |  |  |
| Less than high school | 84 | 16 | 0 | 29 |
| High school graduate | 77 | 23 | 0 | 30 |
| Some college | 67 | 33 | 0 | 27 |
| College graduate | 73 | 27 | 0 | 10 |
| Postgraduate training | 78 | 22 | 0 | 4 |
| Number |  |  |  | 1,818 |
| Chi probability |  |  |  | 0.0000 |
| **Sex** |  |  |  |  |
| Male | 76 | 24 | 1 | 49 |
| Female | 76 | 24 | 0 | 51 |
| Number |  |  |  | 1,807 |
| Chi probability |  |  |  | 0.1108 |
| **Age** |  |  |  |  |
| 18–25 | 69 | 30 | 1 | 24 |
| 26–35 | 71 | 29 | 1 | 26 |
| 36–45 | 78 | 22 | 0 | 20 |
| 46–55 | 81 | 19 | 0 | 14 |
| 56–65 | 85 | 14 | 1 | 11 |
| 65+ | 91 | 9 | 0 | 5 |
| Number |  |  |  | 1,840 |
| Chi probability |  |  |  | 0.0000 |
| **Income** |  |  |  |  |
| Less than $5,000 | 85 | 15 | 0 | 20 |
| $5,000–$10,000 | 80 | 20 | 0 | 20 |
| $10,000–$20,000 | 74 | 25 | 1 | 28 |
| $20,000–$30,000 | 74 | 26 | 0 | 19 |
| $30,000–$40,000 | 64 | 36 | 0 | 8 |
| $40,000–$50,000 | 68 | 32 | 0 | 4 |
| $50,000+ | 44 | 56 | 0 | 2 |
| Number |  |  |  | 1,768 |
| Chi probability |  |  |  | 0.0000 |

Source: Southwest Voter Registration Education Project 1984 exit poll.

Walter Mondale received more support in 1984 from California Latinos than did Jimmy Carter in 1980 and that President Reagan lost ground among Latinos. Both pollsters show that Latinos increased as a proportion of the state's total electorate. (See table 6.)

**Table 6**
Latino Vote for President in California Exit Polls, 1980 and 1984

|  | NCB News | | ABC/WP | CBS/NYT | | SIN[a] |
| --- | --- | --- | --- | --- | --- | --- |
|  | 1980 | 1984 | 1984 | 1980 | 1984 | 1984 |
| Democrat | 59% | 76% | 57% | 52% | 57% | 49% |
| Reagan | 33 | 24 | 42 | 37 | 43 | 51 |
| Other | 8 | 0 | 1 | 11 | 0 | 0 |
| Number | 144 | 206 | 95 | 140 | 216 | — |
| % of electorate | 5 | 7 | — | 4 | 6 | — |

Note: ABC/WP-ABC/Washington Post; CBS/NYT-CBS/New York Times; SIN-Spanish International Network.

[a] Sample size not reported.

SVREP conducted an exit poll in six selected high-density Hispanic precincts in East Los Angeles, California (Norwalk and Santa Fe Springs). Although the sample was not chosen to be representative of a larger population, the results are strikingly similar to those of Mexican American voters surveyed in Texas. Three in 10 Mexican American voters in the East Los Angeles precincts (28%) voted for Ronald Reagan.

*New York Puerto Ricans.* New York state has the third largest number of Hispanics eligible to vote in the nation or slightly more than a million. Almost 6 in 10 of these are of Puerto Rican origin, 2% are of Mexican origin, 6% of Cuban ancestry, and 35% are Hispanics of other national origin. Because of the heterogeneous character of the Hispanic population and the small sample size, the statewide network polls of Hispanic voters must be interpreted with care.

Both the NBC and CBS/New York Times exit polls show the Democrats losing ground in New York state from 1980 to 1984, although their estimates vary wildly because of small samples. NBC shows a drop in the percentage voting Democratic from 78% in 1980 to 68% in 1984; CBS/New York Times shows a drop in Democratic support from 67% to 46%. The Spanish International Network (SIN) exit poll shows 41% supporting Ronald Reagan in 1984. (See table 7.)

SVREP provided assistance to the National Hispanic Women's Center in conducting 2,096 exit poll interviews in 23 predominately Hispanic election districts in four New York City boroughs: the

Bronx, Brooklyn, Manhattan, and Queens. Some 1,502 Hispanics were interviewed, 73% of whom were Puerto Ricans.

**Table 7**
Latino Vote for President in New York State Exit Polls, 1980 and 1984

|  | NBC NEWS | | CBS/NYT | | SIN[a] |
|---|---|---|---|---|---|
|  | 1980 | 1984 | 1980 | 1984 | 1984 |
| Democrat | 78% | 68% | 72% | 47% | 59% |
| Reagan | 19 | 32 | 25 | 52 | 41 |
| Other | 3 | 0 | 3 | 1 | 0 |
| Number | 120 | 75 | 21 | 66 | — |
| % of electorate | 4 | 3 | 1 | 3 | — |

Note: CBS/NYT-CBS/New York Times; SIN-Spanish
[a] Sample size was not recorded.

The Puerto Rican vote for president was strikingly similar to the Mexican American vote in Texas and California: 27% supported Ronald Reagan.

*New York City Dominicans.* Dominicans comprise 14% of the Hispanic sample or 207 voters in the New York City exit poll conducted by the National Hispanic Women's Center. Dominican support for President Reagan was slightly higher than among Puerto Ricans: 4 in 10.

*New York City Cubans.* Cubans are only 5% of the New York Hispanic sample. Hence, the results for the 79 Cubans interviewed in the National Hispanic Women's Center exit poll are not as reliable as the results for Puerto Ricans and Dominicans. The findings, however, are interesting in that they contrast sharply with results for other Hispanics polled in New York City. Six in 10 Cuban New Yorkers voted for President Reagan.

*Union City, New Jersey, Cubans.* Two predominately Cuban precincts in Union City, New Jersy, were included in the survey by the Cuban-American Committee and 126 Cubans were interviewed. As many as 87% of them supported President Reagan.

*Florida Latinos.* Some 60% of Latinos of voting age in Florida are of Cuban origin, 10% are Puerto Rican, 8% are of Mexican origin, and 25% are of other Spanish origin, mostly from Central America and the Caribbean.

Only two networks conducted exit polls with large enough samples to isolate the Latino vote in Florida. Both polls show strong support by Cuban voters for President Reagan—nearly 7 in 10 Florida Latinos in the NBC poll and by more than 8 in 10 Latinos in the SIN poll. (See table 8.)

**Table 8**
Latino Vote for President in Florida, 1984

|                  | NBC NEWS | SIN[a] |
|------------------|----------|--------|
| Democrat         | 32%      | 17%    |
| Reagan           | 68       | 83     |
| Number           | 116      | —      |
| % of electorate  | 4        | —      |

[a] The Spanish International Network sample size was not reported.

*Miami Cubans.* As in Los Angeles, the SVREP Miami sample is peculiar in that only five precincts of high Hispanic density were chosen. The Cuban-American Committee of Washington, D.C., conducted the polling among 392 Cuban and 79 other voters.

Nine in 10 Cuban voters (93%) in the Miami barrio precincts said they voted for President Reagan.

The sharp differences in presidential preferences found between Cuban voters and Mexican American or Puerto Rican voters serve to underline the necessity of treating Hispanic subgroups separately in polling analyses.

### Party Identification: Is There a Latino Realignment?

Much has been made in the press recently about a party realignment taking place in the national body politic. The question of whether such a realignment is occurring is beyond the scope of this paper and far more complex than can be addressed in a descriptive piece such as this. Political scientists themselves are divided on the questions: about a third say there is clear evidence of a major party realignment among the electorate, another third do not see evidence of realignment, and a final third see a dealignment occurring whereby voters cease to adhere to party labels and loyalty.

While the question of realignment certainly deserves more extensive analysis than an examination of opinion polls, polling data go beyond the ephemeral realm of voting; they provide information about party identification over time.

**Table 9**

Exit Poll Estimates of Party Identification by Race, 1980 and 1984

| | NBC NEWS | | CBS/NYT | | ABC/WP | | LAT | SIN |
|---|---|---|---|---|---|---|---|---|
| | 1980 | 1984 | 1980 | 1984 | 1980 | 1984 | 1984 | 1984 |
| **Whites** | | | | | | | | |
| Democrat | 35% | 28% | 40% | 34% | 36% | 33% | 26% | |
| Republican | 29 | 35 | 31 | 39 | 30 | 36 | 34 | |
| Independent | 26 | 29 | 26 | 27 | 29 | 28 | 40 | |
| Else/don't know | 10 | 8 | 3 | 0 | 5 | 3 | — | |
| Number | 10350 | 9920 | 13562 | 8010 | 7642 | 8851 | 5331 | |
| **Blacks** | | | | | | | | |
| Democrat | 74% | 75% | 69% | 77% | 75% | 75% | 81% | |
| Republican | 5 | 6 | 9 | 7 | 7 | 6 | 4 | |
| Independent | 13 | 10 | 16 | 16 | 15 | 16 | 15 | |
| Else/don't know | 8 | 9 | 6 | 0 | 3 | 4 | — | |
| Number | 930 | 1167 | 1458 | 801 | 731 | 825 | 772 | |
| **Latinos** | | | | | | | | |
| Democrat | 61% | 59% | 63% | 56% | 62% | 61% | 52% | 67% |
| Republican | 10 | 17 | 18 | 27 | 18 | 21 | 20 | 25 |
| Independent | 14 | 17 | 18 | 17 | 13 | 16 | 28 | 6 |
| Else/don't know | 15 | 7 | 1 | 0 | 7 | 2 | — | 2 |
| Number | 233 | 350 | 323 | 219 | 170 | 278 | 254 | 2145 |

Note: Column headings refer to the following pollsters: CBS/NYT-CBS/*New York Times*, ABC/WP-ABC/*Washington Post*, LAT-*Los Angeles Times*, SIN-Spanish International Network.

Table 9 presents data on party identification by race for 1980 and 1984 from the various network exit polls. The party identification of whites clearly shifted from predominantly Democrat to predominantly Republican with no appreciable change in percent independent.

But 3 in 4 blacks identify as Democrats and that proportion seems to have remained fairly stable from 1980 to 1984. The percentage of blacks identifying as Republican ranges from 4% to 7% and seems to have decreased slightly since 1980.

Once again, given the small samples of Latinos, the proportions vary wildly from one poll to the next. The pecentage of Latinos identifying as Democrat in 1984 ranges from 52% to 67%; Republican, from 17% to 27%; and independent from 6% to 17%.

The changes from 1980 to 1984 in Latino party identification are not very large, but a pattern is clearly evident. There is a slight increase in Republican affiliation—up some 3 to 9 points. The polarization between Latinos and whites is the most striking pattern, however. While Republicans outnumber Democrats among whites, Latinos remain Democratic by a margin of between 2 and 3 to 1.

**Comparison of Latino National Origin Groups**

Differences in party identification among the various Latino national origin groups are clearly evident from the SVREP exit poll. The nine subgroups surveyed are ordered in the stub of table 10 from most Democratic (top) to most Republican (bottom). Cuban Americans have a strong identification with the Republican party. As many as 2 in 3 Cubans surveyed in Miami and 2 in 5 Cubans polled in New York and half of New Jersey Cubans identify as Republican. Only 2 in 10 Dominicans identify as Republican and fewer than 1 in 10 Puerto Ricans and Mexicans identifies as Republican.

*Subgroups of Texas Mexicans.* The SVREP Texas sample of Mexican American voters is large enough to conduct an analysis of subgroup differences in party preference. Table 11 presents the differences by education, sex, age, and income.

No gender gap in party preference is found among Texas Mexicans. Most men and women identify as strongly Democratic, 1 in 4 as independent, and fewer than 1 in 10 as Republican.

**Table 10**

Party Identification of Latino National Origin Groups in 1984

|  | Demo-crat | Republi-can | Indepen-dent | Other | Not Sure | *N* |
|---|---|---|---|---|---|---|
| Midwest Mexicans | 74% | 5% | 17% | 1% | 5% | 703 |
| East Los Angeles Mexicans | 76 | 7 | 15 | 0 | 3 | 223 |
| Midwest Puerto Ricans | 75 | 10 | 10 | 1 | 5 | 533 |
| New York City Puerto Ricans | 72 | 10 | 12 | 0 | 6 | 1,106 |
| Texas Mexicans | 68 | 6 | 22 | 0 | 3 | 1,863 |
| New York City Dominicans | 52 | 21 | 19 | 1 | 9 | 211 |
| New York City Cubans | 40 | 40 | 18 | 0 | 1 | 79 |
| New Jersey Cubans | 29 | 50 | 18 | 0 | 5 | 120 |
| Miami Cubans | 11 | 69 | 13 | 0 | 1 | 391 |

Source: Latino exit poll coordinated by Southwest Voter Registration Education Project, November 6, 1984.

Note: Categories have been collapsed from original questions. "Democrat" is "Strong Democrat" and "Not So Strong Democrat"; "Republican" is "Strong Republican" and "Not So Strong Republican"; "Independent" is "Independent Closer to Democrat," "Strictly Independent," and "Independent Closer to Republican."

Party preference is clearly related to age among Mexican Americans in Texas. Youngest voters (18–25 years of age) are about half as likely to identify as strong Democrats as the oldest voters (age 65 or older). However, less than 10% of voters in each age category identifies as Republican. A larger proportion of "weak Democrats" or "independents closer to Democrat" are found in the under-45 age groups.

This same general pattern of differences in strength of party preference is found among the various education and income subgroups of Mexican American voters. Those without a college education are more likely to be strong Democrats, as are those in the lower income categories. With the exception of the highest income group, there is not a clear pattern of increased Republican identification as one goes up the socioeconomic scale. Only among those with an annual family income of over $50,000—comprising 2% of the Mexican American voters—was the proportion identifying as Republican greater than 10%.

**Table 11**
Party Identification by Education, Sex, Age, and Income
among Texas Mexican Voters, 1984

| | Strong Demo-crat | Weak Demo-crat | Independent Demo-crat[a] | Indepen-dent | Independent Repub-lican | Weak Repub-lican | Strong Repub-lican | Not Sure/ Other | % of Group |
|---|---|---|---|---|---|---|---|---|---|
| *Education* | | | | | | | | | |
| Less than high school | 72 | 9 | 5 | 3 | 2 | 2 | 4 | 5 | 29 |
| High school graduate | 57 | 11 | 11 | 5 | 6 | 2 | 4 | 4 | 30 |
| Some college | 44 | 14 | 15 | 10 | 8 | 5 | 3 | 2 | 27 |
| College graduate | 47 | 14 | 20 | 4 | 8 | 2 | 4 | 2 | 10 |
| Postgraduate training | 46 | 13 | 21 | 8 | 6 | 1 | 1 | 4 | 4 |
| Number | | | | | | | | | 1,824 |
| Chi probability | | | | | | | | | 0.0000 |
| *Sex* | | | | | | | | | |
| Male | 56 | 11 | 12 | 7 | 6 | 2 | 3 | 3 | 49 |
| Female | 56 | 13 | 11 | 5 | 5 | 3 | 4 | 4 | 51 |
| Number | | | | | | | | | 1,813 |
| Chi probability | | | | | | | | | 0.3151 |

*Continued on next page*

| | Strong Demo-crat | Weak Demo-crat | Independent Demo-crat[a] | Indepen-dent | Independent Repub-lican | Weak Repub-lican | Strong Repub-lican | Not Sure/ Other | % of Group |
|---|---|---|---|---|---|---|---|---|---|
| *Age* | | | | | | | | | |
| 18–25 | 43 | 16 | 11 | 8 | 7 | 3 | 5 | 7 | 23 |
| 26–35 | 49 | 10 | 18 | 5 | 8 | 2 | 5 | 2 | 26 |
| 36–45 | 58 | 12 | 10 | 7 | 3 | 3 | 4 | 3 | 20 |
| 46–55 | 67 | 12 | 7 | 5 | 2 | 1 | 3 | 3 | 14 |
| 56–65 | 73 | 8 | 7 | 2 | 4 | 3 | 2 | 2 | 11 |
| 65 + | 81 | 6 | 4 | 2 | 1 | 2 | 1 | 3 | 5 |
| Number | | | | | | | | | 1,843 |
| Chi probability | | | | | | | | | 0.0000 |
| *Income* | | | | | | | | | |
| Less than $5,000 | 69 | 10 | 7 | 2 | 2 | 1 | 3 | 5 | 20 |
| $5,000–$10,000 | 60 | 13 | 9 | 3 | 2 | 4 | 4 | 7 | 20 |
| $10,000–$20,000 | 53 | 9 | 15 | 8 | 7 | 2 | 3 | 3 | 28 |
| $20,000–$30,000 | 51 | 14 | 11 | 6 | 6 | 3 | 6 | 4 | 19 |
| $30,000–$40,000 | 46 | 13 | 17 | 9 | 9 | 5 | 2 | 0 | 7 |
| $40,000–$50,000 | 45 | 15 | 13 | 10 | 12 | 3 | 2 | 1 | 4 |
| $50,000 + | 26 | 19 | 11 | 5 | 21 | 0 | 18 | 0 | 2 |
| Number | | | | | | | | | 1,773 |
| Chi probability | | | | | | | | | 0.0000 |

[a] "Independent Democrat" indicates "Independent, closer to Democrat"; "Independent Republican" indicates "Independent, closer to Republican."

Source: Southwest Voter Registration Education Project, 1984 Exit Poll.

## Conclusions

The secondary analyses of national and state exit polls provides both substantive and methodological conclusions. The findings reveal that:

Latino support for President Reagan nationwide was between one-third and slightly less than one-half, according to the national network exit polls.

President Reagan gained support from 1980 to 1984 among Latinos, but the gain was not as great as his increase among white voters. Thus, the polarization along racial/ethnic lines in the vote for president increased from 1980 to 1984.

There were large differences between Cubans and other Latinos in their vote for president and party preference. Cubans voted for President Reagan by a large margin and identify as Republican; a large majority of other Latinos voted for Walter Mondale and identify as Democrats.

Differences among Texas Mexicans were evident in degree if not kind of support for president and party by age, education, and income. Older Texas Mexican voters and those with less education and income were more strongly Democratic. No gender gap in party affiliation was found among Texas Mexican voters. A slight shift toward identification with the Republican party was evident among Latino voters nationally from 1980 to 1984, but there was no compelling evidence of realignment in party identification among Latino voters in the exit poll data.

Some methodological lessons to be learned from this study are as follows:

Latinos are not one but multiple electorates and should be treated as such in polling. To lump them together as a single electorate in the analyses is to blur the differences among the various Latino national origin groups.

Because of the large variation in results of the various national network polls, it is important that the sampling among Latinos be increased to achieve greater reliability. To continue to draw small Latino samples will only perpetuate faulty and unreliable information among those who are seeking data on the Latino vote. However, since the variation among the national exit polls was greater than one might expect to occur because of random sampling error, simply drawing larger samples may not ensure reliable results. Pollsters may have to examine more closely the Latino electorates and stratify their samples to insure an adequate oversampling of Latinos.

Special attention should be given in polling Latinos to their cultural and linguistic differences. Further research is needed on the impact of such aspects as the language of the interview and the ethnicity of the interviewer.

# Political Preferences of Latinos, Blacks, and Whites during the 1984 Campaign

James Shriver III, *Gallup Poll*

The following charts on the 1984 presidential election were prepared for presentation at the conference "Ignored Voices: Public Opinion Polls and the Latino Community." Because of time and other constraints the charts were not presented at the conference. They are thus submitted for inclusion in the conference report.

For many years, the Gallup organization has conducted 20 or more national door-to-door opinion surveys each year. Each survey has comprised a minimum of 1,500 personal interviews with adults, 18 and older, conducted in more than 300 locations across the United States. The area probability sampling procedure produces an approximation of the adult population of the United States living in private households. It excludes persons living in institutions such as prisons or hospitals or on military bases. The Gallup Poll has a record of great accuracy in political surveys—in the 1984 presidential election, the Gallup Poll's preelection survey findings exactly matched the election outcome.

According to the Bureau of the Census, Latinos comprise about 7% of the adult U.S. population; thus approximately 100 Latinos should be found in each 1,500-case Gallup personal interview survey. In fact, our surveys sometimes fail to include the appropriate numbers of Latinos, an experience shared and discussed by other conference speakers. These deficiencies, when they occur, are satisfactorily remedied in the weighting process.

The relatively small number of Latino respondents in any one survey obviates reporting their behavior and opinions with a satisfactory degree of reliability. The problem is exacerbated by the frequent need to introduce additional variables such as political party affiliation or voter registration into the analytical process, further reducing the number of qualified Latinos. The problem of reliability can be seen in table 1, which compares the

percentages of Latinos and the total sample approving of Ronald
Reagan's handling of his job as president, in personal interview
surveys conducted in 1985.

**Table 1**
Reagan Performance Ratings
(% approving)

| Interviewing Dates | | Total Sample | Latinos |
|---|---|---|---|
| 1985 | September 13–16 | 60 | 66 |
| | August 13–15 | 65 | a |
| | July 12–15 | 63 | 52 |
| | June 7–10 | 58 | 46 |
| | May 17–20 | 55 | 50 |
| | April 12–15 | 52 | 58 |
| | March 8–11 | 56 | 41 |
| | February 15–18 | 60 | 61 |
| | January 25–28 | 64 | 44 |
| | January 11–14 | 62 | 51 |

[a] Not available.

To overcome the wide survey-to-survey variability in the small
Latino subsamples, undoubtedly a result of sampling error, we
have combined data sets to produce the charts and tables in this
report. Despite the obvious drawback of sacrificing the time-frame
reference—one cannot follow a trend when all of the data accumulated over a period of time are compressed—it is hoped the
charts and tables that follow will provide some useful information
for scholars of Latinos' participation in the political process.

The Gallup Poll began asking a Latino identifier question in its
personal interview omnibus surveys in September 1983. The question asked in each survey since then is this one:

Are you, yourself, of Hispanic origin or descent, such as Mexican,
Puerto Rican, Cuban, or other Spanish background?

In general, the presentation in this paper follows a chronological
sequence, starting with data on the Democratic nomination
choices derived from surveys conducted in late 1983. Next are the
nomination showdown tests between Walter Mondale and John
Glenn, in late 1983 and early 1984, when it appeared that the
Democratic nomination would go to one of these two front-
runners. Then data are presented on simulated presidential elections (trial heats) between President Reagan and several

Democratic hopefuls. Finally, trial heats between the Reagan-Bush and Mondale-Ferraro tickets, conducted from mid-July 1984 up till the election itself, are analyzed.

Also included are congressional test elections, perceptions of the "most important problem" facing the nation and the political party better able to handle that problem, and several charts relating to respondents' perceptions of their financial situation. Finally, President Reagan's job performance ratings (or popularity) during the second and third quarters of 1985 and political party affiliation during the same period are examined. For each chart and table, Latinos' opinions are compared with those of blacks and whites in the same data set.

Democratic Nomination List
(Based on Democrats)

Survey Dates: October 7–December 12, 1983
Number of Interviews:  Latinos  187
Blacks  424
Whites  2,023

The Question: "Which one of the persons on this list would you like to see nominated as the Democratic Party's candidate for president this year?"

At this early stage in the Democratic nomination campaign, Walter Mondale enjoyed a large lead among Latinos and whites, with Senator John Glenn placing a strong second among the latter.

**Table 2**
Democratic Nomination
(Based on Democrats)

|  | Latinos | Whites | Blacks |
|---|---|---|---|
| Mondale | 40% | 42% | 35% |
| Glenn | 15 | 25 | 8 |
| McGovern | 9 | 9 | 3 |
| Jackson | 8 | 2 | 34 |
| Cranston | 6 | 4 | 3 |
| Hart | 3 | 3 | 1 |
| Askew | 1 | 2 | a |
| Hollings | a | 1 | a |
| Don't know/none | 18 | 12 | 16 |
| Total | 100% | 100% | 100% |

a Less than 1%.

Blacks' preferences were evenly divided between Mondale and Reverend Jesse Jackson. It is generally conceded that the nomination choices at this point were primarily a function of name awareness.

Mondale versus Glenn
(Based on Democrats)

Survey Dates: November 11, 1983–February 13, 1984
Number of Interviews:       Latinos              179
                            Blacks               456
                            Whites             1,972

The Question: "Suppose the choice for president in the Democratic convention this year narrows down to Walter Mondale and John Glenn. Which one would you prefer to have the Democratic convention select?"

Mondale was the overwhelming choice over Glenn among all three ethnic groups. Glenn fared somewhat better among whites, garnering 31% of their nomination votes, than he did among Latinos (21%) or blacks (16%). Roughly 1 Latino in 6 (16%) was undecided between the two men.

Reagan versus Mondale
(Based on registered voters)

Survey Dates: September 16, 1983–July 16, 1984
Number of Interviews:       Latinos              657
                            Blacks             1,663
                            Whites            13,934

The Question: "Suppose the presidential election were being held today. If President Reagan were the Republican candidate and Walter Mondale were the Democratic candidate, which would you like to see win?"

Registered Latinos were closely divided between Mondale (50%) and Reagan (43%), while Mondale received the lion's share (84%) of blacks' votes. On average, Reagan enjoyed a comfortable 18-point advantage over Mondale among white voters during this period.

Reagan versus Hart
(Based on registered voters)

Survey Dates: March 16–July 2, 1984
Number of Interviews:      Latinos        222
                                    Blacks        622
                                    Whites    4,928

The Question: "Suppose the presidential election were being held today. If President Reagan were the Republican candidate and Gary Hart were the Democratic candidate, which would you like to see win?"

The results of these contests were virtually a carbon copy of those pitting Reagan against Mondale. Senator Gary Hart was the narrow choice of Latinos over Reagan, 49% to 39%. Among whites Reagan held a slightly smaller edge, 54% to 40%, over Hart than he had over Mondale. Blacks came down strongly on Hart's side, 79% to 11%.

Reagan versus Jackson
(Based on registered voters)

Survey Dates: October 7, 1983–July 2, 1984
Number of Interviews:      Latinos        312
                                      Blacks        721
                                    Whites    6,084

The Question: "Suppose the presidential election were being held today. If President Reagan were the Republican candidate and Jesse Jackson were the Democratic candidate, which would you like to see win?"

Although Latinos displayed somewhat more enthusiasm for Reverend Jesse Jackson than did whites, in a composite test election Latinos chose Reagan over Jackson, 54% to 33%. Whites voted for Reagan (76%) almost as monolithically as blacks voted for Jackson (83%).

Reagan-Bush versus Mondale-Ferraro
(Based on registered voters)

Survey Dates: July 13–October 29, 1984
Number of Interviews:        Latinos            420
                             Blacks           1,192
                             Whites           9,591

The Question: "If the Republican ticket of Ronald Reagan and George Bush were running against the Democratic ticket of Walter Mondale and Geraldine Ferraro, which would you like to see win?"

In the final stages of the campaign Latino voters were evenly split between the Democratic and Republican tickets, 48% to 45%. (The 3-point difference is statistically inconclusive.) In a close approximation of the actual election outcome, 61% of whites backed the Reagan-Bush ticket while 34% chose Mondale-Ferraro. Blacks opted for the Democratic ticket by a huge 83% to 10% margin.

Congressional Trial Heats
(Based on registered voters)

Survey Dates: April 6–October 1, 1984
Number of Interviews:        Latinos            186
                             Blacks             508
                             Whites           4,146

The Question: "If the elections for Congress were being held today, which party would you like to see win in this Congressional district—the Democratic Party or the Republican Party?"

While Democratic congressional candidates were narrowly outpolled by Republican candidates among whites, 49% to 44%, 87% of blacks and 62% of Latinos voted for Democrats; 7% of blacks and 29% of Latinos voted for Republicans.

Most Important Problem

Survey Dates: November 18, 1984–May 20, 1985

Number of Interviews:    Latinos       504
                         Blacks        980
                         Whites      8,125

The Question: "What do you think is the most important problem facing this country today?"

International affairs, including the situation in Central America, and unemployment were named by similar proportions of Latinos as the most important problem facing the nation. Whites were preoccupied with the fear of war and other international problems, plus a variety of domestic problems including the budget deficit. Blacks' attention centered on unemployment, with the high cost of living and international tensions also prompting considerable concern. (See table 3.)

**Table 3**
Most Important Problem

|  | Latinos | Whites | Blacks |
|---|---|---|---|
| Fear of war/international tensions | 27% | 29% | 16% |
| Unemployment | 26 | 19 | 38 |
| High cost of living/inflation | 16 | 12 | 14 |
| Excessive government spending/budget deficit | 7 | 14 | 4 |
| Economy in general | 6 | 7 | 7 |
| Drug abuse | 6 | 2 | 4 |
| Crime | 6 | 3 | 4 |
| Poverty/hunger | 5 | 4 | 9 |
| Moral, religious decline | 1 | 4 | 2 |
| All others | 21 | 20 | 12 |
| Don't know | 1 | 3 | 5 |
| Total | 122% | 117% | 115% |

[a] Totals add to more than 100% because of multiple responses.

Party Better Able to Handle
Most Important Problem

Survey Dates: November 18, 1984–May 20, 1985
Number of Interviews:        Latinos            504
                             Blacks             980
                             Whites           8,125

The Question: "Which political party do you think can do a better job of handling the problem you have just mentioned—the Republican Party or the Democratic Paty?"

Consistent with their political affiliation and preference for Democratic congressional candidates, Latinos came down on the side of the Democratic party as better able to resolve the problems they deemed most urgent. However, about 1 Latino in 4 (24%) cited the Republican party as better in this respect. Although few blacks chose the GOP (9%) over the Democratic party (64%), whites gave the Republican party the edge (37%) over the Democratic party (29%).

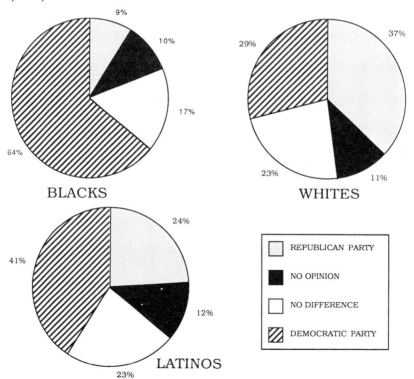

Fig. 1: Party better able to handle most important problem

### Financial Situation Now versus Year Ago

Survey Dates: March 16, 1984–March 11, 1985
Number of Interviews:         Latinos              456
                              Blacks               851
                              Whites             6,653

The Question: "We are interested in how people's financial situation may have changed. Would you say that you are financially better off now than you were a year ago, or are you financially worse off?"

Latinos' responses to the first of two related questions on their economic outlook placed them once more squarely between the optimism expressed by whites and blacks: 34% of Latinos said they were better off now than a year ago while 43% of whites and 23% of blacks felt the same way. Conversely, 29% of Latinos, 47% of blacks, and 23% of whites, respectively, felt they were worse off now than a year ago; 35% of Latinos, 28% of blacks, and 33% of whites felt their financial situation had not changed.

### Financial Situation One Year from Now

Survey Dates: March 16, 1984–March 11, 1985
Number of Interviews:         Latinos              456
                              Blacks               851
                              Whites             6,653

The Question: "Now looking ahead—do you expect that at this time next year you will be financially better off than now, or worse off than now?"

Perhaps surprising, in the light of their varied responses to the previous question, the three ethnic groups shared roughly the same perceptions in their financial outlook for the future, with whites only marginally more optimistic than either Latinos or blacks: 47% of Latinos and blacks felt they would be financially better off in the next year, compared to 54% of whites. Only 13%, 17%, and 12% of Latinos, blacks, and whites, respectively, felt they would be worse off.

Overall Financial Outlook
(Composite of two previous questions)

When the two questions were combined to provide an overall index of economic outlook (looking back and looking ahead), Latinos
again fell midway between whites and blacks.

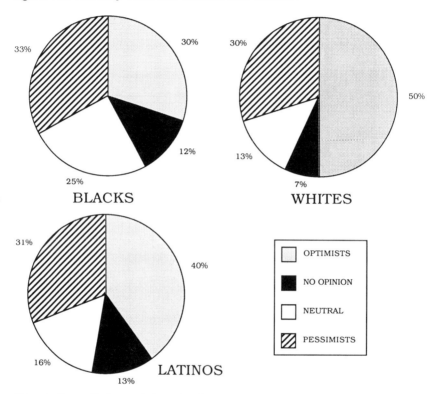

Fig. 2: Overall financial outlook


Reagan Performance Ratings

Survey Dates: April 12–July 15, 1985
Number of Interviews:       Latinos        334
                            Blacks         634
                            Whites       5,396

The Question: "Do you approve or disapprove of the way Ronald
Reagan is handling his job as president?"

|  | Latinos | Blacks | Whites |
|---|---|---|---|
| Approve | 52% | 22% | 61% |
| Disapprove | 32 | 67 | 30 |
| No opinion | 16 | 11 | 9 |
| Total | 100% | 100% | 100% |

## Political Party Affiliation[a]

Survey Dates: April 12–July 15, 1985

| Number of Interviews: | Latinos | 307 |
|---|---|---|
|  | Blacks | 617 |
|  | Whites | 5,147 |

The Question: "In politics, as of today, do you consider yourself a Republican, a Democrat, or an Independent?"

|  | Latinos | Blacks | Whites |
|---|---|---|---|
| Republican | 24% | 10% | 36% |
| Democrat | 45 | 73 | 33 |
| Independent | 31 | 17 | 31 |
| Total | 100% | 100% | 100% |

[a] Omits persons naming other parties or none.

# Comments on Papers Presented by the Panel on Latinos and the 1984 Election

F. Chris Garcia, *University of New Mexico*

## Comments on "Latinos and the 1984 Election: A Comparative Perspective," by Bruce E. Cain and D. Robert Kiewiet

My comments on the paper by Bruce Cain and Roderick Kiewiet will be directed primarily at methodological considerations. They state that the purpose of their paper is "to point out the complexities, advantages, and disadvantages of a comparative approach to minority politics, using the Caltec 1984 poll as an example." For example, they comment on in-person versus telephone interviews, indicating the general advantages of in-person interviews. However, in the case of minority opinion research the balance may shift toward telephone interviews. As the authors point out, the presence of a stranger in the neighborhood of recent immigrants (or, for that matter, even a well-established ethnic minority neighborhood) is likely to arouse suspicion. Of course, the ideal solution would be to hire a member of that ethnic group who has access to or is well known in the neighborhood.

Although the problem of "differential incidence" of telephone ownership might be a major problem in interviewing minorities, in our survey research projects we have found less of a problem with the differential refusal rate. In fact, we have found that we have easier access to minorities when the proper techniques and interviewers are used than we do to many elements of the majority population. The authors did discover that based on their experience "refusal rates were no higher among Latinos than among whites," and that has been our experience in New Mexico over the past several years. Cain and Kiewiet mention the use of Hispanic and Asian surname computer dictionaries to yield subsamples of minorities. I suspect that in some Latino areas, such as northern New Mexico, there is considerable imprecision using surnames to find ethnic respondents because of a relatively high rate of transethnic marriages over the generations.

The authors matched their data on Latinos, Asians, and blacks against that in the 1980 Census. I am not sure how useful this comparison is. There are potential problems, not the least of which is that the Census material is now six years old. The Latino population under study is currently in great flux, and there probably have been tremendous changes within that group. Another inherent problem is that the census identification of minorities was accomplished through a self-identification question while the opinion surveyors in this report apparently used Spanish surnames; thus somewhat different target groups are being compared. In other words, it is not clear that Cain and Kiewiet should fault themselves as they do for possible oversampling or undersampling. Some of the "discrepancies" between the two sets of data may simply be the result of the time and methodological differences in the two samples.

The authors speculate about the nonrepresentativeness of the more politically active or attentive respondents participating in opinion surveys and the likely exclusion of those who are less politically attentive. This is an important bias to consider when interpreting survey results which are generalized to the entire population. However, that bias is probably less problematic when one is investigating, or trying to project, political behavior such as participation in elections. In this case, the biasing characteristics of the opinion sample are precisely those which are found among persons most likely engaging in overt, active political behavior. Therefore, the activist bias in the sample actually may strengthen any electoral projections or hypotheses about actual political behavior. The difficulty arises primarily when one attempts to generalize not to a select, more active group of political actors but to the less attentive, less active general population.

The authors use a key phrase when they write that "the circumstances of minorities in California vary considerably." They state that, "generally speaking [but not always], the longer individuals have been in the country, the more linguistic and cultural differences lessen, and associated problems (of discrimination) recede." While this is true at a very general level, there are so many variations in this process of acculturation and assimilation and consequent levels of discrimination—even within one ethnic group from region to region and locality to locality—that one must have specific knowledge of these variations. This is necessary in order to interpret correctly not only opinion poll results but also to analyze variations within a single ethnic cultural group. In fact, this point is evidenced in the authors' placement of Latinos in the lower left quadrant of their matrix—that is, recent immigrants and lower socioeconomic status—because this is more true of Latinos in California, particularly Southern California, than in other areas such as New Mexico and the Rio Grande Valley of Texas.

Their findings comparing attachment to the United States are interesting in ways other than those which the authors point out. For example, many Latinos, at least Mexican Americans, are so close to their country of origin that it is much easier for them to be "attached" to the country of origin, as is indicated by their maintenance of social links with persons in the mother country. Yet, Cain and Kiewiet did not find this attachment to be any stronger than that among the white foreign-born or Asians. This is in itself a very interesting finding.

Concerning the use of non-English or English language, one major reason for ethnic differences may be the larger linguistic environment or language ambience in which ethnic groups exist. Obviously, Latinos live in an environment which has many reinforcements for the use and maintenance of the Spanish language—such as Spanish language media and proximity to Spanish-speaking countries—while this is less the case for Asians and blacks in the United States. The findings of support by black Americans for bilingual education programs are intriguing and pose a host of questions. For instance, what language(s) are they considering for bilingual ballots?

It is unfortunate that the exact questions asked the respondents in these opinion surveys have not been provided. Their inclusion would have been very informative and useful in analyzing the results of this research. For example, in the bilingual education question, were certain languages specified or simply "bilingual education"? On the immigration question, "amnesty for illegal immigrants," did the queston simply use such broad general phrases or were more specific references made to particular people, particular times, particular amnesty plans, and so forth?

It is not immediately obvious why the authors think that Latino and Asian communities ought to have a "common perspective" on immigration-related issues, since there are so many differences in the historical experiences and current social and economic situations of these two groups.

Although most of the response differences in this study seem to be significant, we should keep in mind that most of these samples, certainly for the Asians and blacks, encompass a sampling error range about 11 points—that is, $\pm$ 5.5% at the .05 level—and that the error range is $\pm$ 4.8% for the foreign-born whites and about

± 4% for the Latino sample. Relatedly, some tests of statistical significance of the findings might have been useful.

The discussion of discrimination and the researchers' selection of two items from among "a number of items in our poll that dealt with the issues of prejudice and discrimination" leads to the suggestion that, instead of selecting or focusing on two individual items, it might have been more revealing had the authors combined several items into a multiitem index of discrimination of some sort.

Throughout the paper it is not clear whether the subsamples are composed entirely of foreign-born persons or whether each subsample includes only a proportion of foreign-born individuals. What percentage of each subsample is foreign-born?

How may the differences between Asians and Latinos on political or partisan questions and the cultural similarities of Latinos and blacks be explained? If these are not foreign-born individuals, it may be due basically to their different political histories, both in terms of quality and length of time in this country. The authors touch only lightly on this and another important related point when they state that "one plausible explanation. . . is that there are important differences in the aggregate socioeconomic circumstances of these groups." Another important (and very little researched) point is the authors' observation that the political norms or values of the societies from which these ethnic groups have come may have residual effects on their political attitudes in this country. Cain and Kiewiet ask a key question when they inquire as to how much Latino attitudes are based on the experience of being a minority group in America per se and how much their attitudes are rooted in the unique cultural values of the Hispanic cultures. Even more specifically, one should try to determine which values are traditional cultural values and which values now a part of the culture stem from Latinos being a distinguishable ethnic minority in United States society. This is a crucially important topic yet one which has been very little studied, certainly by political scientists. There has been some work on this by sociologists and social psychologists, but even that is relatively limited.

The authors' major findings are well summarized in their conclusion. They state that there must be a great deal more reseach conducted on the attitudes, beliefs, and values of ethnic minorities in the United States, and that this is certainly true of the Latino community which is very underresearched at this time. Moreover, one cannot dispute the point that many of these studies ought to be done from a comparative perspective. One must remember that in studying the Latino community itself there is a great deal of room for comparative analysis because of the great variations within the Hispanic group. Latinos' political-historical experiences vary tremendously from one area of the country to another. Not only have the experiences of Latinos in this country varied greatly depending upon their settlement location, but there are even cultural differences in the regions of the country from which they came. Additionally, there are differences in the rates of acculturation and assimilation along with increasing variations among other socioeconomic characteristics, including socioeconomic class, religion, occupation, age, and, always important, generation of residence or recency of immigration to the United States.

The kind of study which Cain and Kiewiet have initiated is certainly a step in the right direction. The authors are aware of many of the methodological difficulties involved in this kind of research and have taken a sensitive position on a very complicated matter. I look forward to reading more of their research results on this very important subject and hope other opinion researchers will follow their direction.

**Comments on "Hispanic Vote Behavior: Selected Findings from Past Research Conducted by Tarrance & Associates," by Lance Tarrance**

It is difficult to offer comments in a concise manner on the Tarrance report, since it consists of bits and pieces of information and because the relationship between them has not been clarified by the author.

In the section entitled "Special leadership survey of Hispanic community leaders (June 1980)," a list of key findings and implications are presented but in a sketchy manner. Although the statements are provocative, there is not enough information provided to allow analysis or commentary. For example, one of the key findings (point 2) states that "the Hispanic leadership is predominantly interested in the local, not state level, of politics." This could have important political implications, yet it is neither elaborated upon nor supported with data. The same is true for point 5 which states, "However, Hispanic leadership concerns for the future and for Texas share a Republican view"—and nothing else. Another interesting "finding" (point 8) is that apparently Hispanic "leadership" in 1980 expressed its voting preferences as follows: Reagan 40%, Carter 36%, Anderson 7%, and Undecided 17%. The fact that South Texas Hispanic leadership as more supportive of Republican candidate Reagan than of incumbent President Carter certainly should have warranted additional commentary. The presentation of statements is followed by some comments, including one which states that "it is likely that Hispanic support for Republican candidates will increase at the local level (for example, mayor and city council) before expanding into state politics at the legislative level." However, again there are virtually no data provided to substantiate this, nor is it explained further. Neither is the reported affinity of Hispanics, according to this study, for Republicans at the national level reconciled with this statement. Moreover, it is not considered that many local offices throughout the country are nonpartisan rather than partisan in nature.

Much of the perceived Republican preference by Hispanic leaders in this study may be attributed to the sampling frame used by the researchers. Hispanic leaders in this study were business owners, professionals, managers, and department heads of business firms, and individuals whom the members of these former groups identified as other opinion leaders. It is to be expected that this leadership segment would be much more Republican-oriented than either the general population or leaders selected from other leadership categories.

Several comments are presented to the effect that Hispanics in Texas are conservative in their ideology, yet little is provided about the way that ideology has been measured or about the particular definition of ideology employed. A chart labeled "Texas Hispanics: Ideology" shows a very small segment of the population (5% to 15% as being "moderate" in ideology whereas "conservative" ideologues numbered 58% in 1980, 45% in 1983, 63% in 1984, and 53% in 1985.

The last part of the paper concerns itself with a "National Hispanic Study (July 1983)" conducted for the Federation for American Immigration Reform (FAIR). Highlights of the survey indicate that Hispanics (and blacks) have a very restrictive view toward immigration, but neither methodology nor data elaborating upon the findings are presented, thus making it impossible for any critical analysis to be conducted.

**Comments on "Latinos in the 1984 Election Exit Polls: Some Findings and Some Methodological Lessons," by Robert R. Brischetto**

Robert Brischetto has provided us with some very valuable data, coming as it does from exit polls of Latinos who have actually cast their ballots. In addition to providing a very valuable service through his extensive secondary analysis of data selected nation-wide from various sources, he has added the results of the exit polls of 6,000 Latino voters coordinated by the Southwest Voter Registration and Education Project. In addition to his valuable data aggregation and synthesis of information, Brischetto has provided many insightful and astute comments on the results and implications of Latino electoral behavior.

Brischetto reminds us that when we are talking about the Latino vote we actually are referring to "a number of Latino electorates" and also points out to us that the Latino community is geographically discrete, concentrated in a few states, and has experienced a tremendous growth relative to the rest of the population. All of these points are very important to any evaluation of the impact of the Latino vote. Most notable is his observation that there was a 77% increase in voting age Latinos from 1970 to 1980.

One should note that more than one-fifth of the Latino/Hispanic voting age population is classified in the "Other Spanish" category, a grouping which is mostly ignored and little understood. Special notice is called to the majority of New Mexico eligible voters who told the census takers that they were "Spanish." It should be noted that this is a special terminology used by the people of Mexican and Spanish heritage in New Mexico based on their long-time residence in the state and their distinctive historical experience. This is a quite different group from the "Other Spanish" found in other states, who are primarily recent immigrants from Central and South America as well as from Spain.

One thing that is evident throughout the paper is the great variation in the results of exit polls. Of course it is difficult to get a very good representative random sample based, as most exit polls are, on interval sampling. And when this is compounded by a relatively small number of Hispanics in the polls, it is not surprising that the percentage of Hispanic voters supporting each of the presidential candidates varies substantially from poll to poll. For example, in California the surveys of Reagan's support by Latinos range from 24% to 51% (Brischetto, table 6). Moreover, CBS shows a completely opposite electoral trend from NBC. From 1980 to 1984 NBC shows a decrease in Reagan support from one election to the other while CBS shows an increase.

Brischetto's report that Cuban American voters supported Reagan at a high level—a rate increase from 67% in 1980 to 93% in 1984—demonstrates again the necessity of treating Hispanic subgroups separately in an analysis of voting behavior.

There is one point with which I must take issue, and that is the characterization of Latino and Anglo voters as being polarized in their support of the Republican presidential candidate. Brischetto uses this term when referring to the percentage difference between the two ethnic groups in their vote for the Republican candidate; it increased by an estimated four to eight percentage points between 1980 and 1984 (Brischetto, table 3). The difference from one election to another is quite small and, given the great variation in exit polling results, it may not be significant. Later, in keeping with his theme, Brischetto notes only slight increases among Latinos in their Republican affiliation from 1980 to 1984 (from 3% to 7% higher), but then states that "the polarization between Latinos and whites is the most striking pattern." Again, this characterization seems at least exaggerated. It should be noted that his data also show that age is an extremely important variable in the level of Hispanic support for Reagan and in GOP identification among Hispanics. The youngest Hispanics are most supportive of the Republican party and presidential candidate. This leads me to conclude that an explanation which is at least equally acceptable to the polarization hypothesis is that Hispanics may be following the same partisan path as Anglos but at this point lag several years behind in Republican preference, perhaps a generation or so. That is, as Hispanics become more assimilated into the economic and political structure of this country, they will be increasingly subject to the same socioeconomic influences and will become increasingly Republican (if the larger society continues to become increasingly Republican). Of course, Latinos are starting from a different base, being much more Democratic and much lower on the socioeconomic ladder. It is at least possible that Republican support among Anglos will plateau and that Hispanic support for Republicans will continue to grow until it reaches or at least approximates that of the Anglo electorate. Consequently, to term this phenomenon, which actually may be a generational lead-lag phenomenon, polarization may be overstating the case and missing a long-term trend.

Finally, one should note that geohistorical or political-cultural differences, even within one nationality group, may be greater than those between nationality groups. For example, although Brischetto does not mention this, his data indicate that there is a greater difference in party identification between East Los Angeles Mexican Americans and Texas Mexican Americans than there is between Midwest Mexican Americans and Midwest Puerto Ricans.

This is a phenomenon that is commonly found in ethnic group political research, for the particular sociohistorical circumstances of a group in a certain region often are the overriding explanatory factors, superseding the more traditional socioeconomic indicators of political orientation.

**Comments on "Political Preferences of Latinos, Blacks, and Whites during the 1984 Campaign," by James Shriver III**

James Shriver recognizes the limitations of his data, which primarily revolve around the small Latino sample size of approximately 100 per survey. While weighting can adjust a subsample to its appropriate proportion in the total sample, it may only magnify any unreliability which originally was produced by the small sample's variation. Shriver has collapsed the results of several surveys taken over a period of approximately one year, realizing that this is not technically without fault. Yet the fact that the Latino population has been recognized by such a well-established institution as the Gallup organization with its sound personal interviewing methodology is still another recognition of the growing importance of the Latino population in the United States.

Collapsing the Latino data produced samples ranging in size from 179 to 657, the latter large number being the sample responding to the question most frequently asked over the series of surveys—that is, the interviewees' choice in the Reagan versus Mondale trial heat. The percentage of Latinos in these combined samples ranges from less than 4% to more than 7% per sample. Hispanic preferences for the presidency show the traditional pattern: Hispanics were more Democratic in their preferences than were blacks but less Democratic than were white voters during the prepresidential election period. It is interesting to note that Latinos shared a majority preference with whites for Ronald Reagan over Jesse Jackson, although by a substantially smaller margin. This fact certainly had relevance for those working to form a "rainbow coalition." The Latinos' in-between position on presidential preference is again illustrated by the Reagan-Bush versus Mondale-Ferraro question. While 61% of the whites favored the Reagan-Bush ticket and 83% of the blacks favored a Mondale-Ferraro ticket, Latinos were split evenly between Reagan-Bush supporters (45%) and Mondale-Ferraro supporters (48%). The midway phenomenon is again shown in preferences for congressional parties. While whites favored the Republican congressional party and blacks heavily supported the Democrats, Latinos were between these two positions, although still fairly heavily Democratic (62%). This in-between position is also noted in the questions on the most important problem facing the country today. During late 1984 and early 1985, white voters primarily were concerned with the international situation. Blacks were concerned foremost with the domestic problem of unemployment, and Latinos were evenly balanced between these two issues. It should be noted that if domestic concerns are collapsed into one variable it far outweighs concern with the international situation for all three groups. In the questions on financial outlook, while Latinos continued to be between the black and white opinions their opinions were substantially closer to those of white voters than black voters. The question on Reagan performance ratings is interesting because among other things it indicates the larger undecided group among Latinos. This may be because Latinos are traditionally Democratic but were generally favorably impressed with Ronald Reagan's performance. With regard to political affiliation or identification, in the spring and summer of 1985 Latinos did not provide either party with majority support: roughly one-quarter identified with the Republican party and almost one-third were neither Republican nor Democrat.

One major observation to be made about the Latino data is that it no doubt obscures significant variations among Latino nationality groupings. It is quite likely that much of the Republican support derives from Cuban Americans and that the Puerto Ricans are most heavily Democratic, with Mexican Americans somewhere in between but probably closer to the Puerto Ricans. Of course, with such small samples, it would be impossible to conduct this very important subgroup analysis.

In sum, the data are interesting and are also supportive of trends reported by other public opinion analysts with regard to Latino political opinions. As a methodologically aggregated grouping, on most issues and political preferences Latinos fall between blacks and whites, although their opinions are usually closer to whites. However, we must remember not only the methodological problems concerning the data, but also that these data are responses to a few discrete opinion questions gathered over a very short period of time rather than comprehensive, in-depth attitudinal information.

## Common Themes and Observations

At this point, I would like to address my comments to some of the common themes woven through the four papers presented on this panel and also to offer some additional observations.

First, we must note that all these papers are comparative. Comparative methodology should be the preferred approach to this kind of research. Simply surveying one population without reference to another group in comparable circumstances may leave as many questions unanswered as it answers. Research comparing a Hispanic group with the majority culture, with other distinctive ethnic cultures, and with other Hispanic groups which vary in terms of national origin, geographical location, or socioeconomic circumstances must be conducted if we are to understand more fully the orientations of Hispanics.

These papers all emphasize either the results of various kinds of opinion polls or discuss survey research design methodology. Hardly mentioned is the actual fieldwork or the administration of these opinion survey projects. Yet this interviewing phase is a crucial link in all opinion survey research. Special attention must be paid to the selection, training, and supervision of bilingual-bicultural interviewers. Their feedback is helpful in modifying and improving our research instruments as well as interpreting the responses.

Moreover, very little has been said about the fine art of analyzing the data. Even the best data may be misinterpreted. Interpretation and analysis must be done by persons with a high level of cultural sensitivity as well as factual knowledge about the communities under study.

A point which is crucial but which is barely touched upon in these papers is the psychological effects of discriminatory experiences on all minorities or, more particularly, on subgroupings within the Latino community. Since persons undergoing systematic discrimination are greatly affected in their attitudes and beliefs, the role that discriminatory experiences have had in promoting similarity or commonality of attitudes among Latinos needs to be explored much further.

The papers I have commented on were written by both academic and commercial pollsters. It is a major step forward for these and other papers by representatives of both groups to be presented at a single conference. More commonly, there is a lack of communication among persons engaged in opinion surveys of the

Latino community. Very little information is shared among commercial market researchers or between this group and academics who are conducting opinion surveys, often in the same communities. I hope that this conference will lead to some institutionalization of mechanisms for us to communicate with one another and to share data which will enlighten each of the participating groups and will improve the information base upon which all of us can draw.

Finally, most of the research done by social scientists and even political pollsters is aimed at dissecting and analyzing data, breaking a population into segments. Of course, this procedure is very common to the scientific way of inquiry. But perhaps as important (and perhaps with more long-range significance), social science researchers and pollsters should integrate the data. Investigators should look for the ties that bind as well as the differences that separate. Politicians, for example, target different electoral segments during their campaigns, but on election day they are concerned only with the total vote. Likewise, persons who are interested in presenting the Latino community as a major force in United States society also should be concerned with the common characteristics that tie the Latino groups together. All of us who do research must be aware of the implications of segmented analysis versus synthesis in our research.

# Exit Polls and the Latino Voter

Warren J. Mitofsky, *CBS News*

Kathleen A. Frankovic, *CBS News*

This paper will discuss problems that affect CBS News/New York Times exit poll interviews with Latino voters. It will review efforts in 1984 primary and general election polls to minimize refusal rates among Latinos, including the use of Spanish-speaking interviewers and Spanish language questionnaires. It will also outline characteristics of Latino voters.

CBS News has been conducting interviews with voters at their polling places on election days since 1967. These voter polls are more commonly known as exit polls. They have been controversial when used to project the election of the next president before every precinct nationwide has closed.

They also have been illuminating. They are the best source of public opinion about how the various voting blocs cast their votes for a candidate and why they did it. They have been used to tell the public that the election of 1982 was not a rejection of Ronald Reagan's policies, even though this was widely expected before the election, and that the election of 1980 was really not a swing to the right but a repudiation of Jimmy Carter.

Exit polls are a better source for this information than preelection polls. When people are interviewed immediately after casting their vote, their motives are still uppermost in their thinking. Furthermore, exit polls measure voter behavior, not opinion. In a preelection poll the researcher does not know if the voter will change her or his mind between the interview and the election and vote for a different candidate. Also, in preelection polls there is no certainty that a potential voter will really go to the polls and cast a vote.

The elimination of these uncertainties and the immediacy of asking about motives for choosing a candidate make exit polls an invaluable tool. It is now possible to make a reliable association between candidate selection and characteristics of these actual voters.

There is another advantage provided by exit polls for studying the electoral process. Exit polls are the first useful means for gathering information about voter blocs that make up only a small proportion of the electorate. The sheer size of a national exit poll sample makes it possible to learn something about the diversity of a relatively small group like Latinos. It has always been possible to design special studies to learn more about Latinos, but always at great expense and with necessary limitations in the design of the study. A national exit poll makes it possible to have a sufficient number of interviews with Latinos to do at least a minimal analysis of the group.

### How A National Exit Poll Is Conducted

A nationwide sample of voting precincts is selected by means of a stratified random design. The effect of the sampling process is that each precinct in the country has a probability of being selected. That probability is proportionate to the number of voters actually voting in that precinct in some recent past election.

Before the election, interviewers collect past voting information and demographic characteristics from each precinct. The data are stored in a computer data bank and used during the processing of the exit poll results.

On election day, one or, in special cases, two interviewers are assigned to work at each sample precinct. They interview every $n$th voter as voters leave the polling place. About 100 voters are interviewed at every precinct. Interviewers start when the polls open and work until the end of the voting day.

After a brief introduction by the interviewer, the voter is handed a questionnaire and asked to complete it and then deposit it in a box. Respondents are not asked their names, nor are they identified on the questionnaire with a code. The responses remain anonymous.

Periodically during the voting day the responses on each questionnaire are read over the telephone to a processing center. The data are accumulated in a computer and estimates are made at the end of the voting day.

In the 1984 general election, the second question on the questionnaire asked:

ARE YOU:
1. White    3. Hispanic    5. Other
2. Black    4. Asian

Responses to this question identified the precincts with Hispanic or Latino voters. There were some Latino voters in 70 of the 176 precincts used for the national level of the 1984 general election exit poll. These 70 precincts were located in 29 states. There were, however, no Latinos in the New Mexico precincts used in the national sample, although New Mexico is the state with the largest proportion of Latino voters. The distribution of Latino precincts across the United States is shown in table 1.

**Table 1**
Percentage of Latinos in 1984 National Exit Poll Sample Precincts

| States | No. of Precincts | % Latino |
|---|---|---|
| | 106 | 0 |
| One precinct in each: Alabama, Arkansas, Indiana, Iowa, Louisiana, Maine, Michigan, Mississippi, New Jersey, North Dakota, Ohio, Oklahoma, South Carolina, Utah, Virginia | 62 | 1–10 |
| More than one precinct in each: California, Colorado, Florida, Georgia, Illinois, Kansas, Kentucky, Maryland, Massachusetts, Minnesota, New York, Pennsylvania, Texas, Wisconsin | | |
| California, Colorado New York | 6 | 11–20 |
| Texas | 1 | 51–60 |
| California | 1 | 61–70 |
| | 176 | |

## Demographic Comparision of Latino and Other Voters

In New York, California, and Texas it is possible to compare several characteristics of Latino and other voters in both their state's primary and the general election. In each of those states, we conducted separate statewide exit polls on the day of the general election. In addition, primary day exit polls were conducted in New York and California, and a special caucus poll was conducted in Texas.

Latino participants in the nominating process are somewhat different from Latino general election voters, but not all that different from state to state. They are not exactly like other voters, but many of the differences can be attributed to their being younger and not as well educated. It seems reasonable to assume that the differences between Latinos and other voters will narrow as the next generation of Latinos participates in the voting process.

The Latino voters are generally younger than other voters in a state. Also, Latino voters who participate in general elections are younger than those who vote in primaries. Although not shown in table 2, a comparison with black voters shows that the Latinos are younger in New York but about the same ages as blacks in California or Texas.

Latinos identify themselves as Democrats in about the same proportion as other Democratic primary voters. In comparison to general election voters, Latinos are more Democratic than all other voters combined, but considerably less Democratic than blacks.

The Latinos in Texas who voted in the Democratic caucus are more liberal than the other caucus participants. They are only slightly more liberal than other general election voters in all three states.

The number of union household members voting in these elections varies considerably from state to state. In all three states' primaries, about 4 out of 10 Latino voters lived in a union household. In New York there was not much variation between the primary and the general election. By contrast, in Texas Latinos were twice as likely to live in union households than the other participants in the caucus. But in the general election, a very small proportion of Latinos or other voters were identified with a union household. It seems that the unions were successful in dominating Latino turnout for the caucus but had no impact on the general election.

The much-heralded registration drives of the 1984 campaign seem to have had more impact on increasing new registration of Latinos than on registering other voters in New York and California, although it had a lesser impact on Latinos in Texas. In Texas, only 10% of Latinos claim to have registered for the first time in 1984, while 18% of blacks signed up, as did 12% of all non-Latinos.

**Table 2**
Latino versus Other Voters in 1984 Primaries and General Election

| | NEW YORK | | | | CALIFORNIA | | | | TEXAS | | | |
|---|---|---|---|---|---|---|---|---|---|---|---|---|
| | Primary | | General | | Primary | | General | | Primary | | General | |
| | Latino | Other | Latino | Other | Latino | Other | Latino | Other | Latino | Other | Latino | Other |
| N (weighted) | 99 (5%) | 1,873 (93%) | 66 (3%) | 2,181 (97%) | 234 (9%) | 2,264 (90%) | 164 (6%) | 2,571 (92%) | 99 (9%) | 995 (90%) | 142 (7%) | 1,833 (93%) |
| *Sex* | | | | | | | | | | | | |
| Male | 48% | 41% | 41% | 48% | 47% | 43% | 55% | 47% | 49% | 41% | 45% | 51% |
| Female | 52 | 58 | 59 | 52 | 52 | 56 | 45 | 53 | 49 | 58 | 55 | 49 |
| *Age* | | | | | | | | | | | | |
| 18–29 | 32 | 16 | 41 | 25 | 20 | 16 | 32 | 22 | 18 | 13 | 36 | 27 |
| 30–44 | 38 | 31 | 29 | 32 | 31 | 29 | 40 | 29 | 31 | 28 | 33 | 36 |
| 45–59 | 24 | 23 | 15 | 22 | 31 | 21 | 19 | 23 | 34 | 23 | 24 | 21 |
| 60+ | 6 | 29 | 15 | 20 | 19 | 33 | 9 | 25 | 17 | 33 | 7 | 16 |
| *Party* | | | | | | | | | | | | |
| Republican | — | 1 | 29 | 33 | 3 | 3 | 22 | 42 | — | 2 | 19 | 34 |
| Democratic | 82 | 81 | 58 | 41 | 86 | 78 | 64 | 39 | 86 | 80 | 59 | 38 |
| Independent | 16 | 17 | 13 | 24 | 10 | 17 | 13 | 17 | 9 | 15 | 21 | 26 |
| *Political Philosophy* | | | | | | | | | | | | |
| Liberal | 35 | 35 | 31 | 24 | 29 | 33 | 25 | 19 | 41 | 26 | 24 | 14 |
| Moderate | 35 | 45 | 33 | 39 | 50 | 48 | 35 | 43 | 41 | 49 | 44 | 38 |
| Conservative | 24 | 14 | 30 | 33 | 19 | 16 | 34 | 34 | 10 | 19 | 28 | 44 |

*Education*

| | | | | | | | | | | | | |
|---|---|---|---|---|---|---|---|---|---|---|---|---|
| Less than high school graduate | 25 | 10 | 30 | 40 | 20 | 8 | 18 | 35 | 38 | 17 | 23 | 38 |
| High school graduate | 28 | 27 | 49 | 37 | 30 | 21 | 39 | 23 | 14 | 21 | 10 | 16 |
| Some college | 23 | 25 | 30 | 22 | 31 | 35 | 23 | 14 | 26 | 24 | 6 | 9 |
| College graduate | 18 | 36 | 26 | 12 | 15 | 32 | 20 | 15 | 19 | 35 | 32 | 12 |
| *Union* | | | | | | | | | | | | |
| Household Member | 37 | 41 | 33 | 26 | 41 | 30 | 27 | 19 | 42 | 21 | 26 | 22 |
| *Income* | | | | | | | | | | | | |
| Less than $12,500 | 46 | 17 | 25 | 21 | 22 | 19 | 24 | 19 | 24 | 20 | 22 | 24 |
| $12,500–$25,000 | 29 | 27 | 11 | 21 | 26 | 26 | 14 | 20 | 25 | 28 | 11 | 22 |
| $25,000–$35,000 | 12 | 19 | 1 | 15 | 20 | 21 | 9 | 21 | 27 | 17 | 3 | 16 |
| $35,000–$50,000 | 9 | 16 | | | | | | | | | | |
| Over $50,000 | — | 13 | | | | | | | | | | |
| *Registered* | | | | | | | | | | | | |
| 1984: For the first time | 14 | | | 10 | | | 13 | 7 | | | 10 | 12 |
| 1984: But not for the first time | 17 | | | 12 | | | 19 | 13 | | | 18 | 16 |
| 1983 or earlier | 59 | | | 74 | | | 65 | 77 | | | 69 | 70 |

*Continued on next page*

| | NEW YORK | | | | CALIFORNIA | | | | TEXAS | | | |
| | Primary | | General | | Primary | | General | | Primary | | General | |
| | Latino | Other | Latino | Other | Latino | Other | Latino | Other | Latino | Other | Latino | Other |
|---|---|---|---|---|---|---|---|---|---|---|---|---|
| *Occupation* | | | | | | | | | | | | |
| Professional/ manager | | | 20 | 31 | | | 13 | 25 | | | 28 | 35 |
| White collar | | | 6 | 12 | | | 7 | 11 | | | 7 | 13 |
| Blue collar | | | 34 | 12 | | | 14 | 6 | | | 14 | 12 |
| Farmer | | | — | 1 | | | 2 | 1 | | | 4 | 3 |
| Housewife | | | 8 | 11 | | | 11 | 10 | | | 16 | 13 |
| Unemployed | | | 11 | 3 | | | 1 | 3 | | | 7 | 2 |
| Retired | | | 1 | 10 | | | 5 | 13 | | | 5 | 8 |
| *Working woman* | 9 | 21 | | | 24 | 25 | | | 27 | 32 | | |
| *Religion* | | | | | | | | | | | | |
| Catholic | | | 67 | 36 | | | 35 | 15 | | | 68 | 13 |
| Baptist | | | 3 | 8 | | | 3 | 8 | | | 5 | 33 |
| Other Christian | | | 9 | 18 | | | 8 | 29 | | | 8 | 32 |
| Jewish | | | 5 | 13 | | | 1 | 4 | | | — | 1 |
| Other | | | 1 | 6 | | | 8 | 12 | | | 3 | 7 |

Note: Dashes represent categories of less than 1%; blanks mean the data were not collected.

**Spanish Ballot Usage in 1984 Primaries**

Spanish language questionnaires were offered to voters in three states during the primary season: California, New York, and Texas. The evaluation data presented here are from the first two states.

In Texas, *no* Latino caucus participants chose to use the Spanish language questionnaire. In California, only 8 Spanish questionnaires were returned from five precincts. In New York usage was slightly higher. One precinct returned 4 (of 330) Spanish questionnaires. Another returned 11 (of 233). And one precinct returned 43 (of 163) Spanish questionnaires.

The refusal rate for the precinct with 43 Spanish questionnaires was 50%. It was much lower (22% and 17%) for the two precincts which had only a handful of Spanish questionnaires. We conducted further analysis of the precinct with 43 Spanish questionnaires. The refusal rate by race was lowest for Latinos, 26% (N = 148); it was very high for both whites, 73% (N = 136), and blacks, 66% (N = 41).

The interviewer was Latino and worked all day in her Lower Manhatten district. She was 48 years old. She was experienced in doing telephone and person-to-person surveys but had never worked on an exit poll before. She said she had few problems and that it was not difficult at all to get people to fill out the questionnaire. Her only comment was that "the questionnaire should be shorter. The people don't like to fill out too much." Her observation is generally consistent with prior exit poll experience. The longer the questionnaire, the higher the refusal rate.

While having a Spanish language questionnaire available in that one precinct seems to have significantly reduced the noncompletion rate among Latinos, in most cases it does not seem reasonable to pursue future use of Spanish language questionnaires. In all the other cases where a Spanish language version of the questionnaire was available, few individuals chose to use them. In California and in the rest of New York state, the additional information gained by providing a Spanish questionnaire was minimal, while in the Texas caucus poll the Spanish language questionnaire provided no new information. The CBS experience is similar to that of other networks, suggesting that Latinos who vote are for the most part fluent in English. To make the use of Spanish questionnaires in our polling effort more efficacious would appear to require drastic changes in the training of the interviewers and more complete research about the polling places where the questionnaires are used.

Examination of the results in the single precinct where a sizable number of Spanish language questionnaires were chosen shows clear differences between Latino voters who chose each questionnaire. The results confirm expectations: the Latinos filling out English questionnaires were much younger than the Spanish questionnaire group. They were also better educated and made more money than their Spanish language counterparts. The English questionnaire Latinos were moderately more likely to vote for Hart or Jackson. Very few people from either group were first-time voters. The English questionnaire Latinos were also more likely to say they didn't vote in 1980 for president, but this could be due to their younger age overall. Detailed results of the comparison between Latinos who used the English language and those who used the Spanish language questionnaire are provided in table 3.

### Refusal Rates in Latino Precincts

New Mexico, which has the highest proportion of Latinos in its population, provides an opportunity to compare the completion rates of Latino and other voters. At the statewide level of our 1984 general election day poll, there were 13 precincts in New Mexico in which Latinos made up at least 40% of the population. Those precincts were scattered throughout the state, and were located in the large cities of Albuquerque and Santa Fe as well as in rural areas. The pattern of refusals in those precincts resembles the pattern of refusals elsewhere, with more refusals in urban than in rural areas, but the difference between Latino and non-Latino refusals varies from location to location.

Exit poll interviewers are asked to record certain types of information about voters who refuse to be interviewed. They indicate, on a separate sheet, the sex, ethnicity, and approximate age of the refuser. Refusers are coded as either males or females; as white, black, Latino, or another race; and as under 30, 30 to 60, or over 60. Previous analyses indicate that interviewers categorize individuals on these characteristics with a high degree of accuracy.

In New Mexico in 1984, voters in the city of Albuquerque were more likely than voters in either Santa Fe or rural New Mexico to refuse to answer the exit poll questionnaire. One-third of the voters approached refused to be interviewed. Among white voters, the refusal rate was 21%; for Latinos, the refusal rate was 39%. This large gap between white and Latino voters was almost entirely due to one large precinct where Latinos made up 86% of the voting

**Table 3**
Spanish-language and English-language Latino Voters
in 1984 Primaries
(%)

| | Latinos with Spanish Questionnaires (*N* = 43) | Latinos with English Questionnaires (*N* = 64) |
|---|---|---|
| *Age* | | |
| 18–29 | — | 25 |
| 30–44 | 9 | 34 |
| 45–64 | 26 | 21 |
| 64 + | 58 | 9 |
| *Sex* | | |
| Male | 35 | 31 |
| Female | 63 | 64 |
| *Education* | | |
| Less than high school graduate | 72 | 22 |
| High school graduate | 14 | 27 |
| Some college | 2 | 23 |
| College graduate | 5 | 17 |
| *Income* | | |
| Less than $12,500 | 60 | 34 |
| $12,500–$24,900 | 9 | 31 |
| $25,000–$34,900 | 5 | 16 |
| $35,000–$50,000 | 7 | 3 |
| Over $50,000 | 2 | 3 |
| *Vote* | | |
| Mondale | 79 | 59 |
| Hart | 9 | 19 |
| Jackson | 7 | 20 |
| Other | 5 | 2 |
| *Vote in 1980* | | |
| Carter | 63 | 66 |
| Reagan | 26 | 9 |
| Anderson | 5 | 1 |
| Didn't vote | 5 | 19 |
| *First time voters* | — | 5 |

population. In that precinct, the morning shift interviewer was non-Latino, while the afternoon shift interviewer was Latino. While both interviewers had exceptionally high refusal rates among Latino voters, the white interviewer's refusal rate (63%) was much higher than the Latino's (50%).

While this suggests that white interviewers may have difficulty in persuading Latino voters to respond to a questionnaire, that may not always be the case, as illustrated by results from another heavily Latino Albuquerque precinct. In that precinct, where a white interviewer worked all day, the refusal rate for Latinos was only 19%. The white refusal rate was 20%, or just about the same. Some 70% of the voters in that precinct were Latino.

In Santa Fe precincts, there was no overall difference in the Latino and non-Latino refusal rate, while in rural precincts there was a significant difference, although overall refusal rates were much lower than in either Albuquerque or Santa Fe. Only 14% of whites in rural Latino precincts refused to be interviewed, while 22% of Latino voters refused. In the two rural precincts where Latinos were more likely than whites to refuse, the ethnicity of the interviewer did not appear to be a factor. We have no information on the interviewer for one of those precincts, but in the other the interviewer was herself a Latina. Detailed information on each of the Latino precincts in New Mexico is provided in table 4. We have learned in the past that younger interviewers may not be as successful as somewhat older interviewers, but aside from that there seem to be no clear patterns that emerge from the detailed precinct information which suggest that Latino interviewers are more successful than white interviewers. If you peruse the data in table 4, you will discover that interviewer perception of ease of interviewing, and even the interviewer's reported experience, is of little help in predicting performance.

No Spanish language questionnaire was made available for general election day respondents in New Mexico. To see whether or not this might have mattered, we analyzed the age characteristics of refusers in the Albuquerque precincts. Our previous experience has been that older people are less likely than younger voters to complete an exit poll questionnaire (in fact, we adjust our results to compensate for the higher refusal rate among older voters). If language was a problem, the difference between the refusal rates of whites and Latinos in the oldest age group should have been much larger than the difference between the refusal rates of the younger age groups. As demonstrated in table 4, there is some support for this hypothesis.

However, the results from the Albuquerque Latino precincts are by no means conclusive. In rural Latino precincts, age of respondent bore no relationship to refusal rates for either whites or Latinos. The results from Santa Fe look very much like those from Albuquerque, although some cell sizes are very small. However, there may be other factors besides language that are important. Older urban Latinos may be generally more hesitant to express their opinions, and may be otherwise more alienated from the American political process than are older whites.

**Table 4**
Refusal Rates in Latino Precincts in New Mexico

| | Refusal Rate | | | | | |
|---|---|---|---|---|---|---|
| | Latino | | White | | Total[a] | |
| | N | % | N | % | N | % |
| ALBUQUERQUE (population 332,000) | | | | | | |
| *Precinct 21* | | | | | | |
| Morning: White female, some reported difficulty getting voters to participate, able to persuade some reluctant people to take part. | | | | | | |
| Afternoon: Young Latina, some reported difficulty, persuasion needed. | | | | | | |
| Both shifts | 190 | 56 | 29 | 21 | 222 | 52 |
| *Precinct 22* | | | | | | |
| Morning: Latina, no reported difficulty, persuasion needed. | | | | | | |
| Afternoon: White female, no reported difficulty, little persuasion needed.[b] | 48 | 10 | 47 | 6 | 98 | 8 |
| Both shifts | | | | | 168 | 18 |
| *Precinct 24* | | | | | | |
| Both shifts: White female, no reported difficulty, persuasion needed. | 110 | 19 | 50 | 20 | 161 | 19 |

*Continued on next page*

*Precinct 26*

| | | | | | | |
|---|---|---|---|---|---|---|
| Both shifts: White female, had some trouble getting people to participate and persuading reluctant people to respond, the only one in the 13 precincts who had trouble distinguishing between voters and nonvoters. | 28 | 50 | 30 | 47 | 59 | 47 |
| | | | | | | |
| ALL LATINO PRECINCTS IN ALBUQUERQUE | 376 | 39 | 156 | 21 | 610 | 33 |

SANTA FE (population 75,000)

*Precinct 61*

Morning: No reported difficulty, no persuasion needed.

Afternoon: White female, had experience with exit polls, no reported difficulty, persuasion needed.

| | | | | | | |
|---|---|---|---|---|---|---|
| Both shifts | 91 | 10 | 85 | 19 | 176 | 14 |

*Precinct 62*

Morning: Experienced with exit polls, some reported difficulty, no persuasion needed.

Afternoon: White female, no reported difficulty, no persuasion needed.

| | | | | | | |
|---|---|---|---|---|---|---|
| Both shifts | 46 | 22 | 119 | 28 | 166 | 26 |

*Precinct 63*

Morning: White female, exit poll experience, some reported difficulty, little persuasion needed.

Afternoon: Latina, no reported difficulty, little persuasion needed.

| | | | | | | |
|---|---|---|---|---|---|---|
| Both shifts | 67 | 42 | 59 | 36 | 128 | 38 |

*Precinct 64*

Morning: White female, exit poll experience, no reported difficulty, no persuasion needed.

Afternoon: White female, some reported difficulty, no persuasion needed.

| | | | | | | |
|---|---|---|---|---|---|---|
| Both shifts | 62 | 40 | 112 | 27 | 166 | 27 |

ALL LATINO
PRECINCTS IN
SANTA FE

| | | | | | | |
|---|---|---|---|---|---|---|
| | 266 | 27 | 375 | 27 | 636 | 25 |

RURAL AREAS

*San Ysidro, Precinct 71* (Sandoval County, Indian reservation area north of Albuquerque)

Both shifts: Latina, exit poll experience, some reported difficulty, some persuasion needed.

| | | | | | | |
|---|---|---|---|---|---|---|
| | 21 | 10 | 71 | 13 | 92 | 12 |

*Lumberton, Precinct 72* (Population 200, in Rio Arriba County in the north)

Both shifts: Exit poll experience, some reported difficulty, little persuasion needed.

| | | | | | | |
|---|---|---|---|---|---|---|
| | 48 | 50 | 7 | 71 | 55 | 53 |

*Tucumcari, Precinct 32* (Population 10,000, in Quay County, borders Texas)

Morning: Latina, some reported difficulty, persuasion needed.

Afternoon: Latina, no reported difficulty, persuasion needed.

| | | | | | | |
|---|---|---|---|---|---|---|
| Both shifts | 113 | 12 | 8 | — | 143 | 15 |

*Continued on next page*

*Tome, Precinct 57*
(Population 400, in
Valencia County, below
Albuquerque)

| | | | | | | |
|---|---|---|---|---|---|---|
| Both shifts | 65 | 29 | 62 | 13 | 127 | 21 |

*Chimayo, Precinct 73*
(Population 2,000, in Rio
Arriba County)

Morning: Young Latina
(23), no reported difficulty, persuasion needed.

Afternoon: No ex-
perience, no reported
difficulty, persuasion
needed.

| | | | | | | |
|---|---|---|---|---|---|---|
| Both shifts | 122 | 17 | 34 | 9 | 156 | 15 |
| ALL LATINO PRECINCTS IN RURAL AREAS | 369 | 22 | 182 | 14 | 573 | 20 |
| ALL LATINO PRECINCTS IN NEW MEXICO | 1,011 | 30 | 713 | 22 | 1,819 | 26 |

Note: Total for each group is the sum of refusals and completes. Missed voters were not included in the refusal rates.

[a] Total column provides refusal rates of all voters, not just Latinos and whites.

[b] For Precinct 22, overall refusal rate by race includes afternoon data only.

**Table 5**
Voter Age and Refusal Rates in Albuquerque Latino Precincts

| | Latino | | White | | Total[a] | |
|---|---|---|---|---|---|---|
| Age | N | % | N | % | N | % |
| 18–29 | 72 | 21 | 31 | 10 | 105 | 19 |
| 30–59 | 231 | 40 | 86 | 21 | 317 | 32 |
| 60 and older | 72 | 58 | 27 | 26 | 111 | 46 |

[a] Total column provides refusal rates of all voters, not just Latinos and whites.

**Conclusion**

The problems associated with conducting exit polls among Latino voters are not unique to Latinos. While it is true that these voters do have somewhat different demographic characteristics than other voters, the differences do not require different survey research methods. Sound methods produce valid data, irrespective of voter characteristics.

Spanish language questionnaires have been used in the exit polls since 1972, but they have marginal effect on improving the exit polls. Too few voters use them to affect the results in any meaningful way. It does not seem that most Latino voters have difficulty with English language questionnaires, except in New York where becoming a citizen is not a requirement for registering to vote. If Spanish language questionnaires are to be used in the future it is clear that the locations for their use must be chosen more selectively, and that interviewer training must be improved.

The use of Latino interviewers also doesn't seem to have a major effect on response rates. Based on the evidence, it is the skill of interviewers that has the greatest effect on refusal rates, not their ethnic or racial background. Selecting Latino interviewers to conduct exit poll interviews at predominately Latino precincts does not necessarily lead to improved response rates.

# Muted Voices—Problems in Polling Latinos

I. A. Lewis, *Los Angeles Times Poll*

The title of this conference is "Ignored Voices" and it's a good title because the voices of Latinos in the United States are often ignored. Partly, I think, that's because the rest of the American society often doesn't take the time or the trouble to listen to those voices. There is certainly not much survey research directed toward Latinos and its quality is often uneven.

But my comments today have to do with the reverse side of that communications failure. My topic might better be called "Muted Voices" or perhaps "Indistinct Voices" because, for a number of reasons which I shall try to detail for you, the voice of the Latino respondent is often very difficult to hear.

As director of the NBC News Poll, director of polling for CBS News, as a partner in the Roper Organization, and director of the Los Angeles Times Poll, I have conducted hundreds of nationwide polls which, of course, included Latinos. In every one of these, to the best of my recollection, Latinos were underrepresented. And I dare say that has been the experience of my colleagues at other national survey research organizations.

To illustrate the reasons for this underrepresentation and also a number of other problems and difficulties that are encountered in polling Latinos, I will devote the major portion of my remarks today to experiences encountered during a study of Latinos that was conducted by the Los Angeles Times Poll in February and March of 1983 as part of a series of newspaper articles about the Latino experience in California which subsequently won a Pulitzer Prize for our newspaper. Although greater efforts were made to interview Latinos for that study than is generally the case in routine statewide or national polls, it may provide a useful case study to determine which techniques have proved successful and which have not.

There are a number of reasons for Latino underrepresentation in survey research, for this muting of the Latino voice. Undoubtedly the most important of these has to do with the language barrier. In the 1983 study, 50% of respondents preferred to be questioned in Spanish. In this respect, Latinos are similar to other Americans of more recent residence whose native language is not English. The difference is that there are a great many more Latinos than, say, Pacific Islanders or Vietnamese. We are told that before long Latinos will constitute the largest ethnic minority in the United States. A failure to attend to so large a segment of society can lead to unfortunate or even drastic results.

Another equally important reason for underrepresentation of Latinos in telephone surveys is economic. Fewer Latinos than the average own telephones and thus they are more difficult to interview in this fashion.

A further reason is cultural. One frequently finds that Latino men prefer to speak for their wives, daughters, and other female relatives, a procedure which is not permitted according to our rules. In addition, we find that there tend to be slightly more Latinos than Latinas in our samples of California. That may not be the case in the Northeast or even in Florida where the Latino family structure is perhaps more stabilized. But I would expect to find the same condition in Texas where one might find a significant influx of Mexican American men who have come north to work and who either will send for their female relatives later or return to Mexico without ever having done so.

Moreover, nearly all Latino respondents appear to be somewhat reticent and uncooperative, possibly because they fear involvement with the establishment which might, in turn, lead to immigration problems. In the 1983 Latino study I mentioned just now, 21% of the foreign-born Latinos who responded admitted that they were undocumented. I cannot guess how many who failed to respond were undocumented.

Moreover, at least in California, the Latino household tends to have an extended character which often includes near-relatives or friends or friends of friends who would not normally answer a ringing telephone or elect to speak with strangers on the phone.

Another reason for Latino underrepresentation in our national samples is undoubtedly demographic, inasmuch as the Latino population is skewed toward younger age groups and thus does not so easily meet the 18-year-old requirement of our sampling procedures. The qualified respondents who are present in the household also tend to be younger and, like most younger respondents, are likely to be more difficult to find at home.

On the other hand, according to our findings Latinos in general are no more likely to be away from home when calls are made even though, being somewhat more downscale as a group, one might expect them to be less frequently away from home. We find that some 55% of Latinos are at home during three of the four days previous to their interview. Perhaps one reason for this is explained by the predominance of children in the household. Typically, only about a third of Latino households in our California samples are without children, and of households with children, more than two-thirds have children under 12 years of age.

Another reason for the underrepresentation of Latinos in public opinion surveys is operational: it is very difficult to find qualified Latino personnel to conduct fieldwork. Difficulties centering on recruitment and training of interviewers have proved to be the most intractable problem encountered.

In our 1983 study, once it had been decided to oversample a large proportion of Latinos, it became apparent that our normal staff of 15 to 20 bilingual interviewers (out of a staff of approximately 200) would be inadequate. We decided to recruit 40 or 50 more interviewers. Calling around to other organizations, we quickly determined that there was no pool of experienced interviewers who could meet our needs and that it would be necessary to train these interviewers ourselves (as, indeed, we do with all our interviewers). This process took far longer than we had anticipated: recruiting occupied the better part of two months. We contacted community groups, ethnic organizations, and churches. We found a few candidates by asking schools and colleges to post notices on their bulletin boards. A local advertising agency that had Latino accounts was able to provide a few leads. We contacted friends, we used word-of-mouth. In all, we contacted more than 20 groups which involved repeated callbacks and repeated referrals for our field supervisor. In the end, a series of ads in the news section of the paper proved most effective. From all this activity, we managed to obtain a list of about 100 potential interviewers.

Next, we personally interviewed each applicant. Most of them had never had any related experience but, during conversation, we were able to evaluate how articulate they were and whether or not our schedules would fit with theirs. They were asked to read a sample questionnaire in both English and Spanish. That proved difficult for many. We were forced to drop a fairly sizable number of English and Spanish illiterates as well as quite a few bilingual illiterates. From the initial list of 100 we selected 40 prospective interviewers for further training.

Each of them came to a four-hour session at which their training manual was explained, key points were emphasized, and the sampling procedure was demonstrated very carefully. The trainees conducted interviews with real respondents and, by means of a loudspeaker attachment which allowed everyone to hear both ends of the conversation, they critiqued each other's performances afterward. Unfortunately, out of this group of 40 only 28 showed up for the first day of interviewing.

All of our interviewers are routinely monitored by supervisors and their performance is rated on a checklist form which becomes part of the interviewer's record. Whenever necessary, the interviewer is counseled immediately after an interview so as to reinforce the learning process. I have reread the monitor reports for this study in preparation for this talk and I must say that they are discouraging. "Was here only one day," says one report. "Paperwork not understood after repeated counseling in both English and Spanish," says another monitor report. "Reads questions in Spanish, talks to himself in English," says another. "Gets many refusals." "Has his girlfriend do the paperwork because he hasn't learned how to do it." "Leads the respondent, paraphrases, skips around among questions." We had to let most of them go. After two months of recruiting, we ended up with fewer than 10 good people.

Needless to say, this part of the study was quite frustrating and cost more money than we had budgeted. Moreover, we failed to achieve our goal of 1,000 Latino interviews: we had to be satisfied with 549, even though we extended our interview period to eight days rather than the five we had originally planned.

Except for one survey that was conducted in Mexico City, the Los Angeles Times Poll has never interviewed Latinos exclusively, preferring to oversample Latinos in our regular studies. For that reason, interviewers begin in English until it becomes apparent that the respondent prefers otherwise. If the interviewer is not bilingual, the telephone number is passed to someone who is and the Latino respondent is called back immediately.

You may have noticed that I have employed the term "Latino" almost consistently throughout my remarks. I have done so by design. One of the questions I have put to Latino respondents is:

People of Spanish origin are often referred to by different labels. What term do you use.?

In California, the most popular term is "Mexican" or its translation "mexicano." I have no doubt these labels are preferred because the majority of these respondents are Mexican. But, of course, I was looking for an all-inclusive term that could be used to refer to all people of Spanish origin. That label proved to be "Latino" which was chosen by 18% of the California sample, a larger number than the 14% who opted for "Hispanic," the 4% who liked to be called "Chicano," and the 2% who preferred "Spanish" or just plain "American."

In past polls, roughly 50% of Latino respondents in California have preferred to be interviewed in Spanish. For obvious reasons, this figure correlates well with the 52% of California respondents who said they were born outside the United States. Of the remaining Latinos who said they were born in the United States, 38% said that neither their parents nor their grandparents had been born in the United States. Only 8% said that both of their parents and all of their grandparents were native to this country.

On the other hand, only 13% of respondents said that English was spoken regularly at home despite the fact that 48% of Latino respondents preferred to be interviewed in English. But only a little more than a third of Latino respondents felt that they spoke English "very well" and another 26% said they spoke English "just well." Thirty-six percent said they spoke English "not well" or "not at all."

The Los Angeles Times Poll always uses a random selection procedure for determining who shall be interviewed within each household. We have had good success using a modification of the Kish selection tables which are based on certain household composition information that must be obtained at the beginning of the interview. On the other hand, we much prefer the last birthday method which seems much less threatening and which allows one to launch more quickly into the body of the questionnaire. We have experience no difficulty with this procedure in Latino households.

It is, of course, always necessary to produce a Spanish-language version of the questionnaire. Although this is a routine procedure for us, it almost always presents a problem. It is my experience that no one who speaks Spanish is ever satisfied with anyone else's translation. Sometimes it is considered "not correct Spanish," other times it is deemed not colloquial enough. Since I speak no Spanish, I have found that the best policy is to begin with a fairly literate translation and then pass it around to different people until there is general agreement that it is colloquial enough.

The method we have used for identifying Latinos in the sample consists of two questions, the first being:

> Are you, yourself, of Latino or Hispanic descent—such as Mexican, or Puerto Rican, or Cuban, or other Spanish background—or not?

We find this more explicit and more productive than another question which we have used in the past:

> Does anybody in your family speak Spanish as a first language, or not?

This question is followed by a second:

> What is your race? Is it white, black, Asian or some other?

As is well known, many Latinos prefer to think of themselves as being of a different race than either whites or blacks, and this leads to such confusing marginals suggesting that Latinos are more than 50% something other than black or white or Asian. We combine the findings from these two questions into a variable which classifies any person as Latino who regards himself or herself as such, regardless of race. The remainder of those who describe themselves as white are therefore non-Latino (perhaps they should be more properly called Anglos—borrowing a term that is perhaps more common in the western part of the country than elsewhere). Something similar can be said for blacks: for us they are non-Latino blacks.

The sampling strategy for the 1983 study was somewhat unusual. In previous studies of special publics—in particular, studies of blacks—we had found that a modified version of the Wachsberg sampling technique was useful. This involves creating clusters of telephone numbers based on "seed" numbers obtained from previous interviews. For this poll, 15 previous studies were reviewed and 1,500 telephone numbers selected from respondents who identified themselves as Latinos. These numbers were considered "seeds" from which a cluster of other telephone numbers was derived by substituting random numbers for the last two digits of the line number. Interviewers were required to identify at least one residence from each cluster before proceeding to the next cluster.

This sampling technique increases the probability of contacting special publics if the targeted group tends to be ghettoized. The logic rests in the fact that once a telephone household has been identified using random sampling techniques, the chances of finding another such household within the same block of 100 telephone numbers is large when people of that characteristic live nearby, since neighborhoods tend to have identical area codes and exchanges as well as similar line numbers. I have used this technique with great success in sampling blacks. It is less effectively employed when sampling Latinos because—in California, at least—Latinos are more widely dispersed throughout the community than are blacks. In a recent study of poor people the same technique was employed with even less advantage. I am led to assume, therefore, that blacks are more ghettoized than Latinos, who are more ghettoized than poor people.

On the advice of Leobardo Estrada, a demographer at the UCLA Graduate School of Architecture and Urban Planning who helped redesign the 1980 Census questions about Latinos, this Wachsberg technique was further modified for the Latino study under question. Because many Latino families in California have acquired an extended nature through the addition of relatives or friends who temporarily or permanently live in the same residence, an attempt was made to arrive at a random distribution within each household by conducting two interviews, one within the "primary" household and one within the "secondary" household.

At the completion of each Latino interview, interviewers were instructed to probe for how many adults lived in the household who were either the head of that household or that person's spouse, parents, or children—that is, the primary household. Next, they were instructed to determine how many adults in the household could not be described as being within this primary group and were therefore members of the secondary household. If the interview had been conducted with a member of the primary household, then a second interview was to be attempted with a member of the secondary household, or vice versa. As usual, random selection within primary or secondary households was required.

Using this procedure, 6% more interviews were obtained than would have been the case had it not been employed. I feel certain that, because of this technique, our sample was a more accurate reflection of the Latino community. Nevertheless, considering the scanty results, I question whether the extended household condition is prevalent enough in California to justify such complexity.

Throughout most of these remarks, I have tended to refer to the Latino community in California as if it were monolithic and single-minded. Of course it is not. Moreover, across the nation there are other Latino communities which are even more richly diverse. We all know that the Mexican American respondent tends to be younger and more Catholic, to marry more frequently than other

Latinos, and to be less rich and less likely to be in a labor union.

On the other hand, there is a regretable tendency on the part of public pollsters to lump all Latinos together and to consider them—if they consider them at all—as one entity. I suppose the reason for that is that so much of public polling is concerned with politics. I would guess that roughly 30–40% of all the questions we ask in the Los Angeles Times Poll are in some way related to politics. And the simple political fact about most Latinos is that they don't vote. In our exit poll of 7,310 voters in the 1984 presidential elections, only 4% described themselves as either Mexican, Puerto Rican, Cuban, or Other Latino. In our California polling, we find that fewer than half of Latinos are even registered to vote. So if Latinos are underrepresented in our samples, one can mollify some concerns with the thought that their numbers do, after all, approximate their strength in at least political affairs.

Although Mexican American Latinos are somewhat more conservative politically, they are at the same time more Democratic in their party affiliation than other Latinos. And that seeming contradiction underscores other contradictions within the Latino psyche which tend to make them a less cohesive group. Also, perhaps Latinos are ignored politically because they tend to split their vote (unlike blacks, for example) and thus have more difficulty making their presence felt politically.

I have left until the end of my remarks the question of using face-to-face interviews rather than telephone interviews for polling Latinos. Of course, much of my experience has to do with telephone interviewing and I am a passionate advocate of the technique, even though there are a great many difficulties involved in this method.

Among the most important are the difficulty of drawing a good sample from among a population that has fewer residential telephones than the average and Latino reticence in using a telephone because of widespread language difficulties. But my feeling is that many of the problems we have encountered using telephone sampling techniques would have been present or counterbalanced if face-to-face interviews had been used. Another great problem—recruiting and training interviewers—is a case in point. I don't really think it makes much difference whether a poor interviewer conducts a telephone interview or a face-to-face interview.

Instead, I would urge you to profit from my difficulties and to persevere. Should you have access to experienced bilingual interviewers in your area, by all means try to recruit them, although I would suggest that they be carefully tested beforehand. Also, prepare to interview for longer periods of time if your object is to gain sufficient Latino respondents. Above all, have patience; certainly the results can be worthwhile. Despite the effort involved, survey researchers must learn to be more skillful at capturing data that can bring new understanding of the vital Latino segment of our society.

# Problems in Polling Latinos: The State of the Art

Joe Belden, *Belden Associates*

There seems to be an assumption in some quarters that in the United States opinion survey methodology is not yet able to measure Latino attitudes accurately. I would rather phrase it like this: In the United States, survey methodology has long existed—and has in fact been used—to poll Latinos properly, but not all opinion researchers have applied the methods properly.

The truth is, however, that we have not known just what the pollsters are doing to ensure that Spanish-speaking populations turning up in their samples are being correctly represented. So I have undertaken to poll the pollsters on their current practices. It is the results of this survey of 112 public opinion research organizations that I am contributing to this symposium.

A newly awakened demand for attention to the problems of polling Hispanics has undoubtedly been engendered by two factors. One is the remarkable growth of our Hispanic population, now said to be above 17 million and apparently destined to be the largest minority by the year 2000. Another factor is the ever-increasing use of the sampling survey in politics, commerce, and social science.

The Hispanic community should indeed see to it that its weight registers properly, particularly in this new age of information that depends so much on such instruments as the opinion sampling survey.

As you will see, the pollsters are paying a good deal of attention to the special problems of polling Hispanics. But devoting particular attention to the Hispanic proportion of the sample is a relative matter: how large must a foreign language group be before it requires special treatment? There are more than 80 language groups in this country—at least that is how many are involved in the bilingual education program. Strictly speaking, every non-English-speaking person should be included in every survey in which she or he happens to fall. Practically speaking, they cannot all be included, but when potentially 1 out of every 10 respondents is Spanish-speaking, we should examine our procedures and determine whether any significant biases are creeping into our results.

What are the problems involved in polling Latinos? I believe they can be categorized into four areas. The most important is probably communications, and you will see that the pollsters I have surveyed agree with this. The survey process includes a series of critical informational transactions: between client and researcher, between researcher and interviewer, between interviewer and respondent, from respondent back to the interviewer, from interviewer back to the researcher, and from the researcher to the client. Most of these exchanges depend on a language-based instrument, the questionnaire. Such factors as question wording and interviewer behavior render the process extremely sensitive. When we introduce a foreign language into the process, the difficulties multiply.

A second problem area is sampling, the procedure through which it is possible to select a relatively small number of respondents to represent the entire population of a barrio, or a city, or a state, or the entire country. To accomplish this reliably, certain rules must apply in sample design. The physical characteristics of the Latino population often require extraordinary design and execution. For one thing, Hispanics tend to cluster rather than disperse throughout the population, and the more clustering the more the researcher has to watch the sampling process. Latinos also tend to have larger families than Anglos, which creates a problem of representation when the basis of selection, as usual, is households, and only one interview is made per household, which is desirable. Obviously, Latinos and others with larger than average families should be weighted up to reflect their greater number of eligible respondents per household. This is something often ignored. Another perennial sampling problem has been the inability to ferret out all illegal residents who fall into the sample, presumably because of their fear of being deported. I do not know of any pollster who knows the answer to interviewing illegal residents in hiding.

Analysis is a third problem area. Here the responsibility for a good job falls first on the editors and coders who must interpret any replies in Spanish into English equivalents; then at a higher level there is usually the need to interpret not only the substance, but the flavor and nuance of Hispanic attitudes, preferences, and intensities, sometimes among several different Hispanic cultures.

An underlying problem in polling Hispanics runs through all the others: personnel. It is a difficulty most commonly felt in finding Spanish-speaking interviewers, either for house-to-house or telephone surveys. Ideally, interviewers should be English-Spanish bilinguals, for they are usually trained and supervised by employees who speak only English. And, preferably, bilingual interviewers should themselves be Hispanic. An even more important reason for using bilingual field-workers is that interviews with U.S. Hispanics are not necessarily all conducted in Spanish. Because our Hispanic community includes persons fitting the complete spectrum of language ability—from Spanish only to English only—I have always preferred to give Hispanic respondents a choice of language for the interview. In a study my company, Belden Associates, did in Miami some years ago, 73% of Latinos preferred to be interviewed in Spanish, but 21% chose English and 6% of the encounters resulted in a mixture of the two. In a San Antonio market study in 1980, a majority of respondents, 68%, used mostly English during the interview, only 22% used mostly Spanish, and 10% used each language about equally. The Texas Poll, now conducted by the Public Policy Resources Laboratory at Texas A&M University, is currently finding that while 13% or 14% of its respondents are Hispanic, only 2% to 5% choose Spanish for the interview when given a choice. In a recent statewide survey in California, Field Research Corporation found that one-third of Hispanics selected English for the interview.

Within a research organization's office it is obviously also important to employ competent bilinguals. Maintaining a staff of researchers who also know both languages fluently places great burdens on research organizations. Unless they become heavily involved in Spanish-language work, I do not see most of them meeting really high standards in this respect within the near future.

Having thus reviewed what appeared to be the major problems in polling Latinos, I decided to find out what pollsters across the country were collectively doing about all of this. So in the summer of 1985 I conducted a survey. First, I mailed a brief questionnaire to a nationwide sampling of public opinion researchers. Let me explain the methods used and then show you the results.

I decided to survey individuals representing organizations currently doing public opinion studies in the United States. (Many opinion pollsters also do market studies, but this survey does not attempt to totally represent market research practice, which includes groups not doing opinion polls.) It is generally accepted that the most complete list of pollsters is the directory of the American Association for Public Opinion Research (AAPOR), which includes the great majority of people in this field, both commercial and noncommercial. So the 1984–85 *AAPOR Directory of Members* became the basis for the sample of polling organizations. From the 1,182 members listed, I selected the 243 whose titles indicated they were decision makers and thus most capable of answering about their practices. Included were those identified as chairman, president, director, owner, partner, executive vice-president, vice-president—research, director of research, manager of research, and the like. Eliminated were those with no title or who were in subordinate or academic positions not connected with a research group. Although the 1983–84 AAPOR membership was 51% commercial and the remainder noncommercial (academic, government, or nonprofit), my selected 243 included 86% commercial, indicating that many of the noncommercial members were interested in public opinion research but not necessarily in survey practice. Only U.S. addresses were used.

The individuals selected were sent a personally typed letter, a one-sheet questionnaire with 15 questions front and back, and a stamped return envelope. A total of 142 questionnaires were returned, or 58.4%. As mail surveys go, that is not a bad response rate, although some surveys attain higher response by means of various incentives or from highly motivated groups (one might expect pollsters to be among the most interested in a high response, since the great majority of them say, in this survey, that they conduct mail surveys).

Discarded as unusable were questionnaires from 11 organizations that do not conduct surveys (question 1), and 19 whose surveys do not cover Hispanics (question 5). The remaining 112 questionnaires became the base for all results reported here, unless otherwise indicated. This sample is 87% commercial and 13% noncommercial, almost exactly reflecting the 86–14 ratio of the questionnaires sent out. Other than that, it would be difficult to ascertain how representative the sample is of American pollsters. To encourage frank replies, respondents were given the option of omitting their names and affiliations. But from the many who did identify themselves, we can be assured that the 112 respondents include a wide variety of organizations, from major ones such as Harris, Yankelovich, Chilton, CBS, USA Today, Sears Roebuck, and the Los Angeles Times, to one-person shops which do only a few projects a year but collectively produce an enormous volume of opinion research. As you will see, the results of the survey are so well-defined that their general direction would be highly unlikely to change if we were to poll the pollsters with a much larger sample or a more elaborate sample design.

The first question asked was: "Does your organization conduct opinion, market, or other types of surveys in the U.S. that are nationwide? Regional? Local?" Of the 112 respondents, 80% do national studies, 71% do regional studies including statewide, and 90% do local polls. From the size of these percentages we can see that many are involved in more than one geographic coverage.

Question 2 asked: "Are any of your survey findings published regularly?" Because most of the organizations represented are commercial, I was struck by the fact that close to half (42%) do publish their polls and surveys. The findings of the majority (57%) who do not release them regularly, I believe we can assume, do have an audience such as a client. And data in the hands of such an audience, limited as it might be, can conceivably be more effective than the Gallup or Harris type of report in the mass media.

Next I asked: "Approximately how many of your surveys in the past twelve months have been by telephone, personal (face-to-face), mail or other method?" Because some responded with a percentage distribution of their methods rather than the number of surveys using each method, I cannot estimate the volume of each type. But the greatest number of organizations, 9 out of 10, are using telephone interviewing. That three-fourths (74%) continue to use a personal or face-to-face approach is encouraging despite the rush to the telephone in recent years. This is especially significant in surveying Latinos, for I believe that they are best interviewed in person, house to house, eliminating the problem of low telephone incidence and reducing suspicions that hamper both sampling and questioning. The only other method used by the majority (67%) is the mail questionnaire.

The questionnaire next informed the respondents that in the remainder of the questions " 'Hispanics' means persons of Spanish origin living in the U.S." and that the "questions deal with surveys of the general population, not with surveys of Hispanics only." The latter admonition was used to let all respondents know that we were concerned with the treatment of Hispanics in the general course of survey research, not when attention to special problems must perforce be paid by doing an all-Hispanic study.

Next, question 5 served to eliminate organizations whose

surveys never include Hispanics. And then the questionnaire went into the substantive matters investigated among our 112 organizations polled.

Question 6 asked: "What do you consider the main problem in surveying Hispanics in the U.S.?" As might be expected, problems of communication were the most often reported, especially language barriers (48%), followed by lack of cooperation including fear of official-sounding strangers (15%). The next most common problems were operational, having to do with general sampling (15%); finding and identifying Latino respondents (11%), due either to low incidence or the possible hiding of undocumented residents; and low phone incidence (11%). The third group of problems dealt mostly with the cultural diversity of the Hispanic community in some areas (14%), which makes it difficult to poll uniformly among Mexicans, Puerto Ricans, Cubans, and others. Frankly, I think the problem of cultural diversity, especially in the use of Spanish, tends to be exaggerated.

Next the pollsters were asked for their opinion on whether the Hispanic population of the country is "now significant enough to require special attention in nationwide surveys of the general public" (question 7). The answer was yes by a two-thirds majority. Here is the first evidence from the survey that there exists widespread consciousness among pollsters of the need to pay attention to these problems. However, a third remain unconvinced or uninformed.

Of course, not every pollster does nationwide surveys, where the problems of polling Hispanics may seem diminished by their yet relatively low incidence in the total population. The real test emerges when researchers have to focus on an area where they will encounter Hispanics with much greater frequency, making up a much more significant part of the sample. So I posed two more questions, asking not what the surveyors think but what they are actually doing. Question 8 asked: "When your universe [population to be surveyed] includes a relatively *large* percent of Hispanics, do you take special steps regarding Hispanics, or do you treat them like any other respondents?" Then question 9 repeated the inquiry but on the premise of the universe being a *small* percent of Hispanics.

When the incidence or percentage of Hispanics is expected to be large, 70% of the pollsters said they take special steps to include them. But when the expected incidence is small, 80% said they do not take special measures, treating Hispanics like any other respondents—which probably means, for one thing, that

Latinos who cannot speak English are omitted from the survey. How can this be so widely condoned when presumably all these researchers know that classically an individual, once drawn into the sample, must be included, no matter who or where the person is? Let me speculate on the rationale. To begin with, the number of Hispanics who should appear in the sample is relatively small; in the normal course of sampling some Hispanics who speak English will be included, reducing the number omitted; many of the missing ones, if interviewed, would express opinions or preferences consistent with those of the non-Hispanic part of the sample; so the remaining dissenting Hispanics are so few that their omission cannot significantly affect the overall results, which are subject to a plus-or-minus tolerance due to size of sample anyway. A simpler way to rationalize this is simply to define the universe as English-speaking adults, let us say, technically absolving one of any obligation to include citizens who cannot speak English.

It is reassuring that 7 of 10 of our pollsters do take special measures to represent Hispanics when the sample includes a substantial Spanish-speaking portion. This is higher than I had expected. We do not know how close to actuality these replies are. Next, with question 10, we asked: "In which of these survey functions do you ever take special steps regarding Hispanics?" The following response indicates that in line with the pollsters' major concerns—communications functions—it is language and field procedures where their main attention lies in surveying Latinos.

| | |
|---|---|
| Question Language | 70% |
| Interviewer selection | 67 |
| Interviewing respondents | 57 |
| Sample design | 54 |
| Interviewer training | 53 |
| Locating, selecting respondents | 47 |
| Interviewer supervision | 38 |
| Coding, editing responses | 36 |
| Reporting, interpreting results | 29 |
| Tabulation | 13 |
| Questionnaire design (format) | 12 |
| Other | 4 |

The last four questions explored survey techniques particularly pertinent to surveying Latinos, to see how much attention researchers are paying to such details. Question 11 discovered that only about a fifth always attempt to interview in Spanish people who speak only that language. About as many say they never interview in Spanish, although all of these had reported earlier that they do surveys where they encounter Hispanics. About half stated that whether they interview in Spanish depends on the survey.

Question 12 asked which of five questionnaire formats were being used when the interviewers were bilingual. The majority (52%) prepare a separate Spanish questionnaire. Twenty percent furnish a separate list of Spanish questions and record answers on the English questionnaire—a rather cumbersome method. I was shocked to learn that 23% allow interviewers to translate the regular English questions into Spanish during the interview; nothing could be more devastating to the quality of the questions. And it was dismaying to find that only 9% have discovered what I consider the best format, a bilingual questionnaire with Spanish questions right alongside the English. This avoids separate forms, flip-flopping from one side to the other, and impromptu translations. The bilingual questionnaire also facilitates the bilingual interview in which both languages are used back and forth. Also, English-only employees in the office do not have to deal with a Spanish questionnaire, since the whole thing is in English, as usual, except for the Spanish questions alongside. This technique requires bilingual interviewers, not just Spanish-speaking, who I believe are essential in what amounts to a bilingual situation, not just a Spanish situation, most of the time.

Another refinement in polling Hispanics in the United States is giving bilingual respondents a choice of language for the interview, or welcoming the use of both. Obviously, this step requires truly bilingual interviewers, not Latinos who speak good Spanish but poor or no English—for there are many Latinos in this country who know English better than Spanish, and with time their numbers are bound to increase. From question 13 we find that only 23% of our pollsters are providing a choice of language when they turn up a Hispanic bilingual. Most of them (46%) say it depends on the survey, which could mean that they do nothing about this most of the time.

Lastly, question 14 inquired whether the researcher weighted the results for Hispanic balance of the sample, which some practitioners hold to be essential when needed. For example, if the percentage of Hispanics in the area being surveyed is known but the survey fails to generate that percentage, the number of Hispanics in the sample may be mathematically weighted up, and then all results are based on the adjusted sample. Such weighting can be done, up or down, for any other characteristic of the sample. My results show that apparently few researchers (5%) follow the practice regularly, although the majority (61%) state it depends on the survey. Nearly a third (29%), however, reported never weighting the sample. Experience shows that practically any survey attempting to sample blacks or Hispanics correctly needs some adjustment. But some researchers continue to boast that their samples are pristine—that is, unadjusted—even if biased.

To summarize the results of the poll of pollsters, it appears that opinion researchers in general appreciate the problems of surveying Latinos, and to me at least a surprising number are following good practice in many ways to meet the challenges. But the results also show that a good many of our researchers are not doing so when surveying Latinos. Perhaps the current state of the art is as good as can be expected until the Hispanic community grows further. Mervin Field, director of the California Poll, made some pertinent comments in this respect when replying to my questions:

> As the Hispanic population grows, it will require more specific attention in some respects (larger market, people with more purchasing power) and less attention in other respects. As Hispanics become more assimilated, they will be treated analytically in more conventional demographic terms, e.g., by income, education, etc., and less as "Hispanics."

A major barrier to better research practice in dealing with the Hispanic population is economic. It simply costs more to use special techniques. Quite often the importance of the Hispanic to the research underwriter does not outweigh the added expense of polling Latinos with all refinements operating. Field says that in marketing studies clients interested in the Hispanic market are making provisions to have this segment of the market properly represented. But it is his impression that in political or public policy studies many research agencies "rely on the principle that, if the respondent cannot be interviewed in English, it is highly likely that the person is a non-voter or incapable of responding to broad public issues."

My survey of pollsters did not go into the issue of whether American society owes foreign language groups a right to be addressed, officially or otherwise, in the language of their country of origin. I did investigate what the Canadian experience has been in dealing with their French-speaking minority. I wrote to a dozen researchers in Canada, and the most succinct reply came from

Hastings Withers, technical director of the Print Measurement Bureau in Toronto, who among other things wrote:

> We in Canada have generally made the political decision to properly measure the consumer habits of French-speaking Canadians, and to do so in French as is appropriate, but in general no such effort is made for other language groups. There are no technical problems that can't be solved; it comes down to whether the survey practitioner or his client, wishes to invest the funds in the survey to include minority language groups.

Withers points out that, although French is the only second language used in survey research, in a city like Toronto the population speaking only Italian or Chinese or Greek or Portuguese is much greater than the population using French—which speaks well for the political and economic clout the French Canadians have attained. This power is explained by another correspondent, Michael Saykaly of Optima Consultants in Ottawa, who says: "Canada has two official languages and francophones, who constitute one-quarter of the population, are territorially concentrated; they control the pivotal province of Quebec which gives them some influence in national affairs."

Saykaly, who is qualified not only as an outside observer but as one who has also lived in the United States, comments on the reasons why the American public, and survey practitioners in general, do not view their Hispanic community in the same way that Canadians view their francophone community:

> (1) Lack of a shared perception that a compact exists between two founding peoples (as exists in Canada).
> (2) Hispanics constitute a much smaller proportion of the total U.S. population than do francophones in Canada.
> (3) Hispanics do not comprise a vast majority of any pivotal state, as do the francophones in Quebec.
> (4) Americans take seriously the "melting pot" tradition which tends to preclude acceptance of a second official language (notwithstanding some "local" recognition such as in New York City, Miami, and Los Angeles).

There may well be other experience from Canada and other multilingual countries that we can apply to the improvement of Hispanic polling in the United States.

# Problems in Polling Latinos: Insights from Surveys of Blacks

James W. Prothro, *University of North Carolina*

Because I have carried out only one study of Latino public opinion and that in a country—Chile—where gringos rather than Latinos would pose special polling problems, I have been concerned about my credentials for this conference on ignored voices. My hope, and that of the conference organizers, is that my more extensive if less intimate experience in surveying the opinions of blacks in the United States offers some lessons that may prove helpful for improving work on Latino opinions. Five common problems or concerns may be noted.

The most immediate parallel with which I am struck is the problem of terminology. That some of the participants in this conference object to being called "Latino" while others abhor "Hispanic" underscores the problem. In the early 1960s, when "Negro" was the accepted term for those now called "black," the pronunciation of the word carried intense affective weight in states of the old Confederacy. Among many southern whites, the correct (long *e* and long *o*) pronunciation was impossible, for it implied some measure of respect for, or at least recognition of, Negroes as fellow human beings. The easy solution was to assume, as most national polling organizations had to, that interviewers would follow local usage. Because pronunciation varied by class, education, and even ideology within sampling points, however, a better solution was needed. In a southwide survey in which I was then engaged, we found the one neutral term for southern whites, with no pronunciation problem, to be "colored people." On the other hand, "Negro" at that time remained the accepted term among blacks (as well as among whites in the rest of the United States) so it was necessary to use different questionnaires with special wording for each race.

In the case of Latino polling, at least the mispronunciation of Spanish terms by Anglos stem more from ignorance than prejudice and hence does not carry the same sort of affect. Although various pejorative terms may be used as substitutes for "Latino" or "Hispanic" in informal conversation, they never, of course, appear in interview schedules. The decision among people of Spanish-speaking origin about which term to use may develop in a manner parallel to that of blacks in the late 1960s. In that period, black leaders began to drop the term "Negro" in favor of "black," the present usage. Today interviewers would lose rapport with many blacks if they said "Negro," just as they would have lost rapport (and perhaps the interview) earlier by saying "black." The transition in usage was under way in 1968. In order to ensure desired usage in an election study that year, we asked blacks in a national sample which term they used; the overwhelming preference was still "Negro." Here is a case in which leaders were ahead of the general public but still able to change general usage; by the next (1972) presidential election, "black" had almost completely replaced "Negro." If Latino/Hispanic leaders are in equal accord, usage may similarly become uniform for members of their community. Or are people of Spanish-speaking origin too scattered geographically and divergent in place of origin to come to agreement? I leave the answer to specialists on the Latino community.

Beyond the obvious question of what to call the group whose opinions are sought, a second concern is the recruitment and training of interviewers who can maximize validity in responses. Granted that record-keeping, following written instructions, and accurate recording of responses are typically middle-class skills, interviewers are almost necessarily middle-class. The possibility of class bias thus pervades survey research. When a large portion of the population being sampled is from lower educational and income strata, the problem is magnified. Any language difficulties contribute further to bias. The appropriateness of recruiting interviewers who can be accepted and understood by respondents thus seems evident. But academics are notorious for their reluctance to take the apparently obvious for granted. In our studies of black political opinions in the 1960s, we felt that respondents might be tempted to overreport political involvement to black interviewers no less than to underreport to whites. We devised a built-in validity test by using a short battery of factual political questions and splitting a pretest sample of blacks between white and black interviewers. In rural areas, black respondents who were interviewed by fellow blacks proved more knowledgeable than those interviewed by whites; race of interviewer made little difference in urban areas.

Because respondents cannot pretend to have information (such as the name of the state capitol or county seat) they do not have, but can refrain from demonstrating information they do have, our findings support the need to match interviewer and respondent characteristics for groups who may feel vulnerable—rural blacks in our 1960s case. Language problems aside, some Latino groups may feel as vulnerable in the United States today as did blacks in the rural South a generation ago.

The thoughtful papers of Joe Belden, I. A. Lewis, Warren Mitofsky, and Kathleen Frankovic suggest a third concern: defining the universe or population to be sampled. The exit polls from which Mitofsky and Frankovic's data were drawn constitute a neat and clear-cut solution; from the universe of actual voters an excellent sample can be drawn with relative ease and with marvelous geographical clustering of respondents. Although administering questionnaires at the polling place offers clear advantages, it is somewhat akin to the longstanding reliance of psychologists on conveniently assembled classes of college sophomores. Some critics argue that, because of the students' role as test subjects, textbooks on general psychology should be entitled *General Psychology of the College Sophomore*. In the same vein, if researchers are concerned with explaining the attitudes of Latino voters, the exit poll is both efficient and convenient. If researchers are concerned with ignored voices, however, the exit poll is of limited help. Adult Latinos in the United States may be considered as four populations for sampling purposes: all residents, legally documented residents, citizens, and voters. Different research purposes will lead one's focus to shift from one to another of these populations. My own interest in voting behavior is so great that I relish data from the last category. All of us should, however, remain acutely aware that such a focus restricts us to a small minority (certainly no greater than a fourth) of Latinos. Interest in ignored voices leads to an expanded definition of the population to be sampled. Indeed, a future orientation would suggest an expansion beyond my listing to include minors. Specialists in Latino problems might benefit from the example of psychologists and conduct more studies in classrooms, in this case in secondary schools with heavy Latino enrollment. Students are even more conveniently available in their classrooms than voters are as they leave the polls.

The problem of making more voices audible leads to my fourth concern, the need for a major investment of funds to examine Latino opinions properly. The cost of a truly comprehensive survey of Latinos would be enormous, but at least one such benchmark study would certainly be worth the investment. Indeed, a comprehensive survey is absolutely essential if we are to know to what degree Latino voters accurately speak for the unheard Latino majority.

The fieldwork required for sampling and interviewing by the face-to-face method has become so expensive that telephone samples are now the norm, as Belden's findings demonstrate. I agree with the accepted wisdom on the general advantages of telephone polling now that 90% of all occupied housing units are reported to have telephones. This conventional knowledge includes findings to the effect that people without telephones in their households do not differ significantly in attitudes, once income is controlled, from those who do have telephones. But these reassuring findings may not uniformly apply to concentrations of special populations such as Latinos and southern blacks. In one county in which I am currently planning fieldwork, for example, the proportion of black households without telephones is over 60%. I cannot believe that, simply by overweighting the lowest income stratum of blacks with telephones, a random sample of telephone subscribers can be taken to represent the opinions of all blacks in such a county. The idea that the views of a majority without telephones can be obtained by weighting the views of some of the minority with telephones strains credulity. A special effort to carry out face-to-face interviews in a sample of all housing units in such areas would not only provide substantive information but also resolve the methodological issue of "virtual representation" of nonsubscribers through the weighting of subscribers.

A final concern is ethical: how can pollsters avoid subjecting Latino respondents to stress? Universities are required to have some sort of committee on the use of human subjects through which research proposals go if they pose any threat to the well-being of those studied. In the zealous effort I have recommended to ensure a representative sample, would Latino residents of ill-defined households feel threatened—either by the attempt to enumerate all individuals in the households or by the questions themselves? Undocumented residents might find questions about voter registration or intention to vote, for example, frightening. Well-trained interviewers can establish a rapport that permits such questions to be raised without a sense of threat. All researchers in this area should ensure that their interviewers are sensitive to this problem. Awareness of this and of the other concerns I have noted

will, I trust, add a representative, audible and confident Latin ac-
cent to the chorus of American public opinion.

# Linking Cultural Characteristics to Political Opinion

Barbara Caplan, *Yankelovich, Clancy, Shulman*

In 1980, Yankelovich, Clancy, Shulman, (YCS) first began conducting research on the Hispanic market. The purpose was, and still is, to provide the business community with information geared to the enhancement of marketing consumer goods and services to this important and growing population segment.

On the surface, such research studies may seem irrelevant or at best tangential to the issues underscored at this conference. After all, what do basic marketing questions have to do with the portrayal of Latino public opinion for the development of public policy and the national political agenda? In what way does insight into issues such as brand loyalty, price elasticity, distribution preference, and so forth relate to the weightier problems of social and political magnitude?

It is the thesis of this paper, however, that there is a relationship between consumer research on the Hispanic market and the conference's objectives. The linkage is operative on a number of levels, and I have selected three areas to discuss that emerge from YCS' consumer studies of interest to this audience. The three are interrelated, but merit separate consideration for the purpose of clarity: the validity and usefulness of treating Hispanics as a distinct population; the characteristics of the Hispanic population; and the implications of YCS' findings for public opinion polling among the Hispanic population.

## The Validity and Usefulness of Treating Hispanics as a Distinct Population

The attention of marketers and advertisers has been drawn to this segment of the population for several reasons; and it is not unreasonable to suggest that their rationale can reinforce and contribute to research capabilities in areas other than consumer studies. First, though relative to the general population Hispanics represent only a small segment—about 16.5 million people today—they are estimated to more than double in numbers by the year 2000. Next, from a marketing point of view, Hispanics represent an attractive market to address because they are highly concentrated geographically and reachable through Spanish media as well as English mass market media. Also, in this business climate where marketers are looking at strategies that piece together small population segments for incremental growth, catering to the Hispanic segment fits into this strategy. Finally, and perhaps most salient to the conference goals, YCS' studies of Hispanics reveal that the Hispanics share unique characteristics that distinguish them from the Anglo mainstream population. More particularly, they are not "hyphenated" American émigrés as much as persons of a "blended" lifestyle.

This last point is an important distinction for marketers, media people, and others who research opinion because it means that they must no longer expect Hispanics to show only clearly Hispanic attitudes in the marketplace; nor, conversely, what might be considered typical of an assimilated American. Rather, they must understand that Hispanics are more likely to feel and act according to the problems and interests found in their blended lifestyles.

In light of the above, it is clear that knowledge about the Hispanic population is necessary not only to those who shape public policy, but also to those who research issues demanding informed understanding. The next point in this paper highlights some of YCS' findings in this regard.

### The Characteristics of the Hispanic Population

Central to YCS' research keyed to the Hispanic population in the United States is the assumption, proven valid over time, that knowledge about the attitudes, values, and lifestyles of this segment is essential to effective marketing. That is, over and above demographic information (income, age, household size, etc.) and market facts (products purchased, etc.), sociocultural characteristics are a prerequisite to a full understanding of consumer behavior. In fact, these very characteristics help to expose the myths that cloud assumptions often distorting a more accurate reading of Hispanic public opinion in general.

In light of YCS' experience in the area of social values and its commitment to their relevance, studies conducted by the firm are notable for their incorporation of such input and its interpretation. SIN (Spanish International Network) commissioned YCS to do two studies, one in 1981 and one in 1984. YCS on its own also developed a study in 1984 entitled "Hispanic Viewpoint." This study was in response to what we saw as a true need for more information about this segment of the population for specific product categories.

What, then, has YCS discovered from its research studies? More particularly, leaving consumer-related behavior aside, what information about social values and cultural commitments among Hispanics contributes to the mandate of this conference? To address these questions what follows are selected findings drawn from the Spanish USA Study commissioned by SIN, chosen for their applicability and possible implications for the broader issues of effective opinion polling. These findings are compared to findings from YCS' 1981 research commissioned by SIN.

## A Brief Look Back at 1981

YCS research in 1981 revealed that the 15 million Hispanics living in the United States were, in fact, a separate, identifiable market. Tied to their ethnic traditions and to the Spanish language, Hispanics regarded themselves as a unique subculture—more Hispanic than American or with equal links to the United States and to their native lands. As consumers, Hispanics were more responsive to new market entries (products, stores, services), more oriented to big national brands than other Americans, and were markedly aware of their combined market power. The almost universal commitment to the Spanish language as the keystone for maintaining ethnic identity was reflected in the widespread use of Spanish-language media, particularly television, even though English media were credited with technical superiority.

Like other immigrant groups before them, Hispanics were committed to upward mobility, to acquiring material possessions—in other words, to pursuing the American dream. And, reflecting the spread of new values during the 1960s and 1970s among American society at large, Hispanics also were supportive of goals which emphasized personal development and expression over and above material success; for example, Hispanics were committed to such self-involved values as physical fitness and the enhancement of personal attractiveness.

While Hispanics in the United States were not homogeneous, the differences among Puerto Ricans, Cubans, Mexicans, and other Hispanics were found to revolve around migration history and the strength of the emotional ties to the homeland. Differences blurred when consumer behavior and media usage patterns were at issue. Thus, it was concluded, the marketer could consider all Hispanics in aggregate as a consumer segment.

### Shifts in the Social Climate, 1981–1984

In the three years between the studies of YCS for SIN (1981–1984), a number of major shifts in the political, social, and economic life of the United States have taken place which are changing the orientation of Hispanics, just as they are causing changes among Americans at large. The following are some of the shifts.

*A Change in the Role of Government.* There has been a gradual but real weakening of the role of the federal government—in fact, of government in general—in the social policy arena. The 1960s and 1970s were decades when American society was strongly committed to pursuing a social agenda, e.g., environmental protection, consumer protection, civil rights, equal opportunity and access for all, improved education, and medical care delivery. But by the late 1970s, United States society grew far more selective about social policy, narrowing the areas for effort and commitment. And, derivatively, support for reducing the role of government grew rapidly. Instead, personal responsibility for one's own welfare emerged as the avenue of the 1980s, and the public exhorted government to support (rather than contain) business in order to ensure economic growth and jobs.

*A Severe Economic Recession.* The recession which began in earnest in late 1980 was an overarching element during part of the period between 1981 and 1984, directly affecting income and employment opportunities but also influencing goals and values. The widespread belief that future economic horizons for the United States were unlimited and easy to realize (assumed in the early 1960s) had spurred the social agenda of the 1960s and 1970s. That belief was being seriously shaken in the late 1970s.

Among the public, earning a living—getting and holding a job—became a foreground issue rather than a given from which one could go on to address social and personal objectives.

*New Social Themes Emerge.* A new set of social values began to crystallize in the early 1980s: a fusion of the new economic focus with the more contained but still vital "focus-on-self" values of the 1960s and 1970s. Themes such as the following were being articulated among all elements of the society.

A new realism. Acceptance of the idea that one cannot be/have/do everything and that, while this sense of limits need not be tragic, new types and levels of effort are required to meet the new social and economic goal.

Cost-effectiveness. Action, purchases, and decisions increasingly were being assessed on the basis of the costs (in time and effort as well as money) required. Ideological reasons for an action were no longer sufficient, nor was habit, a sense of comfort, etc.

Increasing reliance on personal efforts, individual actions, merit. The focus-on-self values of the 1960s/1970s were based on the assumption of economic "entitlements," growing out of affluence, which permitted attention to inner life and needs and to feelings of well-being. In the early 1980s, the self (rather than groups or institutions) continued as a focus. Faith in the self to master the more difficult economic conditions became the issue in a generally more competitive society.

Commitment to strategic thinking. Merit/winning was seen increasingly as the result of strategic, pragmatic thinking—not as the outcome of embracing ideological, moralistic positions.

*Central and South America Became Big News.* Directly relevant to Hispanic Americans, the years between 1981 and 1984 saw South and Central America (and Cuba) become dominant elements in the daily news, highlighted by troubled economic conditions in Mexico and in South America.

While a three-year span is rather short for anticipating major changes in attitudes and behavior, enough had occurred since 1981 to warrant updating the earlier report. The 1984 findings for all Hispanics, in aggregate, are presented in the following sections.

**Social Values among Hispanics, 1984**

New values and beliefs were emerging in 1984 among United States populations. While many Hispanics were college educated,

in good jobs, and with above average earnings, the economic indices for Hispanics in aggregate continued to show a gap in earnings and standard of living. Therefore, it may be useful, as a frame of
reference, to present the insights emergent from YCS' 1984 social
values tracking research about the new social values among the
lower middle class.

Among the roughly 20% of the population who were somewhat
disadvantaged in education, and who therefore were in lower-
paying jobs, the 1984 data showed:

A renewed commitment to trying to move up the socioeconomic
ladder via individual effort.

A rejection of economic benefits and opportunities that were not
based on merit.

Realism about what could be achieved, given their competitive
liability, and about the level of effort that had to be expended.

Renewed emphasis on education as the road to upward mobility.

Focus on the future, rather than living for the moment.

All in all, there was a sense of seriousness of purpose and of
commitment to sustained individual effort. In contrast, there were
not signs of moves to antiestablishment political action, nor of
heightened commitment to organized confrontations of employers. This Lower-middle-class segment was, if anything, more
demanding on the educational system to maintain standards
and rigor, so that any degrees attained would be meaningful and in-
dicative of acheivement.

The values and beliefs of Hispanics were shifting in lockstep
with the general population. Hispanics, even more than Americans
in general, were conscious that the economic realities of the 1980s
had introduced hurdles which made getting ahead more difficult.
More than in 1981, Hispanics were moving to curtail time and
money spent in pursuit of new experiences, of excitement and sen-
sationalism. (We had already seen evidence of efforts among
Hispanics to temper their general responsiveness as consumers.)

Hispanics were also beginning to pull back a bit from their
focus-on-self commitments, e.g., to fitness programs and even to
physical enhancement. But, living day by day in a self-denying
mode appeared to generate the need for an occasional shot in the
arm. More than in 1981, Hispanics reported that they needed the
kind of lift that occasional spending for intangibles and pleasures
can provide.

Hispanics continued to hold more traditional views about sex
roles, but there were early signs of an increasing scope for women.

One of the factors that contained Hispanic household income (relative to the population at large) was the lower proportion of Hispanic homemakers who worked outside the home. Clearly, the presence of several young children (Hispanics have more children than other Americans) was one deterrent to women entering the labor force. Also a factor was the evidence that among Hispanics—more than among other Americans—masculinity itself was based on being the breadwinner. Over half of Hispanics defined masculinity in this way, compared to 1 in 3 among the population at large—and these statistics were the same in 1984 as in 1981.

Having an income-producing wife, therefore, appeared to be a violation of basic sex roles in the thinking of Hispanics, more so than among all Americans at this time. (It was, however, only about 15 years ago that Americans in general reported the same ideas about the roles of men and women that Hispanics are articulating today.)

While the idea of "choice without penalty" for women was still relatively undeveloped among Hispanics, the 1984 evidence does suggest the gradual assumption of more aggressive roles by Hispanic women in, for example, influencing big ticket purchases. It may be that modifications in sex roles among the Hispanic community will take place first within the family, and then be noted in the employment arena.

**Cultural Commitments Among Hispanics**

*Strong Ties to Country of Origin.* Of Hispanic adults aged 16 years or more, only 1 in 3 was born in the United States. Of those who had immigrated, only 20% had been in the United States for as long as 20 years. Thus, almost half (44%) were immigrants who had arrived more recently than 20 years ago—24% as recently as within the past 10 years.

*National Origins not Homogeneous.* Mexicans dominated with 60% of Hispanics being of Mexican origin. Puerto Ricans represented about 15%, Cubans 5%, and about 20% of Hispanic Americans were rooted in a wide range of other countries: El Salvador, Guatemala, Nicaragua, Panama, Costa Rica, Dominican Republic, Colombia, Peru, Argentina, Ecuador, Bolivia, Chile, Uruguay, Spain, and the Philippines.

*Rise in Hispanic Identification.* The 1984 research revealed an increase over 1981 in the sense of unity and specialness among Hispanic Americans. This heightened ethnic orientation may have been, in part, a response to the more constricted, difficult economic climate—a form of clinging together in times of adversity. It was in line with the increase in "local parochialism" among the population at large, noted since the 1980 recession. Apparently, in times of stress, allegiance to and identification with smaller geographic units (neighborhoods and cities, not the country as a whole) appears to surface and grow. The rise in Hispanic identification may also reflect the present focus of United States foreign policy on Central America and Cuba which could be stimulating feelings of separateness. This growing sense of unity, of coming together, was evident in many areas.

*Reduced Differences between Nationalities.* There was a distinct blurring of differences in the way Hispanics of varying nationalities felt about each other—how Mexicans felt about South Americans, Cubans about Puerto Ricans, etc. In the scant three years between surveys, the reduction in these differences was so great that each deserves the examination which follows.

"The way we speak Spanish." Although Spanish in the United States reflected the speech of a score of Hispanic countries, localized patterns of speech, slang, etc. were felt to be a lessening barrier between Hispanics of these different national origins. In the 1981 study, 42% of Hispanics cited "The way we speak Spanish" as a meaningful difference; in 1984 only 34% did.

"The music we prefer." Music and songs can be distinctive among nations, and in the 1981 study 35% of respondents mentioned this as a difference; in 1984 only 29% did.

"The foods and drinks we like." In 1981, 30% mentioned food and drink as differences; in 1984 only 21% did.

"Holidays, festivals and celebrations." Here, too, there was a feeling that such observances were an evaporating difference between nationalities. In 1981, 26% described them as a difference; in 1984 only 18% did.

Job opportunities. Prospects for employment, as a difference, showed the second greatest decline between the two studies. In 1981, 24% called it a difference; in 1984, only 16% did.

Religion, beliefs. In the field of religion, 19% termed it a difference in 1981; in 1984, only 15% did.

Art, literature. The greatest rate of reduction in what Hispanics termed differences among nationalities was in art and literature. In 1981, 24% mentioned it; in 1984, only 14% did.

In summary, in 1981, 61% of Hispanics felt that there was a great deal of difference, or some important differences, between Hispanic nationalities. In 1984, this figure had shrunk to 50%.

*Self-description.* In 1984, compared with 1981, more Hispanics thought of themselves as Hispanics first, and Americans second.

|  | 1981 | 1984 |
| --- | --- | --- |
| Hispanic first, American second | 46% | 50% |
| Equally Hispanic and American | 42 | 36 |
| American first, Hispanic second | 12 | 14 |

*Preserving Hispanic Culture.* There was a significant increase in the desire to perpetuate Hispanic traditions through succeeding generations.

|  |  | 1981 | 1984 |
| --- | --- | --- | --- |
| "We should pass on to our children a sense of belonging to our religious and national tradition." | Agree/Strongly Agree | 89% | 94% |
|  | Strongly Agree | 37 | 46 |

This growing emphasis on traditions was also evident in Hispanics' desire to see their culture appreciated by others.

|  |  | 1981 | 1984 |
| --- | --- | --- | --- |
| "Hispanics are demanding respect for and recognition of their culture more than they used to." | Agree/Strongly Agree | 87% | 86% |
|  | Strongly Agree | 30 | 36 |

*Spanish Language.* The Spanish language was increasingly seen as the most important mechanism for preserving Hispanic culture/identity. More than 8 of 10 Hispanics identified Spanish as the key to maintaining and fostering their cultural identity. At a substantially lower level, 5 out of 10, three additional culture-preserving mechanisms were cited: religion, music, and the traditional Hispanic respect for elders.

|  |  | 1981 | 1984 |
| --- | --- | --- | --- |
| Aspects of Culture or Traditions Most Important to Preserve | The Spanish language | 81% | 84% |
|  | Religion/church | 51 | 53 |
|  | Care or respect for elders (net) | 58 | 52 |

| | | | |
|---|---|---|---|
| Respect for elders or parents | | 53 | 47 |
| Care for elders or older people (stay with family) | | 43 | 38 |
| Music | | 54 | 49 |
| Commitment to family | | 50 | 43 |
| Holidays and celebrations | | 41 | 37 |
| Food and beverages | | 46 | 36 |
| Love for life or know how to enjoy life | | 42 | 28 |
| Art and literature | | 48 | 28 |

From 1981 to 1984, there was no sign of increased commitment to mastery of English at the possible expense of Spanish; the commitment to Spanish was stronger if anything. Current language skills aside for the moment, bilingualism was the predominant goal—about 3 out of 4 seeing mastery of both English and Spanish as the ideal. Fluency in Spanish supersedes fluency in English as a goal, 20% to 6%.

| | | 1981 | 1984 |
|---|---|---|---|
| Current Language Skills | Bilingual | 47% | 45% |
| | Fluent in Spanish; enough English to get by | 20 | 23 |
| | Know only Spanish | 23 | 20 |
| | Fluent in English; enough Spanish to get by | 9 | 9 |
| | Know only English | 1 | 3 |
| | Fluent in Spanish | 90 | 88 |
| | Fluent in English | 57 | 57 |
| | Speak only Spanish at home | 45 | 44 |
| Language Goals | Bilingualism | 79 | 74 |
| | Fluency in Spanish | 14 | 20 |
| | Fluency in English | 7 | 6 |

*Media Trends.* Hispanics were spending more time with television and radio, less time with print.

| | Weekly Hours | |
|---|---|---|
| | 1981 | 1984 |
| TV | 19 1/2 | 22 |
| Radio | 15 | 17 |
| Print | 6 1/2 | 6 |

*Spanish Language Media.* There was an increase in the expressed need for Hispanic media. In 1981, 63% believed Spanish
language media were very or extremely important, whereas in 1984
66% felt this way.

There was an increase in the percentage of Hispanics watching
Spanish television, and a decline for Spanish radio and print.

---

Use of Spanish Media in one week

|       | 1981 | 1984 |
|-------|------|------|
| TV    | 68%  | 73%  |
| Radio | 75   | 70   |
| Print | 53   | 46   |

---

### The Implications of YCS' Findings

Throughout the SIN 1984 study, a recurring and overriding factor
was the strength and the endurance of the Spanish language.

This more than any other characteristic is the unifying force link-
ing Hispanics of all nationalities. More of them think of
themselves as Hispanics first, Americans second. They place
greater importance on perpetuating the Hispanic culture and
language throughout succeeding generations, and are expressing
a greater need for Hispanic media.

There is an awakening realization of their economic and political
clout—of the benefits of pulling together to reach common objectives.

This trend toward unity is particularly evident in the way
Hispanics of various national origins feel about each other. They
now see far fewer differences among each other—in the way they
speak Spanish, in employment opportunities, in art and literature.

This homogenization within the Hispanic population is reminis-
cent of the development of America itself—a populace that
despite a diversity of nationalities and interests eventually
became a national market.

In a similar vein, those who research Hispanic opinion for the
shaping of public policy can adapt some of the findings presented
here for their unique purpose. On an obvious level, the growing
cohesiveness of diverse Hispanic groups suggests the reliability
and practicality of sampling from a general Hispanic population,
rather than designating individual subpopulations to be sampled.

In addition, and by way of conclusion, it seems fair to say that knowledge about the social values and cultural commitments of the Hispanics compared to those of white mainstream America is an essential backdrop to research design and interpretation. Opinions about social and political issues do not operate in a vacuum. How people react and respond to research inquiries is very much colored by the unique and shared experiences that define them as an important segment of the United States population.

# Polling Latinos

Curtis B. Gans, *Committee for the Study of the American Electorate*

It took a long time for me to define what my role here would be. I am not, strictly speaking, involved with survey research. I have commissioned two polls—one on who the nonvoters in America were in 1976 and one on who the new registrants were in 1984—and for reasons outlined in detail at this conference, I was not able to discern from those surveys any useful information about Latinos. I am not an academic, although we at the Committee for the Study of the American Electorate believe we do a number of things with as much rigor and at least as much relevance as academics do. Bluntly, I was not sure I had enough expertise to make a contribution to this conference. But I did work out a role that might be useful—to serve as a rapporteur and critic of what happened at this conference and to submit a post-conference paper.

I will try not to reiterate what so many others who have preceded me have already said so eloquently about the complexities of polling the Latino community: about the issue of sample size sufficient to encompass differing national backgrounds, age groups, places of birth, and the like; of questionnaire design; of in-person versus phone surveys; of language, and so forth.

I have, as a nonpsephologist, only four things to add to that discussion, one of which is minor. First, I believe that the work of the Southwest Voter Education Registration Project has been enormously useful, but I believe it is time they question whether the use of Spanish surnames is an adequate basis for determining accurately who are actually Latinos. As Representative Garcia pointed out this morning, the editor of an important Latino publication is a Puerto Rican whose name is Jewish.

Second, I would caution against typecasting people as liberal and conservative based on self-attribution. Attitudes toward issues are by far a better basis for judging liberalism and conservatism than are self-ascribed words. For decades we have had more people describe themselves as moderate and conservative than liberal while, with the exception of the last five years, the nation has plunged ahead in a generally liberal direction.

Third, I think that in discussing the outlook of a population or a segment of the population more has to be done to place a particular response to a question at a particular time in a political context. It may be true, as has been suggested here, that younger Latinos are becoming socially more conservative than previous generations, but one wonders whether that would be true in a time of economic crisis or whether they might at such a time perceive themselves more liberally inclined on both economic and social issues.

Finally, once we have added up all the things that need to be done in order to adequately inquire into Latino views and opinion, it would also be useful to try to quantify the cost of such an effort, for that is a relevant consideration in seeing what can be done and how.

Now I would like to deal with two issues that I believe have not been dealt with adequately at this conference. Not enough has been said about the purpose of polling the Latino community. And too little has been said about the financial means for doing so.

Until the major television networks began using a perfectly valid polling tool called the exit poll for the purpose of telling people how they voted while they were still voting and network anchor people continued to tell people their vote mattered while network actions in projecting poll results before polls closed told them it didn't, I thought the best example of abuse of polls was practiced by Lyndon Johnson. During the early stages of the war in Vietnam, he was constantly confronting doubters of his policies with polls plucked out of his pocket showing overwhelming public support of the war. In the later stages of the war, he ceased doing this, in part because the polls no longer supported the policy he was pursuing. There are those, including myself, who believe he would have been better served if he had adopted policies which would have allowed him to pull out the poll results in the second half of his term rather than the first and that the nation would have been better served also.

But this illustrates the cardinal caveat about polls. They do not lead to what is right. Vietnam was wrong despite the early support and the late opposition. A majority may now support prayer in the schools, but that does not mean it is consonant with the First Amendment to the Constitution. A majority opposes even the limited involvement we now have in Nicaragua, but it continues apace. The choice of the correct policy, for better or worse, will not be solved by polls but by the exercise of leadership, which is why we indeed elect people to office—not simply to represent the electorate, but, in their wisdom, to make choices for that electorate, choices which they will be held responsible for at the polls.

And while there is legitimate use for polls to find out what the public wants in the way of products, or how those products may be sold, or even how candidates may be elected, the purpose of this conference is none of these, but rather to find out the uses of polling techniques which might serve to assist the Latino community.

It seems that the most important function of such polls would be their use in conjuntion with substantive—that is, non-opinion—research on what the Latino community in all its forms needs. How can the condition of the individual Latino be bettered? What does he or she perceive as primary needs? What government policies would be perceived as best suited to meet those needs?

Polling of this sort should attempt to ascertain not simply how the Latino community as a whole perceives its needs, but how the various subgroups within the community perceive their needs. It should also find out how those perceived needs (as Bruce Cain and Roderick Kiewiet described in their poll) dovetail with the perceived needs of other minorities. And how those perceived needs fit in with the perceived wishes of the totality of the electorate. (And it cannot be emphasized enough that such agenda building should dovetail with substantive research about the real agenda and that some effort must be made while pursuing Latino needs to see how they fit in with a national agenda. For the public is being increasingly buffeted by the centripetal forces of hyphenated American interests, which at some point must be translated into a common interest.

Also, I believe the purpose of polling should be to find out the political tolerances of advocacy. Leaders can lead only so far before they are cut off from their constituency and are subject to replacement. Thus, it is important to find out how real needs and perceived demand fit into the public's perception of what it will tolerate in political program, advocacy, and taxation, to mention a few factors.

It is also my belief that it is useful and proper to test rhetorical and programmatic approaches to solving real problems in order to test what the public will accept and how it should be politically packaged to gain the maximum acceptance.

Having said all of this, we come to my second major concern, the question of cost. Adding the agenda described for getting adequate responses from the Latino community to the agenda I have set forward in terms of purpose would mean polling subsets within the Latino community, polling the Latino community along with other minorities, and obtaining sufficient oversampling in national polls.

I know of no polling outfit that would be willing to undertake such surveying on a pro bono basis. Exit polls theoretically have a sufficiently large sample, but because of time constraints they are limited in the nature of the questionnaire they can put forward and, in any event, they do not poll nonvoters. I had a discussion just before this meeting with the chief of the New York Times survey unit who said he did not perceive it to be in his immediate interest, nor that of anyone else he could think of, to create the type of oversample which would be necessary to poll adequately the Latino community. Nor have any private pollsters volunteered out of the goodness of their hearts to conduct such oversamples in their surveys.

Given the growing nature of the Latino community in America, this remains an important item on the national agenda for the development of sound public and political policy and this conference is an important first step in the recognition of this problem. But unless or until there is a substantial commitment to this effort from both the collective foundation community and others in the corporate and political world to provide the wherewithal to make such an effort possible, it will not happen.

Which brings me to a final thought that I believe should be explored. One of the problems of conducting each poll individually is the large overhead cost such polling entails when private for-profit institutions conduct them. It seems to me that such overhead costs might be alleviated, and the possibility of constructive longitudinal research enhanced, if nonprofit polling capacities would address the agenda or subportions of it.

# An Assessment of Data Resources on Latinos in the United States

Armando Valdez, *Stanford University*

The presence of Latinos in the national consciousness has grown steadily in the past 20 years. In large part, this presence reflects an increasing awareness of the nation's fastest growing linguistic and cultural minority and its potential impact on our economic and political institutions. Research on Latinos also has experienced an increase commensurate to the group's salience on the national agenda. For example, the social and economic programs of the War on Poverty created a need for reliable data on Latinos and others. The rise in ethnic and social consciousness in the 1960s and 1970s and the increased number of Latino scholars writing during this period further enlarged the amount of social research on Latinos. In the 1980s, we are experiencing an unparalleled demand for information about this group. However, the costs of collecting data have escalated at an alarming rate while research funds have drastically diminished. As a consequence, available data resources on Latinos in the United States have gained a growing importance; secondary analysis of available data is an attractive and often necessary option.

In 1983–84, the Stanford Center for Chicano Research conducted a national search for existing computerized (that is, machine-readable) data files on Latinos. The goal of the project was to identify and profil publicly accessible, numeric data files on Latinos to facilitate secondary analysis of these data by a broad range of researchers, including demographers, economists, sociologists, statisticians, political scientists, policy analysts, and historians. The product of this effort was the *Latino Data Directory*, an on-line database on 119 subjects from 220 different data sources.

This directory is publicly accessible to anyone with the capability of achieving remote access to the mainframe computer at Stanford University. Unlike commercial databases, which charge an access fee and other user charges, access to the *Latino Data Directory* on-line file is free. The users' only costs are the CPU costs and regular connect charges, which are nominal in comparison to those for commercial databases.

This paper examines the status of available data resources on Latinos based on the *Latino Data Directory*. Although not conclusive, the directory represents a comprehensive sampling of the majority of the available data resources in the country. Before proceeding, the manner in which the directory was compiled, its contents, and its structure will be described.

**Development of the Latino Data Directory**

A national search for publicly accessible data files took the form of identifying potential data sources from available catalogues and data directories as well as major survey research and polling newsletters. Surveys and polls conducted in areas with significant concentrations of Latinos were selected as potential data sources. It was assumed that only a few of these studies or polls focus exclusively on Latinos, but that most others incorporate Latinos as part of the sample. This procedure yielded approximately 600 potential data files. Undoubtedly, there are countless other data resources that include Latinos, yet many of them are proprietary data collected for the sole use of a particular agency or corporation and are not accessible to others. Still other data files do not have sufficient documentation to permit their use by other scholars or analysts and thus are not often archived in major data depositories where they can be readily accessed. Thus, the pool of available data files on Latinos represents the subset of all the identified files that met the public accessibility criteria.

A preliminary review of the estimated 600 data files identified as potentially including Latinos reduced the pool by almost half. A large number of data files, especially public opinion polls, did not have sufficient documentation to permit secondary analyses. Another large subset of data files did not use an ethnic identifier in classifying their sample. A common practice among these data sources was to identify the sample only by race and other demographic characteristics. In the absence of an ethnic identifier, the Latino sample remained submerged in the broader race classifications of the sample population and could not be explicitly identified.

Having thus reduced the number of potential data sources to approximately 300, the next step was to profile specific features of these data files that would permit researchers, analysts, and policymakers to determine the appropriateness of any given data file/data set for secondary analysis. Among the 26 attributes profiled for each data file are the universe, sampling units, study design, data collection period(s), geographic area covered, number of variables, major variables, number of Latinos in the sample, file structure and size, mode of access, and cost. For the most part, only some of these file attributes were mentioned in directories or catalogues. In most cases, a letter was sent to the investigators requesting additional file information. In cases where a response was not received within a month of the request for information, a follow-up telephone call was used to collect these data. This process of developing a profile further reduced the number of data sources to 220. About 35% of the data files were excluded due to insufficient file information available or the lack of response from the investigators.

The resultant *Latino Data Directory* lists available data on Latinos for a wide range of subjects including civic participation, economic behavior, political opinions and attitudes, attitudes toward the military, and opinions on U.S. energy policy and auto safety. The directory also identifies data resources on Latino socioeconomic status, including nativity, housing, educational attainment, labor force status, participation in government cash benefit programs, and health status.

### Significant Omissions from the Directory

The *Latino Data Directory* is significant for what it omits as well as for what it includes. While only 220 data files are profiled in the *Latino Data Directory*, many other data sources were carefully examined but not used for a variety of reasons, the most prominent being that many studies and polls fail to identify the ethnicity of respondents. The directory also reflects the absence of Latino data from some of the better-known national surveys and polls and documents the extent to which Latinos are "invisible" in major national studies. Many prominent data sources identify only the race of respondents; they do not code for the respondent's ethnicity, making it impossible to identify Latino respondents.

A partial listing of major national surveys that do not code their sample for Spanish-origin ethnicity include:

Political Participation in America (1972), a national, cross sectional survey of approximately 1,000 respondents conducted by Verba and Nie on which their classic work, *Participation in America* (1972), is based.

Panel Study of Income Dynamics (1969–82), an annual survey of a national cross section of 5,000 families conducted by the Institute for Social Research at the University of Michigan for various federal agencies. The study oversampled low-income and black families. The study lists Spanish-American as an interviewer-coded race category during the first years but omits even that obtuse form of identifying Latinos after 1973.

National Senior Citizens Survey (1968, 1971), a survey of 3,995 respondents using a multistage area probability sample conducted by the University of Michigan. The survey only coded for race of the respondents as black, white, or other.

Survey of Consumer Attitudes and Behavior (1953–76), a national survey conducted quarterly since the mid-1960s of 1,200 to 1,600 respondents using a cross-sectional design conducted by the Survey Research Center at the University of Michigan. The survey only coded the respondents' race.

### Ratings of Data Resources

This section discusses the adequacy of the available data resources listed in the *Latino Data Directory*. The data resources are grouped as national, state and regional, and local sources. The adequacy of the Latino sample is determined by the combination of sample size, sampling design, and ethnic identifiers used to classify the Latino sample.

A major consideration in any form of survey research is to select a sample in a manner that reduces error. The various types of probability sampling designs limit the range of sampling error to a far greater extent than nonprobability designs. There is also an inverse relationship between sample size and sampling error. The larger the sample, the smaller the sampling error. Furthermore, in the case of Latinos—who manifest a wide range of national origins, race, surnames, and language preferences—the use of ethnic identifiers that reflect this diversity is well advised. Experience has shown that the terms "Spanish-surname" and

"Spanish-speaking," for example, exclude countless Latinos who either do not speak Spanish as their primary language or do not have Spanish surnames because of intermarriage and assimilation. Latinos also fall into a range of racial groups, so that many Latinos are encompassed in each of the racial categories of white, black, and other. For these reasons, a broad set of national origin/ancestry ethnic identifiers increases the likelihood of correctly identifying Latinos in a sample population and thereby increasing the size and reliability of the sample.

Given these considerations, a large Latino sample size does not in itself translate into an adequate sample. For purposes of making some determination about the adequacy of the Latino sample in a national study, a weighted sample of 6.1% will be deemed as the threshold above which a Latino sample is rated as adequate. A sample derived by some form of probability and the use of an ethnic identifier that classifies national origin and ancestry will also be factored into an assessment of the adequacy of the data resources.

*Best National Data Sets.* As shown in table 1, the High School and Beyond 1980 and 1982 data files have an adequate Latino sample. The 1982 senior cohort file for the High School and Beyond Survey tops the list of major national studies with large Latino samples. This is followed by the 1982 sophomore cohort file for the High School and Beyond Survey. Both of these surveys employed a two-stage, stratified probability sampling design. They also used an array of 10 different ethnic identifiers for Latino ancestry and origin. The manner in which the Latino sample was derived and classified is very appropriate and thus the Latino sample is quite adequate.

The National Longitudinal Surveys of Labor Market Experiences ranks next as having the most adequate Latino sample. A total of 15% of the national probability sample is Latino. Four specific ancestry and two national origin identifiers are used to classify the Latino sample population. The size of the Latino sample, the study design, and the classification scheme used also make this data source very adequate.

The Current Population Survey: Annual Demographic File is the product of a national survey conducted each March by the U.S. Bureau of the Census. The design and ethnic identifiers are very good; the sample size is 10% for the March 1982 survey and ranges at that level most years. This file ranks next among the best available data resources on Latinos.

The American Freshman Study (1984), the Supported Work Study (1975–79), the Survey of Income and Education (1976), and the Food Stamp Household Study (1981) all have Latino sample sizes exceeding 10%. They employed various nonprobability sampling designs and are thus not rated as high as the other studies with sample sizes in the same range.

Of these four studies, the Survey of Income and Education (SIE) employed a stratified cluster design which yields good reliability. Thus, of the four nonprobability designs, SIE ranks highest, followed by the American Freshman Study, the Food Stamp Household Study, and the Supported Work Study, respectively.

A caveat is in order here. The rankings suggested above are based on very specific criteria adopted for this paper which emphasize aspects of the studies that render the data reliable and hence generalizable to the nation's Latino population. Inferences about the quality of the data collection and analysis procedures of these studies are not made. Neither is an attempt made to rank the significance of the topic addressed or the relevance of the studies themselves. The *Latino Data Directory* does not contain such information.

*Other National Data.* Table 2 shows six other data sources that exceed the 6% threshold for adequate Latino sample size in national studies discussed earlier. Of these, four employed a probability sampling design: the Health and Nutrition Examination Survey II (HANES I) (1975–80); the Health and Nutrition Examination Survey I (HANES I) (1971–75); the Quality of American Life (1971); and the American National Election Study (1980). The HANES II employed seven ethnic identifiers in contrast to only two (Mexican and Spanish) for HANES I. With a combination of an 8.8% Latino sample, a probability sampling design, and a reasonably adequate set of ethnic identifiers, HANES II ranks at the top among the six studies in table 2 with Latino sample sizes below 10% employing a probability design. The Quality of American Life Study ranks next, followed by the American National Election Study. Despite the 7.7% Latino sample size and the probability sampling design, HANES I used an inadequate set of ethnic identifiers and thus ranks fourth in a field of four data sets using a probability design. The National Medical Care Utilization and Expenditure Survey (1980), which is a longitudinal panel study, used four ethnic identifiers and thus ranks next. The Safe School Study (1976–77) employed a stratified sampling design yet used Spanish as the only ethnic identifier. The data from the Safe School Study have to be regarded as marginal.

**Table 1**

Major National Studies with Latino Samples over 10%
(Presented in Descending Order of Latino Sample Size)

| Data Source | Design | Sample Size | | | Latino Ethnic Identifiers |
| | | Total | Latino N | Latino % | |
|---|---|---|---|---|---|
| High School and Beyond Senior Cohort (1982) | longitudinal study; two-stage stratified probability sample | 11,995 | 2,918 | 24.3 | Chicano, Mexican, Mexican-American, Cuban, Puerto Rican, Other Latin; American, Latin, Hispanic, Spanish origin |
| High School and Beyond Sophomore Cohort (1982) | longitudinal study; two-stage stratified probability sample | 29,373 | 5,220 | 17.7 | Chicano, Mexican, Mexican-American Cuban, Puerto Rican, Other Latin; American, Latin, Hispanic, Spanish origin |
| The American Freshman: National Norms for College Freshmen (1966–84) (1984) | stratified sample of college students | 300,000 | 48,000 | 16.0 | Mexican-American, Chicano, Puerto Rican |
| National Longitudinal Surveys of Labor Market Experiences (1979–82) | national probability sample | 12,686 | 1,924 | 15.1 | Chicano, Mexican, Mexican-American, Puerto Rican, Other Hispanic, Other Spanish |
| Supported Work Study (1975–79) | interviews with individuals having persistent problems holding jobs; sample drawn from 10 major urban cities in nation | 6,500 | 780 | 12.0 | Hispanic, Latin |

| Survey | Design | | | | Groups |
|---|---|---|---|---|---|
| High School and Beyond Students Survey (1980) | longitudinal study; two-stage probability sample | 58,270 | 6,698 | 11.5 | Chicano, Mexican, Mexican-American Cuban, Puerto Rican, Other Latin; American, Latin, Hispanic, Spanish descent |
| Survey of Income and Education (1976) | stratified multistage cluster design | 151,700 households | 16,809 | 11.0 | Central/South American, Cuban, Chicano, Mexican, Mexican-American, Puerto Rican, Other Spanish |
| Characteristics of Food Stamp Households (1981) | simple random selection of households | 7,742 | 800 | 10.3 | Hispanic |
| Current Population Survey: Annual Demographic File (March 1982) | probability sample | 162,703 | 16,153 | 10.0 | Central/South American, Cuban, Chicano, Mexican, Mexicano, Mexican-American, Puerto Rican, Other Spanish |
| High School and Beyond Parents Survey (1980) | longitudinal study, two-stage probability sample | 6,564 | 648 | 10.0 | Chicano, Mexican, Mexican-American Cuban, Puerto Rican, Other Latin; American, Latin, Hispanic, Spanish descent |

Source: Compiled from the *Latino Data Directory* (1985).

**Table 2**
Major National Studies with Latino Samples under 10%
(Presented in Descending Order of Latino Sample Size)

| Data Source | Design | Sample Size Total | Latino N | Latino % | Latino Ethnic Identifiers |
|---|---|---|---|---|---|
| Health and Nutrition Examination Survey II: Children Ages 6 Months–11 Years (1975–1980) | probability sample | 6,839 | 607 | 8.8 | Chicano, Cuban, Mexican, Mexicano Mexican-American, Puerto Rican, Other Spanish |
| Health and Nutrition Examination Survey I: Children Ages 1–11 Years (1971–1975) | probability sample | 4,972 | 385 | 7.7 | Mexican, Spanish |
| Quality of American Life (1971) | multistage area probability sample | 2,164 | 158 | 7.3 | Central American, Cuban, Chicano, Mexican, Mexican-American, Mexicano, Puerto Rican, Other Spanish |
| National Medical Care Utilization and Expenditure Survey (1980) | longitudinal panel study, household interviews | 17,123 | 1,192 | 6.9 | Cuban, Mexican, Mexican-American Puerto Rican, Other Spanish |
| Safe School Study (1976–77) | stratified sample of principals, students and teachers at 642 junior and senior high schools | 31,373 | 2,121 | 6.7 | Spanish |

| Survey | Sampling method | | | | Subgroups |
|---|---|---|---|---|---|
| American National Election Study (1980) | panel study, multistage, three-wave probability sample | 3,587 | 242 | 6.7 | Mexican-American, Chicano, Puerto Rican, Other Hispanic |
| Health and Nutrition Examination Survey II (1975–80) | probability sample | 20,322 | 1,189 | 5.8 | Chicano, Cuban, Mexican, Mexicano Mexican-American, Puerto Rican, Other Spanish |
| National Survey of Family Growth (1976) | stratified multistage probability sample | 8,611 | 481 | 5.6 | Cuban, Mexican, Chicano, Mexican-American, Puerto Rican, Other Spanish |
| National Survey of Attitudes toward Social Security (1979) | random area sample: East, Midwest, South, and West | 1,549 | 84 | 5.4 | Hispanic |
| National Survey of Family Growth (1973) | stratified, multistage probability sample | 9,797 | 489 | 5.0 | Cuban, Chicano, Mexican-American, Puerto Rican, Other Spanish |

Source: Compiled from the *Latino Data Directory* (1985).

Of the remaining four data sets listed in table 2 that fall below the 6% threshold criterion, three employed a probability sampling design as well as a reasonable set of ethnic identifiers: HANES II complete file (1975–80), the National Survey of Family Growth (1976), and National Survey of Family Growth (1973). All three are within one percentage point below the adequate sample-size threshold; yet their design and ethnic identifiers suggest that, while not entirely adequate, these data sets should not be dismissed entirely. Conversely, the National Study of Attitudes toward Social Security employed a random sample and used Hispanic as the only ethnic identifier. These factors relegate it to the category of marginally adequate data.

*Marginal National Data.* Another category of national data sets is shown in table 3. These data sources all fall below the acceptable level of Latino sample size for a national study. Yet the 16 studies listed depict the extensive array of topics for which Latino responses have been recorded. Twelve of them employed some form of probability sampling design. Of these, only 3 used an adequate set of ethnic identifiers. Therefore, while it is not reasonable to expect these data sources to provide adequate profiles of Latinos, they reveal tendencies and plausible hypotheses to examine in further studies. The range of topics addressed by these data sets includes attitudes and perceptions of women, drug abuse and health status, consumer attitudes, family profiles and perceptions about the quality of one's life, and perceptions on political, social, and economic institutions. As such, the Latino data from these sources should not be regarded as conclusive but rather tentative or suggestive.

The *Latino Data Directory* contains still another subset of national data sources as shown in table 4. These are studies, mostly attitude surveys, with unspecified Latino sample sizes. The available documentation is not sufficiently detailed to provide this information. In fact, polls sponsored by media organizations were particularly prone to this deficiency. One curious data set in this group is the 1981 Annual Housing Survey. The 1980 Annual Housing Survey (shown in table 3) has a sample 1.25 times the size of the 1981 survey. It has 2,745 Latinos or 3.4% of the total sample. The 1981 survey has a better set of ethnic identifiers for Latinos, but the number of Latinos in the sample is unspecified in the available documentation for that data set. However, it is reasonable to expect that the Latino sample is in the 3% to 4% range based on 1980 and earlier Annual Housing Surveys. In all

**Table 3**

Major National Surveys with Latino Samples under 5%
(Presented in Descending Order of Latino Sample Size)

| Data Source | Design | Sample Size | | | Latino Ethnic Identifiers |
|---|---|---|---|---|---|
| | | Total | Latino N | % | |
| Health and Nutrition Examination Survey I: Children Ages 1–11 Years (1971–75) | probability sample | 23,808 | 1,121 | 4.7 | Mexican, Spanish |
| National Women's Study (1975) | geographically stratified probability sample | 1,522 | 62 | 4.7 | Mexican, Chicano, Central/South American, Cuban, Puerto Rican |
| General Social Survey (1980) | stratified multistage probability sample | 1,468 | 59 | 4.0 | Mexican, Puerto Rican, Spanish, Other Spanish |
| National Household Survey of Drug Abuse (1982) | probability sample of households | 5,624 | 220 | 3.9 | Hispanic |
| General Social Survey (1982) | stratified multistage probability sample | 1,506 | 51 | 3.4 | Mexican, Puerto Rican, Spanish, Other Spanish |
| Annual Housing Survey (1980) | based on 1970 Census, with updated sample of addresses | 79,976 | 2,745 | 3.4 | Chicano, Mexican, Puerto Rican, Other Spanish |
| American National Election Study (1982) | random probability sample, post-election computer-assisted telephone interviews | 1,418 | 47 | 3.3 | Chicano, Mexican, Puerto Rican, Other Spanish |

*Continued on next page*

| Data Source | Design | Total | Latino N | Latino % | Latino Ethnic Identifiers |
|---|---|---|---|---|---|
| American National Election Study (1978) | panel study; random probability sample of 432 congressional districts | 2,304 | 73 | 3.2 | Puerto Rican, Mexican, Other Spanish |
| Myth and Reality of Aging (1974) | multistage, random cluster sample | 4,254 | 129 | 3.0 | Spanish-American |
| Survey of Consumer Finances (1983) | random sample | 3,824 | 109 | 2.8 | n.a. |
| Survey of Consumer Attitudes (Monthly) (1946–84) | random sample | 700 | 20 | 2.8 | n.a. |
| Quality of American Life (1978) | multistage area probability sample | 3,692 | 103 | 2.7 | Central/South American, Cuban, Mexican, Puerto Rican, Spanish |
| High School Seniors Cohort Study (1973) | representative sample of high school seniors | 16,929 | 441 | 2.6 | Mexican-American, Chicano, Puerto Rican |
| National Fertility Study (1975) | longitudinal national probability sample | 3,403 | 70 | 2.0 | Mexican, Puerto Rican, Spanish Other Latin-American |
| Growth of American Families (1960) | area probability sample | 2,684 | 50 | 1.9 | Central/South American, Mexican, Puerto Rican |
| National Survey of the Aged (1975) | multistage area probability sample of households | 2,143 | 25 | 1.2 | Chicano, Mexican, Puerto Rican |
| Virginia Slims' American Women's Opinion Poll (1972) | multistage area probability sample | 4,020 | 19 | 0.5 | Puerto Rican |

Source: Compiled from the Latino Data Directory (1985)

**Table 4**

Major National Polls and Surveys with Unspecified Latino Sample Sizes

| Data Source | Design | Sample Size | | Latino Ethnic Identifiers |
| | | Total | Latino | |
| --- | --- | --- | --- | --- |
| Annual Housing Survey (1981) | based on 1970 Census with updated sample of addresses | 60,408 | n.a. | Central/South American, Chicano, Cuban, Mexican, Mexican-American, Puerto Rican, Other Spanish |
| Federal Employee Attitudes Survey (1979) | stratified random sample | 13,862 | n.a. | Hispanic-origin |
| Youth Attitudes Tracking Study (1975–83) | random-digit dialing household survey of adults ages 16–21 | 5,000 males 5,000 females | n.a. n.a. | Hispanic |
| CBS/New York Times Election Surveys (1980) | random probability sample | 500–2,000 | n.a. | Hispanic |
| Los Angeles Times National Survey on Economy and Domestic Politics (1982) | probability sample | 1,592 | n.a. | Hispanic |
| Los Angeles Times National Survey on Nuclear Weapons Controversy (1982) | probability sample | 1,503 | n.a. | Hispanic |

Source: Compiled from the *Latino Data Directory* (1985).

likelihood, the 1981 Latino sample is larger than in previous survey years due to the enhanced ethnic identifiers used in 1981.

The CBS News/New York Times Survey and the Los Angeles Times National Surveys employed a probability sampling design, yet used the term "Hispanic" as the sole ethnic identifier and are thus likely to have a very inadequate Latino subsample.

### State and Regional Data

The *Latino Data Directory* profiles various state and regional surveys, predominantly public opinion polls. The major regional and state surveys are shown in table 5. Among the topics covered by the state and regional data sources listed are general profiles, health status, attitudes toward marijuana, the so-called California tax revolt, energy use patterns, state policy issues, and regional travel patterns. Of the 12 data sources listed, 8 have a Latino sample size above 6%. While this threshold does not hold for state and regional data (the threshold varies according to the geographic scope of the study and the total number of Latinos residing in that area), it nevertheless provides a point of reference for comparison. Actually, in states with more Latinos a probability sample may be expected to approximate the proportion of Latinos in the state.

As shown in table 5, the Study of Mexican Origin People in the United States (1978), commonly known as the National Chicano Survey, focused exclusively on Chicanos and thus has a 100% Chicano sample. It employed a stratified, multistage area probability design which permitted the identification of an exclusively Chicano sample. By contrast, the Los Angeles Times California Latino Poll (1983) has a probability sample of 1,498 persons yet ended up with only 422 Latinos, or 28.2% of the total sample. Moreover, the Los Angeles Times Poll used the term "Hispanic" as the sole ethnic identifier whereas the National Chicano Survey used a set of eight ethnic identifiers. This comparison illustrates the impact of sampling designs and ethnic identifiers on the size of the Latino sample.

The two most recent studies listed in table 5 both deal with health. In addition, both used only one Latino ethnic identifier. The Colorado Health Survey (1983) used the term "Hispanic" while the California Hypertension Study (1983) used the term "Latino." The Colorado study has a smaller total sample yet ended up with a comparatively larger Latino sample than the California study despite the fact that both used a random sample design. In large part, this is a result of the population on which the study focused. The Colorado study restricted the target population to the medically indigent while the California study drew its sample from the state's entire adult population.

The California Poll data sets from 1971 to 1984 cited in table 5 employed a cross-sectional design and three ethnic identifiers. The 15-year average Latino sample size is 9.6%. Despite the marginal design, these data sets have an acceptable sample-size range and focus on a great variety of salient public issues. In the aggregate, they permit an assessment of public opinions and perceptions over a considerable period of time.

**Local Area Surveys**

A number of local surveys conducted principally in cities in the Southwest are also included in the *Latino Data Directory*. A sampling of such studies is shown in table 6. Among the topics covered by these local area surveys are family characteristics, income and household expenditure patterns, political attitudes, voting patterns, attitudes toward undocumented immigrants, and general policy surveys.

Three of the seven data files listed in table 6 have an exclusively Chicano sample: the Austin Family Survey (1971), the Mexican-American Political Attitudes and Behavior Survey (1983), and the Survey of Chicano Business People Attitudes on Undocumented Workers (1982). These surveys employed nonprobability sampling designs. The Austin Family Survey and the Survey of Chicano Business People Attitudes on Undocumented Workers used the term "Mexican-American" as the sole ethnic identifier. The Mexican-American Political Attitudes and Behavior Survey (MAPABS) used six ethnic identifiers.

It is interesting to note that the 1983 MAPABS derived its sample from lists of Spanish-surnamed voters while the 1981–82 MAPABS used a systematic random sample design in San Antonio and a multistage cluster design in East Los Angeles. These latter surveys, as a set, have a 74% Latino sample in contrast to the 100% sample of the 1983 survey. All of the MAPAB surveys used a set of six ethnic identifiers, yet in the 1981–82 survey the ethnic identifiers served to screen and classify the sample whereas the 1983 survey employed the ethnic identifiers to classify the respondents' self-identification.

**Table 5**
Major State and Regional Surveys
(Reported in Descending Order of Latino Sample Size)

| Data Source | Geographic Scope | Design | Sample Size | | | Latino Ethnic Identifiers |
|---|---|---|---|---|---|---|
| | | | Total | Latino N | % | |
| Mexican Origin People in the United States (1978) | California, Texas, Arizona, New Mexico, Colorado; Chicago and Oklahoma City SMSAs | stratified multistage area probability sample | 10,574 | 10,574 | 100.0 | Central/South American, Cuban, Mexican, Mexicano, Puerto Rican, Spanish, Latin American |
| Los Angeles Times California Latino Poll (1983) | California | probability sample | 1,498 | 422 | 28.2 | Hispanic |
| Colorado Health Survey (1983) | Colorado | random sample of medically indigent households | 1,000 | 280 | 28,0 | Hispanic |
| California Hypertension Study: Combined File (1983) | California | random sample of California adults | 6,381 | 954 | 15.0 | Latino |
| Public Attitudes toward Marijuana (1976) | California | representative cross-sectional design | 1,033 | 129 | 12.5 | Mexican-American, Other Spanish |

| | | | | | | |
|---|---|---|---|---|---|---|
| California Polls (Field Institute) (1971–84) | California | cross-sectional poll | 1,124 (15 year average) | 109 | 9.6 | Central/South American, Mexican, Other Spanish |
| California Tax Revolt Study (1979) | California | random sample | 1,788 | 149 | 8.3 | Mexican-American, Other Latin-American |
| Florida Annual Policy Survey (1982) | Florida | two-stage random digit dialing telephone survey | 1,086 | 73 | 6.7 | Hispanic origin |
| Florida Energy Survey, Wave II (1981) | Florida | two-stage random digit dialing telephone survey | 800 | 30 | 3.8 | Hispanic origin |
| Los Angeles Times Poll (1979–82) | California | probability sample of California voters | 1,473 | | n.a. | Spanish speaking, Hispanic |
| Bay Area Travel Survey (1973–74) | San Francisco (California) Bay Area | random sample | 5,171 | | n.a. | Mexican-American, Other Spanish-American |
| Bay Area Survey II (1972) | five San Francisco (California) Bay Area counties | probability sample with oversample of blacks | 963 | | n.a. | Mexican-American, Other Spanish-American |

Source: Compiled from the *Latino Data Directory* (1985).

**Table 6**
Selected Local Area Surveys

| Data Source | Geographic Scope | Design | Sample Size | | | Latino Ethnic Identifiers |
|---|---|---|---|---|---|---|
| | | | Total | Latino N | Latino % | |
| Austin Family Survey (1971) | Austin, Texas | survey of married Mexican-American couples | 348 | 348 | 100.0 | Mexican-American |
| Mexican-American Political Attitudes and Behavior Survey (1983) | Phoenix, Arizona | telephone survey of Spanish-surnamed registered voters | 419 | 419 | 100.0 | Chicano, Hispanic, Latino, Mexicano, Mexican-American, Other Spanish |
| Survey of Chicano Business People (Attitudes) on Undocumented Workers (1982) | Austin, Texas | random selection from 1980 *Mexican-American Directory* | 73 | 73 | 100.0 | Mexican-American |
| Mexican-American Political Attitudes and Behavior Survey (1981–82) | San Antonio, East Los Angeles | systematic random sample in San Antonio; multistage cluster sample in East Los Angeles | 1,215 | 903 | 74.3 | American, Chicano, Hispanic, Mexican-American, Mexicano, Other Spanish |
| Seattle-Denver Income Maintenance Experiment (1970–76) | Seattle, Denver | longitudinal survey of low-income households | 6,630 | 2,135 | 32.2 | Chicano |
| Los Angeles Metropolitan Survey VIII (1973) | Los Angeles County | multistage stratified probability sample | 1,028 | n.a. | | Spanish-surname |
| Los Angeles Metropolitan Survey IV (1972) | Los Angeles County | multistage stratified probability sample | 1,006 | n.a. | | Spanish-surname |

Source: Compiled from the *Latino Data Directory* (1985).

The Seattle-Denver Income Maintenance Experiment (1970–76) is a longitudinal survey of low-income households in these two cities. Despite its use of a nonprobability design and only one ethnic identifier, the large number of Latinos in the sample (2,135 persons) offsets much of the expected sampling error. The data set is thus quite adequate for use in secondary analyses if one handles the data with some cautious skepticism.

The Los Angeles Metropolitan Area Surveys (1972, 1973) employed a stratified probability sample and include over 1,000 respondents. While the size of the Latino sample is not specified and the term "Spanish-surnamed" is the sole ethnic identifier used, the strength of the design suggests that a reasonable Latino sample size is included in the survey and is likely adequate for secondary analyses.

## Conclusion

An overview of the data files in the *Latino Data Directory* suggests two tendencies. First, an extensive record of Latino opinions, attitudes, and status on a great variety of subjects has been compiled over the years. Second, the adequacy of this public record varies greatly.

The 220 studies listed in the data directory represent a significant investment in both time and resources. The cost of conducting these studies ranges from $20,000 to $2 million each. Assuming an average cost of $60,000 per study—a modest estimate—the aggregate cost of this corpus of data is $13.2 million. With this level of investment, one would expect a solid foundation of data resources upon which Latino research could build. However, the quality of the data is so uneven that a considerable amount of effort remains ahead. The truly adequate data resources are few.

The systematic omission of Latinos from many major studies conducted by otherwise first-rate organizations is an acute problem that plagues the development of adequate Latino data resources. This assessment of the *Latino Data Directory* poignantly reveals that many researchers either entirely overlook the value of enumerating Latinos in their sample population or do not enumerate Latinos in meaningful ways. These practices are so common, yet can be so readily corrected, that their prevalence suggests a deep-rooted and virtually impervious bias in the research community.

It is not as if the research community and funding agencies are unaware of this issue. In the past decade, several significant attempts have been made to alert federal agencies about this deficiency. In 1974, the report *Counting the Forgotten* by the U.S. Commission on Civil Rights decried the absence of adequate data on the nation's minority population. Also that year, Congressman Edward R. Roybal attached a rider to a House appropriations bill encouraging enumeration of Hispanics in federally funded studies. While this initiative was never enacted, it signaled a concern about the availability of adequate Latino data resources on which to formulate social policy. In 1976, the so-called Roybal Amendment (P.L. 94-311) was enacted and required the Department of Labor to collect Hispanic unemployment data and further required other departments to collect and publish "statistics which indicate the social, health and economic conditions of Americans of Spanish origin or descent." Despite this legislative effort, the problem persists. In 1978 a report by the Civil Rights Commission, *Improving Hispanic Unemployment Data: The Department of Labor's Continuing Obligation*, noted a failure to comply with the provisions of P.L. 94-311 to improve Latino data collection and reporting procedures by the Labor Department. More recently, a task force on Latino data needs convened by the Ford Foundation in 1983–84 reported that the issue of enumeration and proper classification of Latinos by federal agencies continued to be a widespread problem.

This brief chronology of attempts to improve the quality of Latino data resources suggests that the problem is a deeply embedded one. Previous efforts to call attention to the problem and to legislate solutions have met nominal success. A much more vigorous and concerted effort to educate researchers and funding agencies and to monitor periodically their progress in developing adequate data resources on Latinos is needed. A well-orchestrated effort to educate researchers and to encourage funding agencies to enumerate Latinos adequately would significantly alter the quality and utility of the next generation of data resources on Latinos. Their value to scholars and policymakers would be incalculable. Failure to upgrade the quality of Latino data resources would be a costly and strategic error to this nation, because social policy on Latinos would continue to be formulated in an environment of inadequate data resources, which would invariably undermine its benefits.

# A Guide to Survey Research on Latino Public Opinion

Elizabeth R. Forsyth, *CMAS, University of Texas*
Cesar M. Melgoza, *CMAS, University of Texas*

Encouraged by the growing size and influence of the Latino community and the increasing public reliance on opinion polls, scholars are now systematically researching Latino public opinions and attitudes. This is a relatively new development, as F. Chris Garcia, Rodolfo O. de la Garza, and Donald J. Torres have shown in *The Mexican American Experience* (1985). Very little was written on Latino political attitudes and behavior prior to 1970 and the vast majority of research has been published in the last 10 years.

The purpose of this guide is to complement Garcia, de la Garza, and Torres' review of the literature on Mexican American political life by expanding the focus to all Latinos, and narrowing the scope to public opinion research based on survey data. Following their lead, this directory covers only the last 10 years. Research appearing before that time has been covered by the 1973 *Social Science Quarterly* special issue on Mexican Americans and by Leo Grebler, Joan W. Moore, and Ralph C. Guzman's classic work, *The Mexican American People* (1970).

This is not a review of the literature but an annotated guide to the scholarly research on Latino public opinion that has appeared in books and academic journals since 1975. It includes research that is explicitly based on surveys of Mexican Americans, Cubans, Puerto Ricans, and other Latinos. It does not include demographic profiles based on survey research, descriptive works that discuss Latino attitudes without reference to survey data, newspapers and magazine articles, or theses and dissertations. With a few exceptions, the research included has appeared in published form.

The citations included in this guide were gathered via a thorough and systematic process. Many of the citations were found by reviewing the literature in major scholarly journals and by sifting through relevant works published as monographs and books. Other indices such as *The ABC of Political Science* and the *American Public Opinion Index* were also consulted. To ensure the complete inclusiveness of this guide, three major databases were searched electronically. They are Sociological Abstracts, Social Science Research, and Public Affairs Information Service.

The search strategy performed using the computerized databases included two groups of concepts necessary for the wide coverage in this guide: These concepts are (*a*) Hispanic(s) or Latino(s) or Chican(o,a,s) or Cuban(o,a,s) or Puerto Rican(s), and (*b*) Poll(s) or Survey(s) or Public Opinion(s) or Attitude(s) or Voter(s).

In effect, literally hundreds of journals and books were searched for articles containing relevant information. Virtually all the information gleaned from the searches was contained in the University of Texas at Austin libraries or owned by the researchers; all of the key articles and books are summarized in this article. It was our intent to make this guide comprehensive, but we suspect we have missed some items. We therefore invite readers to send information on any items that we have overlooked.

The aim of this bibliographic guide is to encourage research on Latino public opinion by highlighting and facilitating access to the work produced since 1975. Times have changed since 1980 when Lawrence Flood reviewed the principal political science journals and found only nine articles on Mexican American politics. The amount of research contained in this directory and the variety of surveys on which it is based indicate the growing scholarly interest in Latino political attitudes and behavior.

Achor, Shirley. *Mexican Americans in a Dallas Barrio*. Tucson: University of Arizona Press, 1978, 202 pp.

The author supplements her participant observation of a Mexican American neighborhood in Dallas, Texas, by interviewing 23 men and women about their socioeconomic characteristics and their attitudes toward, and opinions on, a wide variety of subjects. The issues addressed include the subjects' expectations for the future, evaluations of specific government programs and actions, attitudes toward family, recognition of Mexican American civic organizations, and perception of principal problems facing their neighborhood.

Alba, Richard. "Ethnic Networks and Tolerant Attitudes." *Public Opinion Quarterly* 42, no. 1 (Spring 1978): 1–16.

Using data from a 1963 survey of Catholic Americans, the author argues for the need to account for cultural change when looking for ethnic differences in survey data. To this end, he analyzes the responses of 10 ethnic groups, including Latinos, to questions about their social networks and their attitudes toward the subjects of free speech and child rearing.

Andrade, Sally Jo, and Marcia G. Torres. *Aspirations of Adolescent Hispanic Females for Marriage, Children, Education and Employment.* Washington, D.C.: Hispanic Youth Employment Center, National Council of La Raza, 1982, 176 pp.

This report to the Hispanic Youth Employment Research Center is based on data from the 1976 National Longitudinal Survey of Labor Force Behavior and the 1980 High School and Beyond Survey. Both surveys provide information on the attitudes of Latino, black, and Anglo youth toward marriage, children, sex roles, education, and employment. The 1976 survey, which was conducted by the Department of Labor, interviewed 12,686 adolescents, 2,002 of whom were Latinos. The 1980 survey, administered by the National Opinion Research Center, interviewed 58,270 high school sophomores, 6,695 of whom were Latinos. In addition to describing the circumstances and attitudes of minority youth, this report discusses the policy implications of gender and ethnic differences.

Antunes, George, and Charles M. Gaitz. "Ethnicity and Participation: A Study of Mexican Americans, Blacks, and Whites." *American Journal of Sociology* 80, no. 5 (March 1975): 1192–1211.

This article uses survey data to test the hypothesis that, when social class is controlled, groups which are the targets of discrimination will participate to a greater degree than Anglos in the social and political process. It analyzes data from a 1969–70 survey of 1,441 Anglo, black, and Mexican American adults concerning their social and political behavior, social attitudes, leisure activities, value preferences, and mental health. The survey was conducted by the National Opinion Research Center and replicates previous studies of blacks.

Austin American-Statesman. Research Department. *A Survey of Mexican American in Austin.* Austin: Austin American-Statesman, Inc., 1981, 40 pp.

In 1982, the Austin American-Statesman, Austin's daily newspaper, interviewed 411 Mexican Americans living throughout the city. This report presents the respondents' principal concerns, their perceptions of discrimination and equal opportunity, their preference for ethnic labels, and their attitudes toward undocumented workers, busing, and policy-community relations.

Other questions inquired about their socioeconomic characteristics and media use. The questionnaire and verbatim responses to open-ended questions are included.

Baird, Frank L. "The Search for a Constituency: Political Validation of Mexican-American Candidates in the Texas Great Plains." *Mexican Americans: Political Power, Influence or Resource*, edited by Frank L. Blair. Lubbock: Texas Tech University, 1977, pp. 77–94.

Utilizing information on the local and county election campaigns of Mexican Americans in five Texas cities, this study seeks to identify and evaluate the qualities most necessary to Mexican Americans for their election to public office. Its data consist of election returns for the years 1968 through 1974, census data, and a survey of 55 Mexican American leaders and candidates in Amarillo, Lubbock, San Angelo, Midland, and Odessa.

Belenchia, Joanne. *Latinos and Chicago Politics*. Blue Cover Series, Chicago Politics Papers no. 3. Evanston: Center for Urban Affairs, Northwestern University, 1979, 27 pp.

This report uses data presented by John Walton and Luis M. Salces in their 1977 work *The Political Organization of Chicago's Latino Communities* to produce a profile of Mexican, Cuban, and Puerto Rican voting patterns in Chicago.

Brischetto, Robert R., and Rodolfo O. de la Garza. *The Mexican American Electorate: Political Participation and Ideology*. Mexican American Electorate Series, Occasional Paper no. 3. Austin: Center for Mexican American Studies, University of Texas at Austin; San Antonio: Southwest Voter Registration Education Project, 1983, 34 pp.

This study constitutes the third project in a series of reports based on surveys of 622 Mexican American citizens of voting age—359 in San Antonio and 263 in East Los Angeles—that were conducted by the Southwest Voter Registration Education Project (SVREP) between November 1981 and January 1982. The report's objective is to assist community organizers and political leaders in understanding the charcter, views, and demands of the Mexican American electorate. This report in particular focuses on Mexican American partisanship, ideology, electoral behavior, and political efficacy with regard to age, gender, marital status, education, employment, income, voter status, and citizenship.

Buehler, Marilyn H. "Voter Turnout and Political Efficacy among Mexican-Americans in Michigan." *Sociological Quarterly* 18, no. 4 (Autumn 1977): 504–17.

The objective of this report is to answer three questions regarding Mexican American political attitudes and participation: (1) Do the terms "apathetic" and "fatalistic" accurately describe the urban Mexican American population? (2) To what extent are low voter turnout and a sense of political powerlessness consequences of the Mexican American subculture? (3) Are differences between Mexican Americans and other groups, and within the Mexican American community, attributable to differences in socioeconomic status, organizational and political participation, and media exposure? The data are drawn from a survey of 465 Mexican American adult males which was conducted in Michigan between October 1967 and March 1968.

Buzan, Bert C. "Chicano Community Control, Political Cynicism, and the Validity of Political Trust Measures." *Western Political Quarterly* 33, no. 1 (March 1980): 108–20.

This article examines the affective and behavioral political orientations within two Chicano communities, one controlled by Chicanos and the other by a coalition of Anglos and Chicanos. Analyzing the responses of Texas high school students to a written questionnaire, the author hypothesizes that Chicanos living in a Chicano-controlled community will be more politically distrustful than Chicanos in a bi-ethnically controlled community.

Cain, Bruce E., and D. Roderick Kiewiet. "Ethnicity and Electoral Choice: Mexican American Voting Behavior in the California Thirtieth Congressional District." *Social Science Quarterly* 65, no. 2 (June 1984): 315–27.

This report examines the impact of race and ethnicity on the 1982 election in Los Angeles' Thirtieth Congressional District. Using data from telephone surveys taken just before and immediately after the election, the authors study Mexican American voting in relation to party loyalty, issues of concern, and evaluation of the candidates.

Cobas, Jose A. "Status Consciousness and Leftism: A Study of Mexican-American Adolescents." *Social Forces* 55, no. 4 (1977): 1028–42.

Using survey data collected on Mexican American high school students in Crystal City, Texas, in 1974, the paper tests a model which posits the effects of ethnic consciousness on "system blame," and of system blame on political leftism. The sample consists of 271 tenth through twelfth grade students. Correlation statistics are presented to test the effectiveness of the model. The authors conclude that, with some exceptions, their results support the model.

Comer, John C. "Street Level Bureaucracy and Political Support: Some Findings on Mexican Americans." *Urban Affairs Quarterly* 14, no. 2 (December 1978): 207–28.

Using a sample survey of Mexican Americans in Omaha, Nebraska ($N = 146$), the author investigates the relationship between Mexican American individuals and the representatives of governmental institutions with whom the subjects had come into contact. The survey is particularly valuable since it offers information on Mexican Americans in a nonsouthwestern region. The data in this survey include measures of satisfaction from specific governmental agencies, of political efficacy, and of voter registration.

Cole, Stephen. *Attitudes toward Bilingual Education among Hispanics and a Nationwide Sample*. New York: Center for the Social Sciences, Columbia University, 1983, 130 pp.

This report presents the findings of two surveys, one of 518 Latinos living in New York and Los Angeles and another of people living throughout the United States. The aim of these surveys was to discover how Latinos feel about bilingual education and how their attitudes differ from those of the general public. After looking at the characteristics that correlate with an individual's attitudes, the author discusses the reasons why individuals do or do not support bilingual education. Appendices include charts presenting the data, the questionnaire used, and a discussion of methodology and sampling problems.

de la Garza, Rodolfo O. *Chicano Political Elite Perceptions of the Undocumented Worker: An Empirical Analysis*. Working Papers in U.S.-Mexican Studies no. 31. San Diego: Program in U.S.-Mexican Studies, University of California, 1981, 24 pp.

This description of how Chicano political leaders perceive the issue of undocumented workers compares their views with the attitudes attributed to the Chicano community by political leaders and scholars. Its purpose is to provide decision makers with accurate information on Chicano attitudes in order to allow them to formulate policies responsive to Chicano interests. The data come from 241 interviews with state and national political appointees, congressional representatives, organizational leaders, and community spokespersons. The interviews, which took place between 1978 and 1980, form part of a larger study of Chicano political elites.

de la Garza, Rodolfo O., and Robert R. Brischetto, with David Vaughn. *The Mexican American Electorate: Information Sources and Policy Orientations.* Mexican American Electorate Series, Occasional Paper no. 2. Austin: Center for Mexican American Studies, University of Texas at Austin; San Antonio: Southwest Voter Registration Education Project, 1983, 26 pp.

This study constitutes the second in a series of reports based on surveys conducted by the Southwest Voter Registration Education Project in San Antonio and East Los Angeles between November 1981 and January 1982. The objective of these reports is to assist community organizers and political leaders in understanding the character, views, and demands of the Mexican American electorate. This report describes information sources (radio, television, newspapers) and policy orientations of Mexican Americans in San Antonio and East Los Angeles to determine whether a correlation exists between them. The authors also correlate information source variables with language ability, age, and education variables to derive fuller understanding of the Mexican American electorate.

de la Garza, Rodolfo O., and Janet Weaver. *The Mexican American Electorate: An Explanation of Their Opinions and Behavior.* Mexican American Electorate Series, Occasional Paper no. 4. Austin: Center for Mexican American Studies, University of Texas at Austin; San Antonio: Southwest Voter Registration Education Project, 1984, 17 pp.

This study is the fourth in a series based on surveys of 359 Mexican Americans in San Antonio and 213 Mexican Americans in East Los Angeles conducted by the Southwest Voter Registration Education Project between November 1981 and January 1982. The report's objective is to assist community organizers in understanding the character, views, and demands of the Mexican American electorate; it builds on previous papers in the series to develop a comprehensive understanding of Mexican American political opinions and behavior, as well as to suggest strategies for increasing Mexican American electoral involvement.

de la Garza, Rodolfo O., and David Vaughn. "The Political Socialization of Chicano Elites: A Generational Approach." *Social Science Quarterly* 65, no. 2 (June 1984): 290–307.

Using information collected in 241 interviews with Chicano political and community leaders, the authors develop and test a generational model to explain the development of contemporary Chicano political elites. This model takes into account the political experiences and motivations of Chicano leaders for the purpose of understanding and predicting how Chicano elites define and carry out their roles.

de la Garza, Rodolfo O., and Janet Weaver. "Chicano and Anglo Public Policy Perspectives in San Antonio: Does Ethnicity Make a Difference?" *Social Science Quarterly* 66, no. 3 (September 1985): 576–86.

This study measures the relative impact of ethnicity and socioeconomic characteristics on Chicano and Anglo attitudes toward various national issues and specific government spending policies. The analysis is based on separate surveys of Chicanos and Anglos that were conducted by the Southwest Voter Registration Education Project in San Antonio.

de la Puente, Manuel. *A Preliminary Analysis of the Occupational Aspirations of Hispanic, Black, and White Youths: The Role of Government-sponsored Employment and Training.* Washington, D.C.: National Council of La Raza, 1982, 86 pp.

The 1979 National Longitudinal Survey of Labor Force Behavior and Youth provides the data for this study of the occupational aspirations of Latino, black, and Anglo youth ages 14 to 21. Approximately 12,700 youths participated in the survey which contains information on the impact of participating in government-sponsored employment training programs on youth aspirations. This study evaluates the results of many of these programs.

Garcia, John A. "An Analysis of Chicano and Anglo Electoral Patterns in School Board Elections." *Ethnicity* 6, no. 2 (June 1979): 168–83.

This examination of Arizona school board elections investigates the extent to which voters prefer candidates of their own ethnic/racial background, the sociopolitical factors that affect these voting preferences, and the degree of polarization among Chicano and Anglo voters. The author uses returns from the Pima County Election Bureau and matches them with demographic characteristics available from the U.S. Bureau of the Census.

_____. "The Political Integration of Mexican Immigrants: Explorations into the Naturalization Process." *International Migration Review* 15 (Winter 1981): 608–25.

This article examines the naturalization of Mexican immigrants as a significant indicator of political integration into the American system. The author extracted 369 Mexican-born respondents from the National Chicano Survey (University of Michigan, 1979) to produce a profile of that population in terms of demographics, labor market experience, immigration background, socioeconomic and political characteristics, and naturalization status. The purpose of this study is to understand naturalization patterns in order to more fully comprehend the Mexican pattern of low naturalization and low political integration into the United States.

————. "Yo Soy Mexicano . . . : Self-Identity and Sociodemographic Correlates." *Social Science Quarterly* 62, no. 1 (March 1981): 88–98.

This study examines the effects of age, state of residence, place of birth, sex, income, and educational attainment on the choice of ethnic labels among Mexican Americans in the Southwest. The labels studied include Mexican American, Chicano, Mexican, Mexicano, and Other Spanish. At the heart of this inquiry is the effort to understand the relationship between concepts such as ethnic identity, cultural loyalty, and cultural assimilation, and sociopolitical attitudes and behavior. The analysis is based on the 1976 Survey of Income and Education conducted in Arizona, New Mexico, California, Colorado, and Texas by the U.S. Bureau of the Census. That survey includes information on education, labor markets, health status, program assistance, and language use.

Glazer, Nathan. "The Structure of Ethnicity." *Public Opinion* 9, no. 5 (October-November 1984): 2–5.

This examination of ethnicity, values, and political choice is based on data collected by the National Opinion Research Center and published as "The Opinion Roundup" in this issue of *Public Opinion*. The data, which are presented in charts, break down the responses of 12 ethnic groups (including Hispanics) to questions about their political and cultural opinions and behavior. The author uses the data to explore the changing values and coalitions which determine the impact of ethnicity on American politics and society.

Girl Scouts of the U.S.A. "The Impact of Minority Presence in Girl Scouting on White and Minority Communities." New York, 1981, 213 pp.

The study examines the attitudes of girl scout members and nonmembers toward minority presence and participation in girl scouting. The study involved 6,000 respondents including 439 Hispanics throughout the USA and may actually be broken down to five studies within one: *internally*, studying attitudes of girl members; girl nonmembers; and adult members. *Externally*, studying attitudes of the general public; and an over-sampling of minorities in the general public. The study was exploratory, not explanatory and the objective was to explore the major social and economic background characters that are related to attitudes about minorities in girl scouting.

Guzman, Ralph. *The Political Socialization of the Mexican American People*. New York: Arno Press, 1976, 266 pp.

This book includes a chapter on Mexican American voting behavior which contributes to its central thesis: that Mexican American political socialization is directly related to the conditions of their social contact with the majority. The author studies Mexican American voter registration patterns using survey data from Los Angeles County and San Antonio that were collected in 1965 by UCLA's Mexican American Study Project.

HACER, Inc. and the National Women's Center. *New York City Hispanics: Who Votes and How?* Washington, D.C.: Hispanic Policy Development Project, 1984, 35 pp.

In November 1984, HACER conducted an exit poll of 1,502 Latinos in New York City. This publication reports the findings of that poll, paying particular attention to the effect of ethnic and gender differences on party affiliation, voting behavior, and opinions on 12 key issues. The ethnic groups interviewed were Puerto Ricans, Cubans, Dominicans, and Others. The issues addressed were U.S. policy toward El Salvador and Nicaragua; normalization of U.S./Cuban relations; talks with Cuba; nuclear freeze; amnesty for undocumented workers; employer sanctions; equal rights amendment; Reagan's economic policies; cuts in federal spending for social programs; and increased spending for bilingual programs.

Hernandez, Andrew. *The Latino Vote in the 1976 Presidential Election: A Political Research Report*. San Antonio: Southwest Voter Registration Education Project, 1977, 22 pp.

This analysis of the national impact of the Latino electorate on the 1976 presidential election is based on the returns in census tracts of 475 precincts in 34 cities. Those returns provide information on the number of Latinos registered in each precinct, the number of ballots cast, and the number of votes received by the major party candidates. Short sections discuss the Latino vote in the states of Arizona, California, Colorado, New Mexico, Texas, New York, Illinois, and Florida.

Hill, Robert B. "The Polls and Ethnic Minorities." *Annals of the Academy of Political and Social Sciences: Polling and the Democratic Consensus* 472 (March 1984): 155–66.

This critique traces the development of polling on racial attitudes and identifies problems inherent in existing polls of minorities. In particular, the critique discusses the selection of study populations; the method of data collection; the selection of polling topics; the use of basic concepts such as beliefs and values; the relationship between attitudes and action; the measurement of overt behavior; the relationship between prejudice and discrimination; and the use of multilevel analysis. The author also offers suggestions for improving minority polling.

Hirsch, Herbert, and Armando Gutierrez. *Learning to Be Militant: Ethnic Identity and the Development of Political Militance in a Chicano Community.* San Francisco: R & E Research Associates, 1977, 146 pp.

Interviews with 726 high school students in Crystal City, Texas, support this discussion of Chicano ethnic and political self-identification. The author's objective is to understand the differences in ethnic self-identification and to examine their consequences for political perception and behavior.

Institute for Puerto Rican Policy. *Puerto Ricans and the 1984 Presidential Race: A Report on the First National Puerto Rican Opinion Survey.* New York: Institute for Puerto Rican Policy, 1984, 13 pp.

The National Puerto Rican Opinion Survey is a poll conducted by the Institute for Puerto Rican Policy of the National Puerto Rican Policy Network, an organization representing the professional sector of the Puerto Rican community. In 1984, 558 Puerto Rican professionals responded to 10 questions posed by the Institute for Puerto Rican Policy. These questions were designed to discover how Puerto Rican professionals were planning to vote in the 1984 election; how they viewed Reagan's economic and political policies; and how probable they felt nuclear war to be. The responses are analyzed by gender, region, and voter registration status. Appendixes contain the questionnaire, the survey results, and a comparison of Puerto Rican responses to those of blacks, Mexican Americans, and the general population.

Jasso, Guillermina. "Attitudes toward International Migration among Texans: Advance Report." Preliminary draft of a report of the Special Assistant to the Commissioner of the Immigration and Naturalization Service, 1979, 29 pp.

In 1978, the Immigration and Naturalization Service conducted a massive survey of the attitudes of Hispanic and non-Hispanic Texans toward immigration. This preliminary report focuses on the attitudes expressed toward six immigration issues addressed by the survey: the granting of amnesty for illegal immigrants; the creation of a temporary resident alien status; the imposition of employer sanctions on those who hire illegal immigrants; a change in the Mexican quota of immigrants; the policy of giving preferential treatment to immigrant family members; and the current level of spending for border enforcement. The responses to each of these issues are broken down by region as well as ethnicity. The findings, the survey methodology, and the procedure followed for interpreting the results are all discussed in detail.

Jennings, James. *Puerto Rican Politics in New York City.* Washington, D.C.: University Press of America, 1977, 275 pp.

Focusing on three types of Puerto Rican leaders, this book employs interviews with 40 Puerto Rican elected and community leaders to study the effect of demographic variables and political structures on leadership styles. Particular emphasis is placed on the relationships of, and between, leaders.

Karnig, Albert K., and Susan Welch. "Sex and Ethnic Differences in Municipal Representation." *Social Science Quarterly* 60, no. 3 (December 1979): 465–81.

This study compares the levels of black, Anglo, Mexican American, male, and female municipal government representation, paying special attention to differences between minority male and female representation and to the question of minority competition. Data come from 1978 and 1979 mail surveys of mayors and city councilmembers in 365 communities around the country. Census data provide figures on income and education.

Kuvlesky, William P. *Gender Differences among Mexican American Youth: A Synthesis of Results from Texas Research, 1967–1980.* San Antonio: College of Business, University of Texas at San Antonio, 1981, 68 pp.

Texas A&M University conducted surveys in 1967 and 1973 of Mexican American high school sophomores in Dimmit, Maverick, Starr, and Zapata Counties, Texas. There were 341 students in the first survey and 379 in the second. This study uses the data from those surveys to explore the differences between Mexican American male and female social orientation and behavior. The questions asked fall into four categories: status projections and values; language use patterns; religious orientation and behavior; and ethnic labeling preferences.

Kuvlesky, William P., and Everett D. Edington. "Ethnic Group Identity and Occupational Status Projections of Teenage Boys and Girls." *Politics and Society in the Southwest: Ethnicity and Chicano Pluralism*, edited by Z. Anthony Kruszewski, Richard L.

Hough, and Jacob Ornstein-Galicia. Boulder: Westview Press, 1982, pp. 67–102.

Focusing on the relationship between occupational aspirations and expectations, this study uses data collected in 1972 and 1973 to compare Mexican American, Anglo, black, and Navajo high school sophomores in Arizona and Texas. The two surveys interviewed 385 Navajo, 192 black, 379 Mexican American, and 331 Anglo teens.

Lamare, James W. "The Political Integration of Mexican American Children: A Generational Analysis." *International Migration Review* 16, no. 1 (Spring 1982): 169–88.

This article explores the importance of national origin in political integration by studying the political orientations of five generations of Mexican American children. In 1978, 700 Mexican American children in the El Paso school system answered a written questionnaire that was designed to measure their assimilation and political acculturation in the United States. This report presents the findings of that survey.

_____ . "Sociopolitical Reactions to Public Policy: Tenant Attitudes about a Relocation Program." *Politics and Society in the Southwest: Ethnicity and Chicano Pluralism*, edited by Z. Anthony Kruszewski, Richard L. Hough, and Jacob Ornstein-Galicia. Boulder: Westview Press, 1982, pp. 237–45.

A 1974 survey of 224 Mexican Americans in El Paso, Texas, provided the data for this assessment of the impact of public policies on sociopolitical attitudes. The author asked lower-income Mexican Americans who had been recently relocated from tenements to public housing how they viewed the government and how they evaluated their new housing and neighborhood. The purpose was to examine their attitudes in relation to the government's relocation policy and their own demographic characteristics.

Lovrich, Nicholas P., Jr., and Otwin Marenin. "A Comparison of Black and Mexican American Voters in Denver: Assertive versus Acquiescent Political Orientations and Voting Behavior in an American Electorate." *Western Political Quarterly* 29, no. 2 (June 1976): 284–94.

Focusing on the distinct political behavior of black and Mexican American voters in Denver's 1971 general municipal election, this study seeks to explain differences in terms of each group's subjective perception of similar social realities. Using a combination of voting results and attitudinal surveys, the authors analyze the patterns of black and Mexican American registration, turnout, vote distribution, and political attitudes that were evident during the election.

MacManus, Susan A. "Identification of Houston's Growth-related Problems." *Houston Initiatives: Phase One Report*. Houston: Rice Center, 1981, pp. 15–17.

Forming part of a larger report, this chapter uses opinion polls conducted since 1975 to identify the attitudes of Houstonians toward growth, their perceptions of Houston's major problems, and their evaluations of the local government's performance. In breaking down the responses by race, the author finds that Anglos, blacks, and Mexican Americans agree on the problems facing Houston, but differ in how they rank the relative seriousness of these problems and in their level of satisfaction with the city's delivery of services.

MacManus, Susan A., and Carol A. Cassel. "Mexican-Americans in City Politics: Participation, Representation, and Policy Preferences." *Urban Interest*, Spring 1982, pp. 57–69.

Based on a 1980 survey of 200 Spanish-surnamed registered voters in Houston, this study explores the political attitudes and policy preferences of Mexican Americans on issues which may be addressed by local officials. The areas examined are the Mexican American community's level of interest in politics; its level of participation in community organizations; its propensity to form alliances with other minorities; and its perception of the major problems facing Houston and the Latino community. In particular, the authors discuss Mexican American attitudes toward citizen-police relations and the provision of tuition-free schooling to the children of undocumented workers.

McKay, Emily, and Raul Yzaguirre. *Recent Hispanic Polls: A Summary of Results*. Washington, D.C.: Hispanic Policy Development Project, 1984, 12 pp.

This report summarizes five major studies on issues of importance to the Latino community: the Southwest Voter Registration Education Project surveys conducted in East Los Angeles and San Antonio between November 1981 and January 1982; the Yankelovich, Clancey, Shulman, Inc. survey market study, "Spanish USA."; the 1983 Public Agenda Foundation survey of elected and appointed Latino officials; the 1983 Coca Cola study of Hispanic markets; and the 1979 National Chicano Survey from the University of Michigan. Issues covered are education, employment, voter participation, immigration, language and media use, and perception of key problems facing the community and of the key institutions addressing those problems.

Martin, George E. *Ethnic Political Leadership: The Case of the Puerto Ricans*. San Francisco: R & E Research Associates, 1977, 148 pp.

For the purpose of testing the applicability to Puerto Ricans of the European ethnic political leadership model, the author interviewed 23 Puerto Rican political leaders in New York City. The interviews took place in June 1974 and were designed to capture the respondents' socioeconomic characteristics and their patterns of political development, activity, attitudes. The questionnaire appears in an appendix.

Melville, Keith, and Harvey Lauer. *Moving into the Political Mainstream*. Washington, D.C.: Hispanic Policy Development Project, 1984, 23 pp.

This is the first part of a two-part report based on a national poll of Latino elected officials conducted by the Public Agenda Foundation in 1983. Questions were put to 444 Latino officials about their perceptions of the principal problems facing Latinos and their opinions of related issues such as the obstacles to increased political participation, low voter turnout, and the effectiveness of institutions serving the Latino community. The questionnaire and the survey results appear in the appendixes.

Melville, Keith, and Harvey Lauer. *Moving Up to Better Education and Better Jobs*. Washington, D.C.: Hispanic Policy Development Project, 1984, 22 pp.

This is the second part of a two-part report based on a national poll conducted by the Public Agenda Foundation in 1983. Questions were asked of 444 Latino officials about their perceptions of the principal problems facing Latinos. In this report, the authors present the officials' opinions on unemployment and lack of job advancement. Specifically, they discuss issues such as undocumented workers, low educational attainment levels, high dropout rates, and language barriers. The questionnaire and the survey results appear in the appendixes.

Miller, Lawrence W., Jerry L. Polinard, and Robert D. Wrinkle. "Attitudes toward Undocumented Workers: The Mexican American Perspective." *Social Science Quarterly* 65, no. 2 (June 1984): 482–94.

This study explores the influence of education, income, and generation on Mexican American attitudes toward undocumented immigrants and U.S. immigration policy. Using data collected in 501 telephone and personal interviews of Mexican Americans in Hidalgo County, Texas, the authors present a brief discussion of the survey design and consider related issues such as job competition, wage scales, employer sanctions, increased enforcement of immigration laws, and the education of undocumented children.

Montenegro, Marilyn. *Chicanos and Mexican-Americans: Ethnic Self-Identification and Attitudinal Differences*. San Francisco: R & E Research Associates, 1976, 74 pp.

The focus of this study is the relationship between Latinos' ethnic identity and the attitudes they hold. Based on interviews with 92 Latinos attending Roosevelt High School in Boyle Heights, Los Angeles, this report correlates the teens' self-identification as Chicanos, Mexican Americans, or Mexicans with their attitudes toward work and material success, service in the armed forces, education, religion, and sexual roles, and their perceptions of discrimination. The aim is to evaluate the diverse responses of Latinos to their position within American society in terms of their ethnic self-concept. Selected U.S. Census data and the survey instrument appear in the appendixes.

National Council of La Raza. *Perspectives on Undocumented Workers: Black and Hispanic Viewpoints*. Washington, D.C.: National Council of La Raza, 1980, 39 pp.

Interviews with minority leaders form the basis of this inquiry into how blacks and Latinos view the issues of immigration and undocumented workers. This is a descriptive rather than an analytical piece and the sample is not identified or described. The issues covered include job displacement, government costs, proposals for curbing immigration, and media coverage.

National Council on the Aging. *Aging in the Eighties: America in Transition*. Washington, D.C., 1981, 170 pp.

This report, conducted by Lou Harris and Associates, examines trends in the aging experience and public attitudes toward older citizen status and problems. The national sample of 3,452 includes 392 Latinos.

Nelson, Dale. "The Political Behavior of New York Puerto Ricans: Assimilation or Survival?" *The Puerto Rican Struggle: Essays on Survival in the U.S.*, edited by Clara Rodriguez, Virginia Sanchez Korral, and Jose Alers. New York: Puerto Rican Migration Consortium, Inc., 1980, pp. 90–110.

This article tests the relevance of assimilation and acculturation concepts for understanding the political behavior of ethnic groups—in this case of Puerto Ricans. The analysis compares the political participation of Puerto Ricans and other ethnic groups using data from a 1973 survey by Columbia University's New York City Neighborhood Project of 379 Puerto Ricans, Cubans, Dominicans, Jews, Irish, and blacks. The forms of political participation explored are voting in local elections, contacting public officials to deal with neighborhood problems, signing political petitions, joining community problem-solving organizations, and attending neighborhood protest demonstrations. The author suggests that research into the ways that culture influences patterns of political behavior may be more useful than reliance on the concepts of assimilation and acculturation.

"One Hundred Influentials and Their Assessment of the Critical Hispanic Issues." *Hispanic Business* 7, no. 9 (September 1985): 18–34.

This article reports the results of a *Hispanic Business* poll of 100 Latino social and political leaders. It presents their demographic profile as well as their responses to questions about language proficiency, economic development, foreign policy, equal rights, trade agreements, domestic policy, affirmative action, and job training.

Ornstein-Galicia, Jacob, and Paul W. Goodman. "Correlating Bilingualism/Biculturalism and Socio-Educational Factors in a Survey of Mexican-American Students at a Southwestern University." *Politics and Society in the Southwest: Ethnicity and Chicano Pluralism*, edited by Z. Anthony Kruszewski, Richard L. Hough, and Jacob Ornstein-Galicia. Boulder: Westview Press, 1982, pp. 197–214.

Based on surveys conducted by the Cross-Cultural Southwest Ethnic Study Center of 301 University of Texas at El Paso students, this article examines student attitudes toward language loyalty and usage. Emphasis is placed on the relationship between language and use of the university as a vehicle of upward mobility.

Pavlik, Thomas J. *Ethnic Identification and Political Behavior.* San Francisco: R & E Research Associates, 1976, 108 pp.

With a view to understanding ethnic political behavior, this study tests assimilation and persistence theories, questions the nature of ethnic identification, and explores its impact on voting, party identification, political efficacy, political alienation, and acceptance of other minorities. Interviews with 354 Mexicans, Irish, Poles, Lithuanians, and Slavs living in Chicago's working-class neighborhoods provide the data.

Peterson, Robert A., and George Kozmetzsky. "Public Opinion regarding Illegal Aliens in Texas." *Texas Business Review* 56 (May–June 1982): 118–23.

This article outlines the major findings of a survey conducted by the Institute for Constructive Capitalism on illegal immigration. The survey was conducted in August 1981 and utilized telephone interviews of 2,041 adult female and male Hispanic and non-Hispanic heads of households selected from throughout the state of Texas. The survey design employed in this survey allows extrapolation of the results to geographic regions both small and large in population size. The survey participants were asked an open-ended question regarding what they perceived as the most important problem facing the state, as well as questions particular to certain aspects of immigration policy proposals. Details on this survey are available in "Concerns, Issues, and Attitudes: A Texas Survey" (Austin: Institute for Constructive Capitalism, University of Texas at Austin, 1981).

Polinard, Jerry L., Robert D. Wrinkle, and Rodolfo O. de la Garza. "Attitudes of Mexican Americans toward Irregular Mexican Immigration." *International Migration Review* 18, no. 3 (Fall 1984); 782–99.

Utilizing data from 341 telephone and personal interviews conducted in Texas' Hidalgo and Travis Counties, this article focuses on the attitudes of Mexican Americans toward issues relating to U.S. immigration policy. The authors examine the relationships between selected variables (such as income, generation, occupation, and region) and Mexican American attitudes toward immigration issues. The issues included are the provision of schooling for undocumented children, the impact of undocumented workers on the employment of Mexican Americans, the enforcement of employer sanctions, and the use of welfare by the undocumented. The thrust of this inquiry is to determine the extent to which Mexican American leadership accurately reflects Mexican American opinion on immigration issues.

Portes, Alejandro. "The Rise of Ethnicity: Determinants of Ethnic Perceptions among Cuban Exiles in Miami." *American Sociological Review* 49, no. 3 (June 1984): 383–97.

This article traces the evolution of ethnic awareness, defined as the perception of social distance and discrimination, that has developed among Cuban exiles in Miami. It is based on a longitudinal study of 590 adult Cuban males who arrived in the United States in 1972 and 1973. The first survey was carried out in those years, and two follow-up surveys in 1976 and 1979. After examining Cuban ethnic awareness, the author investigates individual differences and discusses the theoretical implications of this study for analyzing differences between labor immigrants and political refugees.

Portes, Alejandro, and Rafael Mozo. "The Political Adaptation Process of Cubans and Other Ethnic Minorities in the United States: A Preliminary Analysis." *International Migration Review* 19, no. 1 (Spring 1985): 35–63.

This article examines the patterns of naturalization, registration, turnout, and voting preference of Cuban Americans in the United States, and contrasts them to those of other Latino groups. The focus is on these patterns as indicators of the integration of Cubans into the American political system. It relies on a variety of data including U.S. Immigration and Naturalization Service reports, Bureau of the Census reports, Metro-Dade Elections Department summaries, and interviews conducted by the authors between 1973 and 1979 of 590 adult male Cuban refugees.

Portes, Alejandro, Juan M. Clark, and Manuel M. Lopez. "Six Years Later: The Process of Incorporation of Cuban Exiles in the United States." *Cuban Studies* 11-12 (January 1982): 1–24.

This report presents the results of a six-year longitudinal study of Cuban exiles for the purpose of profiling recent Cuban immigration. The authors interviewed 590 recently arrived Cuban males in 1973 and 1974 and repeated the interview in 1976 and again in 1979 and 1980. This analysis focuses on the 1979-80 survey, which located and interviewed 70% of the original sample. The questions asked fall into four general categories: residential patterns; education and knowledge of English; attitudes toward self and the host society; and employment and income.

Portes, Alejandro, Robert N. Parker, and Jose A. Cobas. "Assimilation or Consciousness: Perceptions of U.S. Society among Recent Latin American Immigrants to the United States." *Social Forces* 59, no. 1 (September 1980): 200–224.

This study examines attitudes held by recently arrived Mexicans and Cubans about U.S. society in order to clarify the state of interethnic relations and to help predict adaptation patterns among recent immigrants. Using data from a survey of 822 Mexicans arriving in El Paso and Laredo, and of 590 Cubans entering Miami, the authors analyze each group's perception of racial discrimination and of the dominant group's attitudes toward them. The initial interviews were conducted in 1972 and 1973 and the follow-up interviews took place three years later.

Ramirez, Albert, and Ruth Chavez. "Family- and Work-related Attitudes and Aspirations of Hispanic and Non-Hispanic Youth." Paper presented at the National Council of La Raza symposium entitled "Hispanic Youth Employment: Research and Policy Issues," May 21–22, 1982, 34 pp.

This inquiry into the attitudes of Latino youth toward work and family tests 12 hypotheses with data from a 1979 National Longitudinal Study of Youths ages 14 through 21. The total sample consisted of 7,795 individuals, of whom 6,143 were white non-Hispanic and 1,652 were Hispanic. The attitudes examined include knowledge of the world of work, commitment to work, willingness to work, attitudes toward sex roles, occupational expectations, and occupational aspirations.

Rodriguez, Roy C. *Mexican-American Civic Organizations: Political Participation and Political Atittudes.* San Francisco: R & E Research Associates, 1978, 94 pp.

In order to measure the political attitudes of El Paso's middle-class Mexican Americans and their involvement in Mexican American civic organizations, the author surveyed 487 people active in LULAC, the Veterans of Foreign Wars, and the Knights of Columbus. The questions were designed to gather demographic information, measure specific political attitudes (response to democratic norms, political chauvinism, regard for the political process, resistance to change, political alienation, political efficacy, feelings on freedom of speech, and liberal-conservative tendencies), and to evaluate political participation and involvement. The questionnaire is presented in an appendix.

Roog, Eleanor Meyer, and Rosemary Santana Cooney. *Adaptation and Adjustment of Cubans: West New York, New Jersey.* Monograph Series no. 5. New York: Hispanic Research Center, Fordham University, 1980, 93 pp.

This effort to assess the adaptation and adjustment of Cubans in West New York, New Jersey, uses information obtained from 300 interviews with Cuban male and female heads of household. It begins with a demographic profile of the Cuban community in

West New York and proceeds to an analysis of the social characteristics affecting occupational mobility and a description of assimilation and adjustment as reflected in cultural behavior, preferences, and attitudes. Special attention is paid to the Cubans' mental health as perceived through their attitudes and behavior.

Rothenberg, Stuart, and Eric Licht, with Frank Newport. *Ethnic Voters and National Issues: Coalitions in the 1980s.* Washington, D.C.: Free Congress Research and Education Foundation, 1982, 148 pp.

This examination of potential voters in terms of their ethnic background and positions on specific policy questions focuses on five ethnic groups: Latinos, Irish, Italians, Poles, and Jews. After a brief look at the political development of these five groups, the authors examine their responses to economic, social, and foreign policy questions. A final section explores the potential for coalitions and suggests ways for interest groups to define and prioritize issues so as to appeal to ethnic constituents. The national sample consists of 1,000 telephone interviews randomly chosen on the basis of ethnic last name. Ample appendixes contain information on the methodology employed, the questionnaire, and supplementary charts.

Tarrance and Associates. See V. Lance Tarrance and Associates and Peter D. Hart Research Associates.

Torres, Marcia G. *Young Hispanic Mothers Enrolled in School and/or Employed Interviewed in the 1979 National Longitudinal Survey of Labor Force Behavior.* Austin: Center for Applied Systems Analysis, 1982, 70 pp.

Forming part of a final report submitted to the Hispanic Youth Employment Research Center, this paper profiles the socioeconomic situation of young Latina mothers and describes their attitudes toward marriage, children, sex roles, education, and employment. The study uses data from the 1979 National Longitudinal Survey of the Labor Force which interviewed 6,288 young females.

Ugalde, Antonio, Frank D. Bean, and Gilbert Cardenas. "International Migration from the Dominican Republic: Findings from a National Survey." *International Migration Review* 13, no. 2 (Summer 1979): 235–54.

Using a combination of U.S. Census data and information contained in a 1974 survey by the Dominican Ministry of Health of 25,000 Dominican households, this article profiles the Dominican migrant to the United States in terms of socioeconomic status, education, occupational status, sex, and age. Though not strictly about Latino public opinion, it does employ an unusual data set to understand why Dominicans emigrate and why some decide to return.

Villarreal, Roberto E. *Chicano Elites and Non-Elites: An Inquiry into Social and Political Change.* Palo Alto: R & E Research Associates, 1979, 167 pp.

Using two separate surveys, one of 201 Chicano heads of household and another of 31 Chicano political leaders, this report studies social and political change in the semirural Chicano community of Beeville, Texas. After measuring the sociopolitical development of Beeville's Chicano community, the author attempts to determine the critical components for predicting degrees of sociopolitical change and to understand the differences between elite and mass political attitudes and participation.

V. Lance Tarrance and Associates and Peter D. Hart Research Associates. *Hispanic and Black Attitudes toward Immigration Policy.* Washington, D.C.: Federation for American Immigration Reform, 1983, 24 pp.

In June and July of 1983, Peter D. Hart Research Associates and V. Lance Tarrance and Associates conducted a national survey of 1,600 blacks and Latinos for the Federation for American Immigration Reform. This executive summary presents the key findings of that study, which was designed to examine black and Latino attitudes toward U.S. immigration policy. They interviewed both citizens and noncitizens about their attitudes toward the immigration issue in general, their perception of the basic direction of U.S. immigration policy, and their reaction to specific policy proposals. The questionnaires, responses, and a description of the survey methodology are included in this report.

Walton, John, and Luis M. Salces, with Joanne Belenchia. *The Political Organization of Chicago's Latino Communities.* Evanston: Center for Urban Affairs, Northwestern University, 1977, 147 pp.

This effort to portray the political organization of Latinos in Chicago is based on interviews with 130 Latino representativs of community organizations. The topics covered in these interviews include the membership, activities, goals, funding, and problems of their organization as well as their own perceptions of community problems, the identity of community leaders, attitudes toward problem-solving strategies, political participation, and socioeconomic background.

Weeks, Michael, and R. Paul Moore. "Ethnicity-of-Interviewer Effects on Ethnic Respondents." *Public Opinion Quarterly* 45, no. 2 (Summer 1981): 245–49.

Similar to previous studies of blacks, this report analyzes the responses of Cuban Americans, Mexican Americans, Native Americans, and Chinese Americans to interviews conducted by individuals from other ethnic groups. It relies on data collected by the Center for Applied Linguistics and the Research Triangle Institute on the English-language proficiency of 1,472 children from non-English-language backgrounds. The Cuban origin respondents were from Miami, the Mexicans from El Paso, the Native Americans from Arizona, and the Chinese from San Francisco.

Welch, Susan. "Identity in the Ethnic Political Community and Political Behavior." *Ethnicity* 4, no. 3 (September 1977): 216–25.

This paper examines the effect of group identification on the political behavior of Mexican Americans with a view to predicting the success of efforts to mobilize Mexican American political activity. Group identification is measured by recognition and approval of Mexican American political leaders and organizations, while political behavior is defined in terms of voting, partisanship, campaign activity, protest activity, and support for protest. The data come from a survey of 8,000 Mexican Americans living in Omaha, Nebraska.

Welch, Susan, John Comer, and Michael Steinman. "Ethnic Differences in Social and Political Participation: A Comparison of Some Anglo and Mexican Americans." *Pacific Sociological Review* 18, no. 3 (July 1975): 361–82.

In an effort to explain the differences in ethnic participatory behavior, this article analyzes Mexican American political and social participation and compares it to that of Anglos and blacks. Only low- and moderate-income Mexican Americans and Anglos are considered in order to control for structural variables. The analysis uses data collected in Nebraska on involvement in political activities ranging from talking with friends to attending a political rally.

Zisk, Betty H. "Chicano Leaders and Urban Politics: A Preliminary Report on Chicanos and Other 'Latino' Minorities." *Mexican*

*Americans: Political Power, Influence or Resource*, edited by Frank L. Baird. Lubbock: Texas Tech University, 1977, pp. 95-108.

This study of the nature of minority leadership compares the experiences of Mexican Americans in Lubbock, Texas, and Santa Ana, California, with Puerto Ricans in Worcester, Massachusetts, and Portuguese Americans in New Bedford, Massachusetts. Interviews with 100 Latino political leaders contributed information on the development of a mass base of support and leadership skills, two variables considered crucial for successful minority leadership. The interviews were supplemented by newspaper accounts and public documents.

## CONFERENCE PARTICIPANTS/VOLUME CONTRIBUTORS

DANIEL J. BALZ is national editor of the *Washington Post*, and is responsible for their coverage of national and electoral politics. In 1984 he covered the presidential campaign, writing on the projections as well as the outcome of the election. During his seven years at the *Post*, Balz has also held the positions of political editor and Southwest bureau chief. Prior to that, he was deputy editor of the *National Journal Magazine*.

JOE BELDEN, retired chair of Belden Associates, Dallas, is one of the pioneers of opinion research in the Southwest. During his 42-year career, he founded the Texas Poll, introduced commercial market research into Mexico, specialized in Spanish language research in U.S. markets, and developed an impressive volume of research for newspapers in this country and Mexico. In 1981, he won the International Newspaper Promotion Association's Goldish Award.

ROBERT R. BRISCHETTO is research director of the Southwest Research Institute (formerly, Southwest Voter Registration Project), a nonprofit, nonpartisan organization devoted to voter education and registration of Hispanics in the Southwest. Dr. Brischetto has supervised numerous surveys of Latinos in southwestern cities and has served as an expert witness in voting rights cases. He is coeditor of the Mexican American Electorate Series.

BRUCE E. CAIN is an associate professor of political science at the California Institute of Technology. He is known for his research and publications in the areas of redistricting, constituency service, and minority representation in the United States and Britain. Dr. Cain has conducted surveys of Hispanics in California and is a consultant for the polling firm of Fairbank, Canapary and Maullin.

BARBARA CAPLAN is vice president of Yankelovich, Clancey, Shulman, Inc., the marketing and social research firm whose 1981 and 1984 studies "Spanish USA" pioneered marketing research focusing on the Latino community. Caplan is responsible for marketing analysis for a broad array of consumer industries. She is directly involved in the YCS Monitor program and provides individual, data-based consultations on specific issues.

ISABELLA C. M. CUNNINGHAM holds the Ernest A. Sharpe Centennial Chair in Communication at the University of Texas at Austin. She writes extensively on consumer behavior, effective selling, and marketing in the United States and Brazil, and in 1981 won the Outstanding Paper Award from the Southern Marketing Association. Dr. Cunningham also serves as a research consultant for corporations, foundations, and nonprofit organizations and as an expert witness in legal cases involving advertising.

RODOLFO O. DE LA GARZA is director of the Center for Mexican American Studies and professor of government at the University of Texas at Austin. He is recognized for his research on Chicano voting attitudes and behavior, U.S.-Mexico relations, and the Mexican political system. Dr. de la Garza is the general editor of the Mexican American Electorate Series and has served as an expert witness in numerous cases involving voting rights litigation.

FRANK DEL OLMO is an editorial writer for the *Los Angeles Times* where he has worked since 1970. He received the 1984 Pulitzer Prize Gold Medal for Meritorious Public Service for the series "Southern California's Latino Community" as well as an Emmy Award in 1976 for "The Unwanted." Del Olmo was voted Outstanding Latino Journalist in 1976 by the National Latino Media Coalition and is recognized as one of the leading journalists writing on Hispanic issues today.

ANGELO FALCON is president and cofounder of the Institute for Puerto Rican Policy, a nonprofit, nonpartisan organization specializing in the analysis of Latino policy issues. His research focuses on Puerto Rican policy in the United States and the criminal justice system. He is a member of Mayor Goode's "We the People 200 Commission" and of the American Political Science Association's Committee on the Status of Chicanos.

ELIZABETH FORSYTH is a freelance editor working in the Washington, D.C., area. She has a master's degree from the University of Texas at Austin and extensive research experience in Latin American studies. Among her activities as a former research associate at the Center for Mexican American Studies, she coordinated the "Ignored Voices" conference. Prior to that she worked in Mexico as a Fulbright Scholar and as a writer for two Mexican ministries: Programming and the Budget, and the Presidency.

KATHLEEN A. FRANKOVIC is director of surveys at CBS News. Her major responsibility is CBS News and CBS News/New York Times national polls and election day polls. She has been at CBS News since 1977 and has written numerous articles on political behavior. She received a Ph.D. from Rutgers University.

CURTIS GANS is director of the Committee for the Study of the American Electorate, a nonprofit, nonpartisan organization researching low and declining voter participation in the United States. A journalist and political activist, Gans is known for his articles in *The New Republic* and *Atlantic*, and for his organization of the Dump Johnson movement and Eugene McCarthy's presidential campaign. He served on the Democratic National Policy Council from 1969 through 1972.

F. CHRIS GARCIA is dean of the College of Arts and Sciences and professor of political science at the University of New Mexico. He is also president of Zia Research Associates, a survey research firm specializing in the Latino Community, public opinion, and voting behavior. Dr. Garcia has published extensively on Chicano politics and the state government of New Mexico, and is on the editorial board of *Political Science*.

CONGRESSMAN ROBERT GARCIA has represented New York's District 18 in the U.S. House of Representatives since 1978. He is currently the chair of the Subcommittee on Census and Population, and was the past chair of the Congressional Hispanic Caucus. Congressman Garcia continues to work toward increasing the participation of Hispanics in the political process and forming a coalition of national Hispanic organizations. He served in the New York State Assembly and Senate for 13 years.

D. RODERICK KIEWIET is associate professor of political science at the California Institute of Technology. He received his Ph.D. from Yale University in 1980. In collaboration with Bruce Cain, he has studied the behavior of major ethnic groups in congressional elections involving Latino candidates. He and Cain were also awarded a large grant by the Seaver Institute to investigate the impact of the rapidly growing Latino and Asian populations upon the future of California politics. The findings reported in this volume are a product of that study.

I.A. LEWIS is director of the Los Angeles Times poll and is a partner in the Roper Organization. Within the field of survey research, he has also directed the CBS and NBC election and polling units. He came to the survey field with 22 years of experience as a reporter, a foreign radio correspondent, and an associate producer and writer for television.

REPRESENTATIVE ALBERT LUNA III has represented Houston's District 143 in the Texas House of Representatives since 1980. He is chair of the Mexican American Legislative Caucus and of the House Committee on Science and Technology. Before being elected, he worked with Vice President Mondale's Task Force on Youth Employment, the ACTION Agency in Washington, D.C., and the Opportunities Industrialization Center in Houston. Representative Luna is a partner in the Apollo Printing Company in Houston.

CESAR MELGOZA is a graduate of the Lyndon B. Johnson School of Public Affairs at the University of Texas at Austin. His research interests are in economic and industrial development and in the political development of the Southwest. His master's professional report "Chicanos in the New Economy: The Impact of Industrial and Political Change in the Southwest" received honorable mention in the Emmette S. Redford Award for Outstanding Research competition at the university. Currently, Melgoza is participating in a program for city management training with the City of San Jose, California.

WARREN J. MITOFSKY is director of the CBS News Election and Survey Unit, and an executive producer of primary and election broadcasts. He developed the vote-estimating models and analysis systems used by CBS, introduced exit polls to the coverage of politics in 1967, and started the CBS News/New York Times Poll in 1975. Prior to working for CBS, Dr. Mitofsky worked for the U.S. Census Bureau where he was responsible for the sample design of many surveys.

HARRY PACHON is executive director of the National Association of Latino Elected and Appointed Officials (NALEO), a nonprofit, nonpartisan organization that addresses public policy and other issues affecting the Hispanic community. He has over 12 years of governmental, private sector, and academic experience in public management and issues affecting the Hispanic community. Dr. Pachon also teaches public administration at Baruch College, City University of New York.

BENJAMIN I. PAGE holds the Frank C. Erwin Centennial Chair in Government at the University of Texas at Austin. He is known for his research and teaching in the areas of policy formation; political economy; public opinion, voting, and elections; and the presidency. He has received numerous grants and awards, most recently, the 1984 Outstanding Book Award from the Policy Studies Organization for *Who Gets What from Government*.

JAMES W. PROTHRO is a professor of political science at the University of North Carolina. He has been director of the Institute for Research in the Social Sciences and the Louis Harris Data Center as well as editor of the *Public Opinion Quarterly* and the *American Political Science Review*. He is recognized for his research on black political participation, voting behavior, and the politics of American democracy.

CONGRESSMAN WILLIAM RICHARDSON represents New Mexico's Third District in the U.S. House of Representatives. He is chair of the Congressional Hispanic Caucus and former executive director of New Mexico's Democratic party. Active in many legislative caucuses and community groups, Congressman Richardson is distinguished by his involvement in Hispanic issues. Prior to his election, he was an international business consultant and university lecturer.

GEORGE C. SHIPLEY is president of Shipley and Associates, a research and consulting firm with a national clientele of both political and corporate accounts. The firm consults and conducts polls for political campaigns at all levels in addition to conducting research for many corporations and trade associations. A former faculty member of the University of Texas at Austin, Shipley specializes in the application of behavioral research methods to marketing and political problems.

JAMES SHRIVER III is vice president of the Gallup Organization, managing editor of the Gallup Poll, and editor of *The Gallup Report*. He has over 20 years of experience as an advertising account and product manager. Since 1975, his responsibilities have included formulating the questions used by the Gallup Poll, writing a newspaper column and *The Gallup Report*, and designing and implementing marketing and opinion research studies.

LANCE TARRANCE, JR., is president of Tarrance & Associates, a research company that analyzes public opinion as it relates to electoral behavior. Conducting surveys and public opinion analysis for political races at all levels, the firm also specializes in corporate public affairs, marketing, medical, and media research. Tarrance has also worked for the Republican National Committee, the Bureau of the Census, and Decision Making Information.

ARMANDO VALDEZ is currently associate director of the Stanford Center for Chicano Research at Stanford University. Dr. Valdez is a communications scholar with a specialty in the production and distribution of knowledge in society. He has published various articles on this subject.